The Four Flashpoints

How Asia Goes To War

Brendan Taylor

16pt

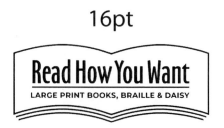

Read How You Want

LARGE PRINT BOOKS, BRAILLE & DAISY

Copyright Page from the Original Book

Published by La Trobe University Press,
an imprint of Schwartz Publishing Pty Ltd
Level 1, 221 Drummond Street
Carlton VIC 3053, Australia
enquiries@blackincbooks.com
www.blackincbooks.com

La Trobe University plays an integral role in Australia's public intellectual life, and is
recognised globally for its research excellence and commitment to ideas and debate.
La Trobe University Press publishes books of high intellectual quality, aimed at general
readers. Titles range across the humanities and sciences, and are written by distinguished
and innovative scholars. La Trobe University Press books are produced in conjunction
with Black Inc., an independent Australian publishing house. The members of the LTUP
Editorial Board are Vice-Chancellor's Fellows Emeritus Professor Robert Manne and
Dr Elizabeth Finkel, and Morry Schwartz and Chris Feik of Black Inc.

A catalogue record for this
book is available from the
National Library of Australia

Cover design by Regine Abos
Text design and typesetting by Tristan Main
Maps by Alan Laver
Cover image © shauni/Getty Images

Printed in Australia by McPherson's Printing Group

TABLE OF CONTENTS

FOREWORD   iv

INTRODUCTION: TICKING TOWARDS MIDNIGHT   ix

CHAPTER 1: RIPE FOR RIVALRY: ASIA   1

CHAPTER 2: ASIA'S CRUCIBLE: THE KOREAN PENINSULA   15

CHAPTER 3: BITTER ENMITY: THE EAST CHINA SEA   60

CHAPTER 4: CHINESE LAKE: THE SOUTH CHINA SEA   95

CHAPTER 5: A COMING CATACLYSM: TAIWAN   135

CHAPTER 6: CAN ASIA AVOID CATASTROPHE?   178

ACKNOWLEDGEMENTS   201

NOTES   204

FURTHER READING   249

BACK COVER MATERIAL   268

Index   271

PRAISE FOR *THE FOUR FLASHPOINTS*

'The map of Asia is dotted with flashpoints, places where national interests overlap and war could all too easily break out. In this informative and carefully argued volume, Brendan Taylor surveys the most explosive of these points, assessing the risks posed by each and proposing ways to damp down the danger that they could someday erupt into conflict. There are valuable insights in *The Four Flashpoints* for strategists, scholars and concerned citizens alike.'
—Aaron L. Friedberg, professor of politics and international affairsat Princeton and former deputy assistant for national security affairsin the office of the US vice-president

'We all know where the most dangerous flashpoints in Asia are, but Brendan Taylor has gone further than anyone in illuminating why they are so dangerous and how we might avoid conflict. He has produced the most gripping scenarios for major power war in Asia in print – as well as the strongest case for the wise statecraft we will need to keep the peace.'
—Michael J. Green, senior vice-president for Asia at the Centrefor Strategic and International Studies and author of*By More ThanProvidence: Grand Strategy and American Power in theAsia Pacific since 1783*

'This book is a clear, calm, rigorous and highly readable examination of the flashpoints that make

Asia so dangerous today. It explains how they evolved, why they matter and how they might blow up. *The Four Flashpoints* is the perfect guide to the looming perils of the Asian Century.'

—Hugh White, professor of strategic studies at the Australian NationalUniversity and author of*Without America: Australia in the New Asia*

For Jenny

FOREWORD

The centenary of the outbreak of World War I provided the occasion to compare events in 1914 and 2014. New histories, such as Christopher Clark's *The Sleepwalkers* and Margaret Macmillan's *The War That Ended Peace,* highlighted how the great powers had stumbled, mistakenly, into a war they either didn't want or thought they could win easily. Several commentators speculated about the parallels between the great powers in 1914 and those of today, particularly in Asia, where mounting rivalries and local disagreements have the potential to provoke much wider conflict, but a strange sense of complacency about this possibility appears to rule supreme.

In 2018, as we celebrate the centenary of the Great War's end, that complacency hasn't dissipated. US President Donald Trump's and North Korean leader Kim Jong-un's exchanges of bombast and diplomatic posturing make for entertaining viewing, but few seriously believe that a major war is imminent. As Brendan Taylor argues in these pages, this pervasive absence of anxiety about Asia's points of tension has resulted in half-hearted efforts to find genuine resolutions to or even conflict-stabilising mechanisms for them. Arguably, the major reason for our lack of unease is that war in Asia is increasingly hard for us to imagine, because peace has prevailed in this region for so long.

There are at least four reasons why Asia's rivalries are more threatening to global peace and order than other regional rivalries. The first is quite simply capacity. Asia's explosive economic growth is providing its great powers with the means to initiate and wage devastating conflict against one another. Arms purchases by all major Asian powers have increased markedly over the past quarter century, even as, due to the growth of their economies, the proportion of their gross domestic product devoted to arms has fallen. The imperative is to expand, particularly given what the neighbours are buying. None seems to have even come close to a sense of adequacy. With each passing year, the arsenals of the Asian powers are deepening and becoming more sophisticated; their war planning and military exercises are proceeding apace.

Second, Asia's centrality to the global economy and global information flows means that a major conflict in this region will cause disruption and devastation in all other regions. So intense would a full-blown conflict in Asia be that the combatants would seek to weaken their adversaries across three undefendable commons: the world's maritime highways, cyberspace and outer space. Control of sea lanes would allow combatants to prevent their enemies from resupplying, particularly with energy, during wartime. Cyberspace and outer space hold the keys to 'blinding' opponents' surveillance and control systems. Major and ongoing disruptions to these three commons, each so critical to the operation of the global economy, would cause incalculable economic damage and distress.

Third, Asian powers' inexperience in recent decades in waging major conflicts arguably makes it more likely that they will stumble into one. For years, Asia's great powers have been acquiring sophisticated weaponry without the chance to test its capabilities and vulnerabilities, or to refine military doctrine governing its use, which has likely led to significant misperceptions of how powerful these great powers are. If such misperceptions are conservative, they can be a stabilising influence; if not, they can be very dangerous. Constant growth and greater sophistication of weapons systems can make deterrent calculations very difficult to make and communicate to rivals.

Finally, even as Asia's countries prosper economically, the emotive forces of history and nationalism are becoming ever more powerful across the region. Governments are burnishing comparisons to past periods of national greatness as a way of bolstering their legitimacy. School curricula inculcate both bitter memories and unflattering stereotypes of neighbours. Seemingly unimportant reefs and islands, or remote borderlands, have become imbued with a sense of national pride and the legitimacy of the state.

For these and a host of other reasons, Brendan Taylor's *The Four Flashpoints* deserves very close reading. As the first comprehensive, comparative account of the rivalries that attend the Korean

Peninsula stalemate, the competition over the Senkaku/Diaoyu islands, the South China Sea stand-off and the status of Taiwan, this book provides a clear menu of the geopolitical hotspots that should most concern world leaders and citizens. While there are plenty of books that examine the *why* of conflict in Asia – the underlying tensions and causes of rivalries – this is the first to systematically survey the *how* and the *where* of the possible outbreak of conflict in Asia.

Taylor provides a careful assessment of the balance of stakes, forces, initiatives and motivations attending each of Asia's flashpoints, in a way that allows the reader to draw their own conclusions about how dangerous each one is. He reminds us of Coral Bell's concept of 'crisis slide', which can see one flashpoint increase the potential for conflict in others through a range of impacts on rivals' behaviour and calculations. And he provides us with a clear hierarchy of what he believes are the most and least combustible of the four flashpoints.

This is exactly the book citizens and policymakers need right now. It is an antidote to the complacent belief that because conflict in Asia has been averted so far, we can discount its potential in the future. Sobering but not alarmist, *The Four Flashpoints* is a reminder that the best hope for peace is a widespread appreciation of just how fragile and contingent it can be.

Michael Wesley
Canberra, July 2018

INTRODUCTION

TICKING TOWARDS MIDNIGHT

As World War II, the deadliest conflict in human history, drew to a close, scientists who had invented the atomic bomb anguished about the social implications of this 'destroyer of worlds'. They launched a pamphlet, which became a magazine, *Bulletin of the Atomic Scientists.* The cover of the inaugural issue carried a simple image of a black-and-white clock, set against a dramatic orange background. Its designer, Martyl Langsdorf, intended the clock to convey the urgency of their concerns. She set the time at seven minutes to midnight.[1]

Every few years since, a panel of esteemed scientists and nuclear experts – which today includes fifteen Nobel laureates – has met to evaluate the greatest threats to the future of humanity. Based on their assessments, the minute hand of the Doomsday Clock is moved back or forward. In January 2018, the hand was moved ahead by thirty seconds, to show two minutes to midnight. The clock has never ticked closer to that apocalyptic hour.

This time has been seen just once before: in 1953, at the height of the Cold War. In late 1952, America obliterated a small Pacific islet known as Elugelab with its first test of a thermonuclear device – a significantly more powerful weapon than the atomic bombs that flattened the Japanese cities of Hiroshima and Nagasaki in August 1945. Within months, the Soviets had tested a thermonuclear bomb of their own. The *Bulletin of the Atomic Scientists* responded to these developments with the direst of assessments: 'Only a few more swings of the pendulum, and, from Moscow to Chicago, atomic explosions will strike midnight for Western civilization.'[2]

Asia barely rated a mention in the evaluation of global threats in 1953. In 2018, this region featured prominently in the expert panel's report.[3] It is not hard to see why.

Asia is at a dangerous moment. China is rising faster, further and across more dimensions of power than any country in history. Its newfound assertiveness is shaking the foundations of the US-led strategic order, which has kept the peace in the region for more than half a century. North Korea has accelerated its nuclear and missile capabilities, posing further challenges to that order. America's Asian friends and allies are edgy. Japan is especially nervous, beefing up its military in response. Geography and a troubled history with China and Korea place it directly in the firing line.

In 2017, the Korean Peninsula drifted treacherously close to conflict. The young, reckless North Korean dictator Kim Jong-un successfully tested an intercontinental ballistic missile, demonstrating that he had the capacity to strike the United States – and half of the rest of the world – with a nuclear weapon. US President Donald J. Trump bit back belligerently with a warning to North Korea not to 'make any more threats to the United States' and pledged to unleash 'fire and fury' upon the Supreme Leader should he threaten the nation. While Trump and Kim appeared to make good in a historic summit in June 2018, their meeting was high on symbolism and low on substance. And North Korea has an abysmal record of sticking to the agreements it makes. With the unpredictable Trump and his hawkish national security adviser, John Bolton, in the White House, any repeat of the duplicity Pyongyang is known for could serve as a trigger for military action.

In Japan, a nationalist government is throwing off the constitutional constraints imposed at the end of World War II. The 'pacifist clause' in Japan's postwar constitution compelled it to renounce the right to war and the military forces to wage it. But Tokyo is unwilling to face Asia's new dangers in this strategic straitjacket. The prospect of Japan developing nuclear weapons is no longer unthinkable. Its defence spending is on the rise, and so too is its appetite for assurance that Washington will side with it in a clash against China, especially in the troubled waters of the East China Sea. A startling 80 per cent of Japanese fear that conflict could erupt in this sea over a set of disputed islands that Japan calls the Senkaku and Beijing the Diaoyu.[4] Ownership of those rocky outcrops would improve either side's ability to control these strategically significant waters and the resources that lie beneath them. With growing numbers of Chinese and Japanese military ships and aircraft patrolling the area, the risk of an inadvertent clash, which would unleash nationalist fervour and could escalate quickly into a major war, is rising.

Nowhere is China's power clearer than in the South China Sea, where Beijing's construction and militarisation of artificial islands has confounded America and its allies. Washington is furious that China has started landing warplanes, including nuclear-capable bombers, on these land features, improving its ability to control this critical maritime gateway. While the United States could take out the artificial islands militarily, to do so would risk war with China. Washington is unwilling to take that chance over distant outcrops. But the alternatives, short of military action, are next to nonexistent; America's new Indo-Pacific commander, Admiral Philip S. Davidson, said as much during his April 2018 confirmation hearing before the US Senate Armed Services Committee.[5]

The United States is also charting an unpredictable course. Its mercurial leader has thrown out the traditional diplomatic playbook. He continues to prod recklessly at the 'One China' policy that has maintained stability across the Taiwan Strait. Trump was the first president-elect to have contact with the leadership of Taiwan since China and America normalised relations in the 1970s. He has signed off on legislation allowing senior US officials to meet with their Taiwanese counterparts, reversing four decades of diplomatic practice.

With independence-leaning forces now in power in Taipei, the ire of Beijing – which regards Taiwan as a renegade province – has been invoked. China's strongman leader, Xi Jinping, forbids any attempt to separate Taiwan from China. Yet most of Taiwan's twenty-three million–strong population believe they already belong to an independent country, and only a shrinking proportion feel any affinity with China. This sentiment is strongest among Taiwanese under forty, where 70 per cent say they would be willing to defend their democratic way of life in the event of a military attack from the mainland.[6]

Given Trump's assertion of an 'America first' foreign policy, the rise of China, a Japanese military on the march and the uncertain spectre of North Korea, it is an open question whether the United States can and wants to maintain power in this economically and strategically vital region. Should the United States, the source of stability in Asia in the post–World War II world, leave or be forced out, what happens next is anyone's guess. Without Washington, which nation, or combination of nations, will move in to fill the power vacuum?

A major war in the Asia-Pacific is more likely than most people assume. The region is in the throes of a 'crisis slide': a period in which the cumulative pressure of crises over multiple tension spots is pushing the area closer to conflict. The outcome of any such conflict remains to be seen, but it will likely shape the world in ways both unimaginable and terrifying.

***

This book answers three questions: How probable is major war in Asia? Where is conflict most likely to originate? And what can be done to prevent it?

Each chapter considers one of four major flashpoints – Korea, the East China Sea, the South China Sea and Taiwan – and examines the sources of tension, the main power players, the missteps and missed opportunities for diplomacy, and the key episodes of escalation over time. It explores the vital interests of these players – the political, economic and strategic interests that they would go to war to defend. These might include an important patch of territory. It could involve the defence of an ally to demonstrate one's reliability as a partner. It could be an economic resource regarded as sufficiently lucrative or critical to national wellbeing to wage war over. Or it could entail something as fundamental as national survival. As the American strategist Bernard Brodie observed, 'the importance of vital interests comes not necessarily from some intrinsic quality, but rather from what we are ready to do about some infringement of them, real or imagined'.[7]

The likelihood of military conflict in each flashpoint is assessed. What might prompt one or more of the key players to use force, and under what conditions? Would the use of force be intentional or inadvertent? How might a military conflict play out, and what would be its costs, both human and financial?

Each chapter also explores the diplomatic possibilities for resolving tensions. How did past agreements come about, and why did they collapse? Are there potential diplomatic avenues that have not yet been opened? Will these minimise the risk of crises, or should such strategies be aimed at management and de-escalation when conflict erupts? In a region that is ripe for rivalry, is there any political appetite for resolving flashpoints diplomatically? The chapters conclude by assessing the implications for that flashpoint's future, and what this means for Asia more broadly.

In a region as combustible as this, it is difficult to provide definitive answers to such questions. History shows us clearly that the consequences of military force or diplomatic intervention are not always apparent in advance. As British prime minister Winston Churchill wrote:

> Never never never believe any war will be smooth and easy, or that anyone who embarks on that strange voyage can measure the tides and hurricanes he will encounter. The statesman who yields to war fever must realise that once the signal is given, he is no longer the master of

policy but the slave of unforeseeable and uncontrollable events.[8]

Yet as the world ticks towards midnight, it is crucial that we examine the circumstances that could lead to a military clash in these areas and the potential consequences – particularly if conflict erupted in multiple locations simultaneously.

War can still be avoided. The final chapter of *The Four Flashpoints* looks at what is needed to arrest the crisis slide in Asia and to construct a stable new order. Each of the four flashpoints has a separate trajectory, despite their interrelation, and needs to be managed differently. Some are more pressing than others. To avoid catastrophic conflict and navigate safely towards a new Asian order, the United States will need to double down on its security commitments to the Korean Peninsula and the East China Sea, where it currently enjoys 'situations of strength', while at the same time easing off on Taiwan and in the South China Sea, where the scales of military power are tipping against it. Is the erratic Trump administration up to the task? For now, it is moving in the opposite direction, and there is no certainty it will find its way forward without blunder.

ASIA'S FLASHPOINTS ZONE

CHAPTER 1

RIPE FOR RIVALRY: ASIA

When the Cold War ended a quarter of a century ago – and in the emerging global stability the Doomsday Clock moved to seventeen minutes to midnight – several commentators were already anticipating a darker future. Princeton professor of international affairs Aaron Friedberg, for instance, characterised Asia as 'ripe for rivalry' and saw the region as destined to become 'the cockpit of great power conflict'.[1]

Commentators such as Friedberg saw three sources of instability.

First, the end of the Cold War between the United States and the Soviet Union made Asia more dangerous because it removed what Australian scholar Desmond Ball called the 'tempering mechanism' for keeping regional conflict under control. What Ball meant was that the division of the world into rival ideological camps imposed discipline at the regional level: countries belonging to the communist bloc generally needed to secure the backing of their Soviet patron before picking a fight with a member of the opposing US-led capitalist camp, and vice versa. With the disintegration of the Soviet Union, and with real doubts over whether America would remain in the region or bank the substantial savings from no longer having to maintain its massive forward military presence, longstanding Asian antipathies that had been temporarily obscured by the superpower stalemate bubbled to the surface. In these, Ball saw 'much fertile ground for regional conflict'.[2]

Second, pessimists saw a deadly downside to Asia's strong economic growth. New regional players, such as China, Japan and India, were on the rise. History shows that such shifts in economic power tend to produce international instability, as leaders draw upon their nation's newfound wealth to build military capability. This dynamic becomes more pronounced when multiple powers are rising simultaneously, as they were in Asia. A multipolar system, comprising several major powers, would be more unstable than the predictable bipolar patterns of the Cold War period, where strategic alignments tended to be less fluid.

Third, unlike in Europe, where an elaborate multilateral framework had been developed after World War II, in Asia such institutional arrangements were in short supply. Supporters of liberalism have long maintained that intergovernmental organisations such as the European Union serve to build trust by improving international communication. They increase opportunities for policymakers to interact, the argument goes, and to gain a more intimate appreciation of the other side's perspective. Such organisations can also potentially be valuable in negotiating and managing international crises. The absence of such mechanisms in post–Cold War Asia reinforced expectations that unadulterated power politics would prevail.

Conflicts left unresolved from the wash-up of World War II did in fact flare on the Korean Peninsula and across the Taiwan Strait during the mid-1990s. This seemed to confirm fears that Asia was heading towards a turbulent future. Yet as the new century turned, there was suddenly less tension in the air in Asia. Washington became increasingly preoccupied with developments in the Middle East as it waged the War on Terror. Beijing launched a charm offensive, designed to woo neighbours with economic inducements and a softer diplomatic approach. It settled long-standing border disputes, sometimes on less-than-advantageous terms, and established a Free Trade Area with the ten members of the Association of Southeast Asian Nations (ASEAN). Smooth-talking ambassadors took the place of table-thumping cadres in key diplomatic posts. The Japanese economy entered its second decade of stagnation, putting paid to predictions of Tokyo's rise.[3]

As the decade wore on, tensions subsided on the Korean Peninsula and across the Taiwan Strait. And by decade's end, commentators were even talking up the prospect of a US–China Group of Two, or 'G2', that would allow the world's two most powerful nations to work collaboratively.[4]

These developments fuelled optimism that the region was set for stability. Some of this commentary grafted old ideas onto the new Asia. The well-established argument that trade prevents conflict was popularly applied. As countries became increasingly intertwined through economic and political alliances, journalists and academics predicted a peaceful region. Leaders, they contended, would be loath to pass up this economic windfall for a costly war.[5] Many viewed the emergence of indigenous multilateral groupings – such as the ASEAN Regional Forum, the East Asia Summit and the ASEAN Defence Ministers' Meeting – as adding ballast to already buoyant economic conditions. Some, such as Australian prime minister Kevin Rudd, even saw potential to build upon these foundations to construct an 'Asia-Pacific community' inspired by the EU.[6]

Other commentators pointed to Asia's distinctiveness from Europe, which they saw as beneficial in establishing a peaceful order. The American academic Robert Ross argued that Asia's stability stemmed from its unique geography. Ross regarded Asia not as a single region but as two separate regions – one continental, one maritime. Asian peace in the twenty-first century was attainable, he argued, due to Chinese dominance of the former and American command of the latter. Because of the physical distance between these two powers, neither threatened the other in quite the same way as more geographically proximate rivals.[7] Scandinavian scholars sought even deeper answers to the puzzle of Asia's peace, pointing to culture as an explanation. The interviews they conducted with scores of Asian policymakers showed that just as personal connections and informal networks – or what the Chinese call *guanxi* – are often critical to doing business in this part of the world, so these qualities of informality and intimacy are central to the avoidance of conflict because of the confidence and trust that personal interactions generate.[8]

But Asia's brief period of stability was a calm before the storm. A succession of crises rocked the region from 2010, as tensions heated up simultaneously on the Korean Peninsula and in the East and South China Seas. North and South Korea were taken to the brink of conflict as Pyongyang sank one of Seoul's navy ships and bombarded the South Korean island of Yeonpyeong. Chinese and Filipino craft faced off at a disputed reef in 2012, as did Chinese and Vietnamese vessels in 2014, after Beijing parked an oil rig in Vietnam's exclusive economic zone. Relations between Beijing and Tokyo also became strained from 2012 after Japan unilaterally 'nationalised' the disputed Senkaku/Diaoyu Islands in the East China Sea.

Against this backdrop, the diagnoses of Asia as set on a course for conflict have resurfaced. Prominent among this commentary is the voice of Harvard professor Graham Allison. He likens Asia's present to the period before the Peloponnesian War that devastated Ancient Greece, as recounted in Thucydides' classic history. Allison argues that just as Athens' rise instilled such fear in Sparta as to make conflict virtually inescapable, so America's apprehension over China creates a similar predicament today. His analysis of instances over the past 500 years where a rising power has threatened to displace an incumbent show that the protagonists have failed to escape what he termed the Thucydides Trap 75 per cent of the time.[9] The British strategic thinker Christopher Coker predicts that such a Sino–American conflict could erupt within the decade.[10] The Australian journalist Richard McGregor believes instead that an Asian version of the Wars of the Roses – those infamous battles for influence in Tudor England – is looming between China and Japan. But America's alliance with Tokyo, he contends, could still entangle it in that conflict.[11]

World leaders have also invoked the Thucydides Trap in relation to Asia. Addressing the sixteenth Shangri-La Dialogue in June 2017, Australian prime minister Malcolm Turnbull observed that 'the rapid rise of a new power, be it modern China or Ancient Athens, creates anxiety'.[12] Chinese president Xi Jinping has championed the idea that Asia needs a 'new model of great power relations' in an explicit counter to such Thucydidean thinking.[13]

The sparks of war: how and why flashpoints matter

The term 'flashpoint' comes from the sciences. A flashpoint is the lowest temperature at which vapours from a liquid will ignite when exposed to a flame. The lower the flashpoint, the more volatile the liquid. Applied to international affairs, flashpoints are geographic areas with the potential to erupt suddenly into violent conflict. Timothy Hoyt, a professor at the US Naval War College, suggests that flashpoints have three common characteristics. First, they have a political dimension, meaning that they 'must be at the forefront of a significant and long-standing political dispute'. Second, geographical proximity is critical – tension spots 'tend to become greater concerns if they are proximate to both adversaries'. Third, flashpoints 'threaten to involve or engage more powerful actors in the international community, raising the possibility of escalation into a broader war'.[14]

Commentators who point to a coming Asian conflict tend to downplay, if not dismiss, the importance of flashpoints. As Allison argues, 'more important than the sparks that lead to war, Thucydides teaches us, are the structural factors that lay its foundations'.[15] What he means by 'structural factors' are those deeper causes of war, such as changes in the balance of military power between nations. While these factors likely form at some distance from – potentially decades before – the onset of conflict, they are considered integral to it. The Australian strategic commentator Hugh White takes a similar stance in his Quarterly Essay *Without America: Australia in the New Asia,* arguing that flashpoints are 'just symptoms' of an underlying Thucydidean rivalry between a rising China and an America in decline.[16]

Structural causes are critical to an understanding of many international conflicts. Yet decision-making in crisis situations is highly complex, as Allison showed earlier in his landmark study of the Cuban Missile Crisis – those fateful thirteen days in October 1962 when America and the Soviet Union came perilously close to world-ending nuclear war.[17] Allison's Harvard colleague Joseph Nye helpfully likens the process of analysing conflict to building a fire. The deeper causes are akin to logs: necessary fuel for the flames but insufficient in themselves to ignite. As Nye puts it, logs 'may sit for a long time and never be lit. Indeed, if it rains before somebody comes along with a match, they may never catch fire.'[18] As important, therefore, is an understanding of the more immediate causes of war – the kindling, the paper and the striking of the match. This is why an examination of flashpoints is so important.

Focusing upon deeper, structural factors often reveals much about *why* a certain war or conflict happened – although typically those factors only become truly apparent with the benefit of hindsight. But it will generally tell us far less about *how* that conflict came about. The Australian historian Christopher Clark explores this subtle but important distinction between the why and the how of conflict in his bestselling account of the events that led to World War I, *The Sleepwalkers: How Europe Went to War in 1914.*

Understanding how, not just why, Asia's major powers might go to war is all the more important to anticipating conflict in a region so diverse. Each of the four flashpoints discussed in this book exhibits a unique dynamic. Each involves a different constellation of key players. Their geography is distinct, with implications for the combustibility of each. History tells us that conflicts escalate more quickly between countries with land borders than between those separated by sea, where the distance militaries need to travel affords more time for diplomacy. And each flashpoint engages the 'vital interests' of Asia's major powers – those political, economic or strategic interests worth going to war over – to quite varying degrees.

Yet the flashpoints are also interconnected, through history, proximity and the potential to erupt into conflict. The cumulative pressure of crises over these flashpoints is pushing this region closer to war.

The four flashpoints: an anatomy

The four flashpoints in this book have traditionally been regarded as Asia's most prominent geopolitical hotspots. More importantly, they are relevant to what the Australian historian Geoffrey Blainey once called 'wide war' – conflict that draws in many nations, especially the leading players in the international system.[19]

To understand the interconnections between them, we need to look to the historical context. All have roots in the aftermath of Japan's defeat in World War II. While Korea, the East China Sea, the South China Sea and Taiwan were disputed areas well before 1945 – centuries before, in some cases – by World War II, they were under Tokyo's control. Korea and Taiwan were Japanese colonies. The Ryukyu Islands in the East China Sea – a chain that includes, for Tokyo, the Senkaku Islands – was part of Japan. Tokyo had also annexed the Spratly and Paracel Islands in the South China Sea.

When forty-eight nations met at San Francisco's War Memorial Opera House in September 1951 to broker peace with Japan, they laid the foundations for what became Asia's US-led security order. Washington used this gathering to help establish new alliances with Japan, Australia and New Zealand, and the Philippines. Similar pacts were forged with South Korea and Taiwan soon thereafter.[20] This 'San Francisco system' of Asian alliances served for decades as the region's security anchor. America received access to Asia's markets, while in return its stabilising security presence facilitated this region's remarkable economic growth.[21]

Yet the San Francisco conference also inadvertently sowed the seeds for conflict in the twenty-first century. The peace treaty it produced required Tokyo to renounce its ill-gotten wartime gains. What it didn't specify was who should fill the vacuum left by Japanese withdrawal in these areas or, in some cases, precisely which patches of land were included in this renunciation. The agreement over the Ryukyu, for instance, stated that the United States was to administer these islands for an unspecified period, after which they would be returned to Japan. Yet when Washington made good on that promise during the early 1970s to ease deepening tensions in the US–Japan alliance, Taipei protested that the Senkaku Islands were not part of the Ryukyu and should be returned to their rightful owner, Taiwan. Beijing had, by this time, also laid claim to the islands, considering Taiwan part of China. Neither Beijing nor Taipei had been invited to San Francisco in 1951 to help clarify these ambiguities, due to confusion over who was the rightful ruler of China following the recently concluded Chinese Civil War.

Such uncertainties also affected disputes over the South China Sea, where Beijing and Taipei – along with Paris and Manila – had claims. Complicating matters still further was the fact that Korea, which Tokyo renounced as part of the treaty agreement, had been split in two at the end of the war.[22]

Each of these four flashpoints has the potential to bring the world's two leading powers, America and

China, into conflict. And the histories of and current tensions in these areas are inextricably linked.

Some might argue that rising tensions between China and India (over their disputed land border and in the Indian Ocean) should also be included in a discussion of flashpoints in Asia. While Sino–Indian war is certainly conceivable – China fought a month-long war with India in late 1962, after all – it is difficult to envisage a scenario today in which such conflict draws in other major players. That may change in the future, particularly once China and India become the world's two leading economies, as they are predicted to do by the year 2050.[23] Until then, however, those areas of Asia most likely to spark 'wide war' lie on the Pacific side of the continent.

The spectre of major war in Asia might still seem outlandish to many, especially in this region of tightly knit economies, where the presence of nuclear weapons renders the costs of conflict almost inconceivable. But that mentality is dangerous. Complacency is one of the main characteristics of crisis slide.

Only last year, knowledgeable observers likened tensions over Korea to the Cuban Missile Crisis of the 1960s – the most dangerous stand-off of the Cold War.[24] As quickly as calm has come to the Korean Peninsula in recent months, it could just as readily unravel. Asia's burgeoning defence budgets, and the growing number of navy ships plying the region's strategic waterways and military aircraft traversing its skies, are ominous signs. And the same is true in each of these flashpoints, contested areas with difficult histories and important strategic implications for the future.

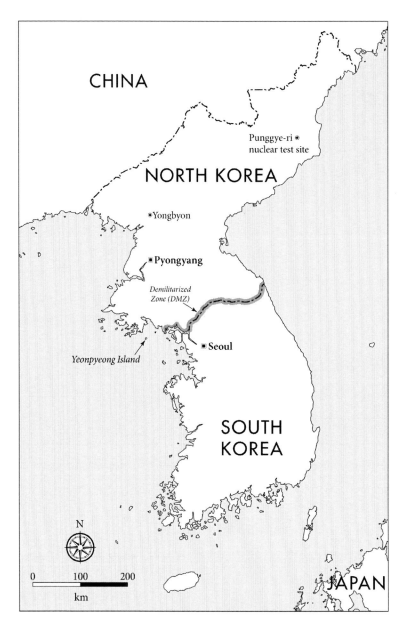

THE KOREAN FLASHPOINT

CHAPTER 2

ASIA'S CRUCIBLE: THE KOREAN PENINSULA

Along the road from Seoul that leads into the heart of the Korean Demilitarized Zone (DMZ) – the strip of land that serves as a buffer between North and South Korea – are ominously named 'rock drops'. Built in the 1970s and 1980s, these slabs of solid concrete are suspended over the road and the railway. Each as large as a house, their purpose is to impede North Korean tank and troop advances: in the event of an invasion, explosives will blast these rocks from their moorings, producing instant barricades. Locals refer to them colloquially as 'North Korean speed bumps'. Adding to this primitive blockade system are rows of 'dragon's teeth'. Standing only three feet tall, these pyramidal concrete pillars resemble those used by Germany during World War II to stymie tank movement and steer them to where they were vulnerable to counterattack.[1]

In an era of precision-guided weaponry, South Korea's rock drops and dragon's teeth have probably outlived their usefulness. Were the North to unleash any of its 4300 tanks upon the South today, American and Korean missiles would almost certainly take out the tanks well before they could be trapped in the South's antiquated barricade system. Yet the rock drops live on as a powerful metaphor. Billboards with sparkling advertisements have been mounted to camouflage these concrete monstrosities as ever-sleeker cars speed by beneath them, symbolising the growing prosperity and technological advancement of Asia's tiger economies. Similarly, belying the economic dynamism in Seoul and other Asian capitals is historical enmity that weighs heavily upon the region's stability. The disgraced former South Korean president Park Geun-hye referred to this startling contradiction as 'Asia's paradox'.[2]

As war clouds darkened over the Korean Peninsula in 2017, fears grew that only devastating conflict could resolve this paradox. In recent months, renewed optimism for a diplomatic solution has lessened these clouds. War cannot be ruled out, but the massive human and financial costs it would entail make it a last resort. Yet a history of failed agreements over the Korean Peninsula points to a challenging road ahead. The best outcome may be a return to tense stand-off and the persistence of Asia's paradox. This seems far from ideal. But North Korea is the land of lousy options.

The DMZ: the scariest place on earth

The Korean Peninsula is rife with contradictions and ironies. Few are starker than that of the Demilitarized

Zone (DMZ) separating the two Koreas. At 240 kilometres long and four kilometres wide, it is visible from space. This mostly mountainous dividing line, aimed at preventing conflict and casualty, has lain largely undisturbed for over sixty years. As a result, the area is home to an array of flora and fauna. Almost 100 species of fish live in its marine ecosystems. Many of its inhabitants are endangered elsewhere; animals that have been all but wiped out beyond the DMZ, such as the Asiatic black bear and the Siberian musk deer, find a reliable habitat within this zone. One of the world's scarcest species of birds, the red-crowned crane (fewer than 3000 survive in the wild), migrates to the area each winter from northern China and southeast Russia. The even rarer Siberian tiger (with a global population of fewer than 600) is also rumoured to roam here, with trackers claiming to have found their prints in the snow and on hollowed-out animal carcasses. It is little wonder that conservationists have been drawing up plans to have this ecological paradise formally designated an international peace park.[3]

History suggests that their prospects for realising this dream are not good. For centuries the Korean Peninsula has been a strategic fulcrum where major power interests have intersected and bloody conflicts raged. The First Sino–Japanese War (1894–95), the Russo–Japanese War (1904–05) and the Pacific War (1941–45) were all products of major powers jostling for dominance over this part of the world. So too was the Korean War (1950–53), out of which the contemporary tensions between the two Koreas arose.

Korea was a Japanese colony from 1910 to 1945, but in one of history's accidents, American and Soviet troops met at the Peninsula's midpoint near the end of World War II, as Tokyo's resistance to their respective military assaults melted away. Moscow and Washington agreed quite amicably to divide the Peninsula at the 38th parallel – the line of latitude 38 degrees north of the equator – and to withdraw their respective forces as soon as a new Korean government had been installed. While those troop withdrawals occurred from 1948 to 1949, agreement over who would govern the country proved elusive. A US-backed government, elected in United Nations–mandated elections, was installed in the South, while a Soviet-backed regime, under the leadership of communist figure Kim Il-sung, seized power in the North. Each side claimed to be the legitimate government of Korea and threatened to use force to depose the other.[4]

Yet both sides needed the support of their superpower patron to launch an invasion. After repeated requests, Kim received approval from Soviet leader Josef Stalin in January 1950. Stalin believed that Washington wouldn't come to the South's aid after US secretary of state Dean Acheson delivered an address in which he intimated that South Korea did not fall within the scope of a new US 'strategic perimeter' in Asia.[5] But when the North launched a surprise attack against

South Korea, Washington felt unable to stand idle. US policymakers feared that America's commitment to Asia would be called into question. Under a United Nations banner, a USled multinational force intervened on the side of South Korea, a development that most historians say caught Stalin completely by surprise.

The Korean campaign started badly for the United Nations Command, as the US-led force was known, who were driven to the bottom of the Peninsula by the advancing North Koreans. It took a daring military manoeuvre from the legendary American general Douglas MacArthur to turn the tide. MacArthur masterminded a surprise amphibious landing at the port of Incheon, which allowed the United Nations Command to trap Kim's Il-sung's troops below the 38th parallel and to make their way up the Peninsula virtually unopposed. As they approached the Yalu River, which separates China from Korea, Beijing began to fear that the American-led advance might not stop at the border. These anxieties drew China into the conflict on the North's side. A bitter stalemate ensued, which ended with the signing of an armistice agreement between North Korea, China and the United Nations Command on 27 July 1953. By this time, close to a million Americans and South Koreans had been killed or wounded defending the South, while an estimated 1.5 million perished on the opposing side.[6]

The DMZ was established as part of the armistice agreement. Ironically, given its name, it was and still is one of the most heavily militarised parts of the planet. At its epicentre is the Joint Security Area (JSA), where the intensity of the tension is apparent. Located not far from the historic village of Panmunjom, where the armistice was signed, the JSA is the only area along the DMZ where troops from the two Koreas stand face to face and routinely look one another in the eye. Famously, for this reason, those on the South Korean side need to stand at a minimum height of 177 centimetres. They all hold a black belt in either taekwondo or judo and routinely strike intimidating martial arts poses; they sport dark sunglasses and are armed with pistols.[7] Their North Korean counterparts are under immense pressure to perform. When one made it to the southern side of the DMZ in November 2017, Pyongyang immediately replaced the remaining thirty-five to forty troops guarding the JSA.[8] The life-threatening injuries the defector suffered in his dash for freedom likely paled in comparison to their punishment.

Beyond the theatre of the JSA, the two kilometres back from the perimeter of the JSA on either side is largely a no-man's-land. The North religiously patrols one patch, the South the other. There is a small village on either side of the DMZ: to the north, Kijŏngdong, the Peace Village (aptly known as 'Propaganda Village' in the South), and to the south, Daeseong-dong, the Freedom Village. The approximately 200 residents of Daeseong-dong must adhere to a nightly curfew to avoid possible abduction by the North. No wonder US president Bill Clinton described the DMZ as the 'scariest place on earth' before he toured it in 1993.[9]

Yet it is only at the outer limits of these two buffer zones that the possibility for conflict is truly apparent. Formidable barbed-wire fences mark these limits. This razor-sharp, rust-coloured wire is punctuated only by watchtowers, from which troops on both sides monitor their respective zones. Immediately behind the barbed wire, two of the world's largest armed forces have amassed much of the firepower at their disposal.

Numerous provocations have taken place along the DMZ since the final shots in the Korean War were fired. One of the grislier occurred on 18 August 1976, when two US servicemen were killed by axe-wielding North Korean soldiers. On that fateful day, Captain Arthur Bonifas and First Lieutenant Mark Barrett were in the JSA as part of a small joint US–South Korean team, near the aptly named Bridge of No Return. The aim of their operation was to trim a tree that was obscuring the line of sight between two observation posts. Pyongyang's rhetoric in the months leading up to the incident had become more bellicose. However, Bonifas was instructed to ignore any harassment from the North Koreans and to terminate the operation only if violence seemed imminent. Several warnings to cease the tree trimming went unheeded, until a group of thirty North Korean soldiers appeared and bludgeoned Bonifas and Barrett to death.

Three days later, the United States and South Korea launched Operation Paul Bunyan, a name inspired by a mythical American lumberjack. In an overwhelming show of military force, an aircraft carrier was deployed into the waters off Korea, and air support was provided for the two platoons of American and South Korean military personnel sent in to cut the tree down to a stump. The United States also moved from DEFCON 4 to DEFCON 3 – the midpoint between its lowest state of military readiness, DEFCON 5, and its maximum state, DEFCON 1, when nuclear war is imminent. No response from Pyongyang, other than a relatively anodyne statement of 'regret' for the incident, was forthcoming.[10]

Deadly provocations have also been initiated below ground. North Korea has a reputation as a country of tunnellers. A retired South Korean general once claimed that there were eighty-four North Korean tunnels running below the DMZ. Whether that was an exaggeration remains to be seen, but four such tunnels have been discovered so far. The third of these, found on 17 October 1978 and known as the Third Tunnel of Aggression, runs 1.6 kilometres long and 73 metres deep. At 2 metres wide, the tunnel could accommodate up to 30,000 troops armed with light weaponry in the event of a North Korean invasion of the South. When the tunnel was discovered, Pyongyang claimed that it was an abandoned coalmine. While coal dust had been smeared around the tunnel's entrance for effect, there is little geological likelihood of coal deposits in the area.[11]

Not theoretical are the thousands of landmines planted in the DMZ by both sides during the Korean War. In the period since, hundreds of South Korean civilians have been killed or seriously maimed disturbing these. In August 2015, Seoul accused Pyongyang of sending soldiers to the southern side of the DMZ to plant fresh landmines. Two South Korean soldiers had lost their legs after discovering these in the worst way possible. Seoul retaliated by resuming the practice, for the first time in eleven years, of mounting loudspeakers to blast a combination of anti-Pyongyang propaganda and South Korean K-pop music – which is banned in the North – across the divide. Pyongyang reacted by heightening its level of military readiness to a 'quasi state of war'. Seoul was given a deadline of forty-eight hours to shut off the speakers, which the North fired upon at one point in the crisis. Tensions were ultimately defused by inter-Korean talks, proposed by Pyongyang, which lasted a marathon forty-three hours. Pyongyang again issued a statement of 'regret' for the injuries suffered and agreed to lift the 'quasi state of war'. In return, Seoul turned off the loudspeakers.[12]

This crisis is a reminder of the Korean Peninsula's fragility. Peace is perilous here because the Korean War never really ended. A demonstration of this occurred in March 2010 when a North Korean submarine fired upon a South Korean naval vessel, the ROKS *Cheonan,* splitting it in two and killing forty-six of its crew. Eight months later Pyongyang was at it again, bombarding the South Korean island of Yeonpyeong, which lies a mere 12 kilometres off the coast of North Korea. Four Koreans (two soldiers, two civilians) were killed and approximately 100 buildings destroyed. The eminently sensible Korea watcher Victor Cha described at the time the danger of tensions escalating into full-blown conflict:

> There is a real possibility of war on the Korean Peninsula. The cause is not a second North Korean invasion of the South like in June 1950, which was successfully deterred by US and South Korean forces. The danger stems from two combustible trends: a North Korea which mistakenly believes it is invulnerable to retaliation due to its nascent nuclear capabilities, and a South Korea that feels increasingly compelled to react with military force to the string of ever more brash provocations like the artillery barrage of Yeonpyeong Island.[13]

Going ballistic: North Korea's nuclear weapons

While the origins of this tension are deeply rooted in the division of Korea following World War II, its character has, as Cha suggests, changed in important ways over the ensuing seven decades. The most significant change has been in relation to nuclear weapons. While Pyongyang's interest in acquiring a nuclear capability can be dated to the mid-1950s, its development of a nuclear program did not begin in earnest until the 1980s, when work commenced on two relatively large reactors. Estimates at the time suggested that these reactors, once operational, would give Pyongyang the capacity to manufacture approximately thirty atomic bombs per year. In early 1992, Central Intelligence Agency director Robert Gates testified before the US Congress that Pyongyang was only months away from having the ingredients to produce a nuclear weapon.[14] This development lit the fuse on the North Korean nuclear crisis of 1993–94, which turned out to be one of the Peninsula's most dangerous moments.

Over the past two decades Pyongyang has undertaken a total of six nuclear tests. The first of these occurred in October 2006. Conducted underground, it yielded a relatively small explosion, equivalent to that produced by 1000 tons of dynamite. To put that into perspective, the Fat Man atomic bomb the United States dropped on Japan in August 1945 was twenty times larger. As such, expert opinion regarded the North's first nuclear test as a fizzer. However, with each ensuing test – in 2009, 2013, 2016 (twice) and 2017 – Pyongyang's nuclear abilities advanced significantly. The blast produced from its latest nuclear test, in September 2017, measured 6.3 on the Richter scale. It caused landslides and the collapse of a tunnel at the test site, reportedly killing up to 200 people.

While its yield remained considerably smaller than the largest weapons in America's nuclear arsenal, experts suggest that Pyongyang is now able to produce a bomb six times more powerful than the Fat Man.[15]

As North Korea's nuclear capabilities have grown, so too has its development of missiles designed to deliver this weaponry. While North Korean missile testing began in the early 1990s – when Pyongyang targeted a medium-range missile at a buoy floating in the Sea of Japan – it has accelerated under the rule of Kim Il-sung's grandson, the enigmatic dictator Kim Jong-un. Since taking the helm in 2011, Kim Jong-un has carried out more missile tests than his predecessors, grandfather Kim Il-sung and father Kim Jong-il, combined. Particularly notable was the successful August 2016 test of a submarine-launched ballistic missile (SLBM). While a technically difficult weapon to master, a capacity for SLBMs could in time give Pyongyang a more potent nuclear force, because submarines are easier to hide and more difficult to detect than land-based launchers.[16]

More startling still was Pyongyang's three test launches of intercontinental ballistic missiles (ICBMs) in 2017. The term 'ICBM' is a relic of the Cold War, used to describe missiles that can fly further than 5550 kilometres – the distance between the Soviet Union and the United States. North Korea's third ICBM test, conducted in November 2017, demonstrated that capacity comfortably. Indeed, experts estimate that this missile has a maximum range of 13,000 kilometres without a payload, and a range of 8500 kilometres when carrying a standard 500-kilogram warhead. Pyongyang likely still has much ground to cover before it can be confident in its ability to deliver a nuclear weapon mounted on this missile. It is difficult in a technical sense to protect a warhead through its high-pressure, high-temperature descent. Most experts agree that more testing is required before North Korea can deliver a nuclear warhead over this distance.[17] Such testing remains unlikely while the current diplomatic negotiations continue.

The Korean Peninsula: a strategic fulcrum

As well as the two Koreas, several major powers – the United States, China, Japan and Russia – have a stake in the Korean Peninsula. Yet it is not always easy for foreign powers to analyse events in the secretive North Korean regime. American intelligence analysts often refer to North Korea as 'the blackest of black holes' given the difficulties of getting a definitive read on Pyongyang's capabilities and intentions. North Korea is one of the most closed societies on earth; it has been nicknamed the 'hermit kingdom'. Its 25 million citizens are brainwashed from kindergarten age and have little, if any, knowledge of the outside world. Pyongyang runs its own internet system, which only allows access to domestic websites and email. North Korea's estimated 3 million mobile-phone users can only make domestic calls. Those who attempt to circumvent these restrictions by tapping into Chinese mobile towers along the border, using phones obtained illegally, face severe criminal charges if caught – under its 'three generations' policy, North Korea punishes not only the perpetrator of a crime but also their entire family.[18]

Despite its firm grip on power, the North Korean regime displays an acute sense of insecurity. This explains its relentless pursuit of nuclear and missile capabilities. Internally, Kim Jong-un faces little threat of popular revolt: there are no known organised opposition movements, and North Korea's impoverished population – which survives on an average yearly income of US$1300 per person – has little energy for insurrection. Kim's biggest internal threat comes from a potential military coup. It is crucial, therefore, to keep the military on side. North Korea's nuclear and missile programs assist with this. As two respected American analysts, Daniel Byman and Jennifer Lind, have observed:

> Nuclear weapons have particular significance in this case because of the ongoing status competition between North and South. The generals can tell themselves: our soldiers are hungry; our tanks are World War II vintage; but we have nuclear weapons – and Seoul does not.[19]

The hermit kingdom also fears external threats, especially from the United States. This insecurity dates from the Korean War, but has intensified in recent years. Pyongyang has watched US-led military interventions against authoritarian regimes in Iraq (2003) and in Libya (2011) and drawn one important conclusion: had Saddam Hussein and Muammar al-Qaddafi persisted with their plans to obtain nuclear weapons, they would still be in power. Speaking after a September 2017 missile test, Kim stated that Pyongyang's ultimate objective is to achieve an 'equilibrium' with the United States in terms of military power, as this is the only way to ensure that an American attack can be deterred.[20] The following month, Kim characterised the North's nuclear program as a 'treasured sword' whose purpose is to protect the country's independence.[21]

Some commentators speculate that Pyongyang's aims are greater and far more sinister than regime survival. This interpretation suggests that Kim's endgame is to reunify Korea on his terms, after removing the American threat by negotiating a peace treaty with Washington. Kim fuelled such speculation with his January 2018 New Year's address, which called for a halt to US military exercises with the South and for Koreans to achieve 'independent reunification'.[22] In the lead-up to the June 2018 summit between Trump and Kim, US defence secretary James Mattis specified that 28,500 American troops stationed on the Peninsula would not be part of the negotiations.[23]

However, Trump hinted at the possibility of withdrawing this presence at a press conference immediately after the summit.[24] Such a withdrawal would remove one obvious impediment to a North Korean attack against the South.

Korean reunification faces further obstacles. With a gross domestic product forty times the size of the North's, South Korea is a much wealthier country. Its defence budget alone is almost as large as the entire North Korean economy. Even if the United States were to abandon South Korea, Seoul has at its disposal a modern armed force that the North would struggle to defeat in conventional combat. South Korea's population is also twice the size of the North's – not to mention considerably healthier – meaning that occupation of this fiercely nationalistic nation would be challenging. Pyongyang could, of course, rely upon its nuclear weapons to decimate its southern neighbour. Yet were it to do so, this would bring South Korea's flourishing economy to a standstill, removing the spoils of war from Pyongyang's perspective. It is also not clear that North Korea's armed forces have the training to operate for sustained periods in an irradiated environment.[25]

This scenario, though, does highlight the considerable stakes involved for South Korea given its location at the front line of this enmity. The elegant glass buildings of its capital, Seoul, located a mere 50 kilometres from the DMZ, could well be destroyed should the Korean Peninsula combust. Estimates produced at the time of the 1993–94 North Korean nuclear crisis suggested that the first ninety days of a conflict on the Korean Peninsula would cost $US1 trillion and up to half a million lives.[26] Those costs would almost certainly be higher today, given the advances that Pyongyang has made in its nuclear and missile programs.

Against that backdrop, South Koreans exhibit striking complacency about the threat posed by North Korea. In polling conducted in 2016 – the same year that Pyongyang conducted two nuclear and more than twenty missile tests – almost 60 per cent of South Koreans believed that war on the Peninsula was 'not likely'.[27] South Koreans have simply learned to live with the threat from the North. Moreover, those in their twenties would rather continue to live with this threat than contemplate reunification. They recognise that reunification would be costly and would require considerable economic sacrifice. While previous generations of South Koreans may have been willing to bear that burden, younger South Koreans are not prepared to pay that price.[28]

American anxiety over this region is in stark contrast to South Korean complacency. During his first State of the Union address, in January 2018, President Trump warned that Pyongyang's 'reckless pursuit of nuclear missiles could very soon threaten our homeland'.[29] Twelve months earlier, in the face of speculation that Pyongyang was on the verge of testing an intercontinental ballistic missile, Trump tweeted belligerently that 'it won't happen'.[30] Yet when Pyongyang defied the US president's predictions and conducted two ICBM tests in July 2017, he responded by threatening to unleash 'fire and fury like the world has never seen' upon North Korea should it persist with its aggressive behaviour towards America.[31] The genuine fear behind Trump's bellicose threats was revealed in January 2018, when US officials mistakenly sent out an emergency mobile-phone alert to Hawaiian residents, warning of an incoming ballistic missile attack. The error went uncorrected for thirty-eight minutes, plunging the state into panic.[32]

While the threat of a North Korean missile strike against the US mainland is new, Washington's desire to address the North Korean problem is not. The George W. Bush administration saw North Korea through the lens of its War on Terror. During his January 2002 State of the Union address, Bush famously referred to Pyongyang as part of an 'axis of evil' that also included Iraq and Iran.[33] Barack Obama, by contrast, saw the Koreas in the context of his signature Rebalance strategy, which was designed to reassure Asian allies of US commitment. This explains why Obama responded to the sinking of the South Korean ROKS *Cheonan* in 2010 by conducting a series of high-profile military exercises with South Korea, much to China's chagrin.[34]

Despite the different emphasis that various US administrations have put on this flashpoint, each has held a similarly negative view of the North Korean regime, and for good reason. The audacious assassination of Kim Jong-un's half-brother, Kim Jong-nam, at Kuala Lumpur International Airport in February 2017 demonstrates that Pyongyang has developed, and shown a willingness to deploy, stockpiles of chemical and biological weapons. In this hit, which was almost certainly orchestrated by North Korean agents, Kim's half-brother reportedly succumbed to a dose of the highly lethal VX nerve agent. The North also has an egregious human-rights record, which includes the widespread use of political prison camps and brutal methods of execution. Again in February 2017, reports emerged that an enraged Kim Jong-un had five senior officials executed with an anti-aircraft gun for providing him with 'false reports' of an unspecified nature.[35] It is little wonder, then, that a United Nations report described North Korea's human rights abuses as 'strikingly similar' to those of Nazi Germany.[36] Washington believes, with some justification, that governments who repress their populations with such extreme measures tend to display similar aggression in their actions on the world stage.

China, meanwhile, has threefold interests in the Korean Peninsula. Beijing and Pyongyang have longstanding strategic ties, forged in blood during the Korean War. Beijing became Pyongyang's most important ally from the 1960s. The relationship was often likened to that between 'lips and teeth' due to its closeness.

Beijing also has a strong interest in North Korean stability, given the 1400-kilometre border the two countries share. Severe political or economic disruption in North Korea, including that caused by an eruption of conflict on the Peninsula, could create a humanitarian disaster for China. In April 2017, Beijing deployed 150,000 troops along this border, ostensibly to conduct military drills but most likely in readiness for the millions of refugees that would come flooding into China in the event of a war.

Last but certainly not least, North Korea acts as an indispensable strategic buffer between China and America's Asian allies. Should the North Korean regime collapse, Beijing's nightmare scenario is reunification of the two Koreas and, with this, the presence of American troops on its doorstep.

But the China–North Korea relationship has come under severe strain in recent years. Kim Jong-un and Chinese president Xi Jinping reportedly dislike each other. Kim executed his uncle, Jang Song-thaek, in December 2013 – Jang was Beijing's closest link to his regime, overseeing North Korea's lucrative coal exports to China and keen to bring Chinese-style economic reforms to the hermit kingdom, and his death highlighted the degree of drift in Chinese–North Korean relations. The more recent assassination of Kim's half-brother can also be read as a slap in China's face. At the time of his death in Kuala Lumpur, Kim Jong-nam was on route to the Chinese territory of Macau, where he had lived for years under Beijing's protection.

This strain has also been evident in diplomatic relations between the two nations. In November 2017, Xi sent the head of the Chinese Communist Party's international liaison department, Song Tao, as an envoy to North Korea, but Kim reportedly refused to meet with him.[37] The younger Kim – unlike his father, who was hosted by Beijing on at least seven occasions between 2000 and 2011 [38] – did not visit China for six years after taking power. His first trip to China, in March 2018, was to meet 'unofficially' with Xi.

China's rise depends upon stability in its immediate neighbourhood. Because Pyongyang's provocations threaten that stability, they have become a source of growing frustration and concern to Beijing. Although North Korea remains strategically important to China, this frustration and concern explains Beijing's apparent willingness to sign up to international sanctions targeting Pyongyang's nuclear and missile programs. So too does the fact that Donald Trump has been dialling up the pressure on President Xi to do more. Successive US administrations have called upon Beijing to exert its considerable leverage against the hermit kingdom, pointing out that China provides the North with an estimated 90 per cent of its food and fuel. While Beijing claims its influence over the regime is limited, Trump – unlike his predecessors – has simply refused to accept this line. Instead, he has called upon

Beijing to put a 'heavy move' on Pyongyang to bring an end to the 'nonsense'. He has threatened to deal 'properly'[39] with the North if China doesn't, and has linked Beijing's performance in this region to American policies elsewhere, namely in the South China Sea and over Taiwan.[40]

Japan, too, has longstanding ties to the Korean Peninsula, having colonised Korea during the first half of the twentieth century. In recent decades, its primary concern with this region has been Pyongyang's burgeoning missile capabilities. Tokyo was caught off guard in September 1998 when North Korea test-fired a medium-range ballistic missile over Japan.[41] Tokyo's fears have only intensified since, with Pyongyang's development of a nuclear-capable missile, known as the Nodong-1, powerful enough to reach all parts of Japan. Further fuelling these fears, Pyongyang test-fired four missiles simultaneously in March 2017. Three of these landed inside Japan's exclusive economic zone, a maritime area stretching 200 nautical miles from the Japanese coastline. Pyongyang claimed that the tests were practice runs for a strike against American military bases in this area.[42]

The following month, Tokyo took the unprecedented step of issuing formal advice to its citizens on how to respond to an incoming North Korean missile. According to this advice, residents might have only minutes to prepare.[43] The growing threat posed by North Korean missiles is now fuelling calls in Tokyo for the construction of missile defences to better protect the Japanese mainland, as well as more powerful missiles to hit back at Pyongyang.

Russia is the other major power with a stake in this region. Its influence on the Korean Peninsula is not what it was during the Cold War when, along with China, it was North Korea's key patron. Relations between Moscow and Pyongyang drifted considerably with the end of the Cold War and the disintegration of the Soviet Union, as Russia sought to cultivate economic ties with South Korea. They came closer in 2000, however, when Moscow and Pyongyang inked a new agreement, the Treaty of Friendship, Good-Neighborliness and Cooperation. In 2011, the two countries undertook to collaborate on a major new gas pipeline. In 2012, Moscow agreed to wipe 90 per cent of the debt owed to it by the North, while the following year a new railway line opened, linking North Korea and the Russian Far East. In February 2016, another agreement was inked, facilitating the deportation of North Korean defectors living in Russia.

Currently, an estimated 30,000 to 50,000 North Korean workers reside in Russia legally. They send much-valued hard currency back to the hermit kingdom.[44] Next to China, Russia is thus the country with the most direct leverage over the North.

However, like Asia's other major powers, Moscow has no interest in seeing North Korea's nuclear and missile capabilities continue to surge forward. Its concern is that other regional powers, namely South Korea and

Japan, might in time respond by developing similar capabilities – or more effective missile defences against them – leading to a destabilising arms race. It is perhaps for this reason that Russia has in recent years shown a greater willingness to support sanctions against North Korea. Moreover, Moscow was clearly startled when in May 2017 North Korea test-fired a nuclear-capable missile that splashed into the sea off the Russian coast – a development Russian president Vladimir Putin described as 'counterproductive, damaging, dangerous'. Putin was careful to caution against using this episode as an opening to 'intimidate' Pyongyang, but the admonition was clear.[45]

Fire and fury: Korea's potential for conflict

In 2017, the Korean Peninsula drifted closer to war than at any time since the North Korean nuclear crisis of 1993–94. Some experts put the odds of conflict as high as 50 per cent.[46] Others, such as former CIA director John Brennan and former Australian prime minister Kevin Rudd, were more conservative in their estimates, suggesting that figure should be in the lower, albeit still significant, bracket of 20 to 25 per cent.[47] Tensions have eased somewhat due to Kim Jongun's 'charm offensive', launched with a high-ranking delegation, including his younger sister, Kim Yo-jong, and a team of telegenic North Korean cheerleaders at the February 2018 Winter Olympics in Pyeongchang, South Korea. In a performance worthy of a gold medal, Kim's move wooed the world, distracting international attention away from Pyongyang's nuclear antics and putting a more human face on the reclusive regime.

But the threat of war has not receded. This region could still take a turn for the worse. Statements from the Trump administration fuel such pessimism. In an extraordinary September 2017 dispatch from his Twitter account, for instance, the US president suggested that his then secretary of state, Rex Tillerson, was 'wasting his time' negotiating with Kim Jong-un – whom Trump referred to as 'Little Rocket Man'. 'Save your energy[,] Rex,' Trump asserted, 'we'll do what has to be done!'[48] Trump's soon-to-be-discarded national security adviser H.R. McMaster was an especially vocal advocate for the use of military force, announcing that Kim Jong-un is 'irrational and undeterrable', that 'there is a military option' to denuclearise the North and that the chances of war are 'increasing'.[49] In January 2018, speculation that proponents of a military solution to North Korea were winning the debate within the administration intensified after Trump's pick for US ambassador to South Korea, Victor Cha, was withdrawn from consideration once he refused to support the prospect of America undertaking military action against Pyongyang.[50] The March 2018 appointment of John Bolton – a 'hawk' who has long advocated force against North

Korea – as McMaster's replacement only fuelled such speculation.[51]

There are several ways the Trump administration could use military force against North Korea. At one end of the spectrum, the United States could launch a full-scale invasion resembling the Korean War. In late 2017, the Pentagon, in a letter to the US Congress, advised that such an offensive was the only way to remove North Korea's nuclear weapons 'with complete certainty'.[52] An invasion on this scale would entail significant military resources. Recent estimates suggest that it would require over 700,000 American troops – more than four times the number deployed to Iraq at the height of that conflict, and more than seven times the number sent to Afghanistan.[53]

Even if the United States were to emerge victorious from such a campaign, it would encounter many of the same challenges as North Korea in attempting to forcibly reunify the Peninsula. Humanitarian relief and postwar reconstruction efforts of unprecedented scale would be needed, particularly if Pyongyang used nuclear bombs or deployed its frightening array of biological and chemical weapons during the conflict. As a November 2017 report by the US Congressional Research Service observes:

> North of the Demilitarized Zone, as many as 25 million North Koreans could be affected by a conflict, which could reduce already scarce food and other essential supplies available to the

general public. Further, approximately 80,000 to 120,000 prisoners in prison camps could be released and may need immediate attention. South of the DMZ [South Korea] could need significant assistance recovering and reconstructing key infrastructure, such as fuel and electricity services, contending with casualties, delivering emergency supplies, and much more ... Some analysts suggest that [South Korea] might also have to prepare for and counter sabotage attempts to foment insurgency by any remaining North Korean [Special Forces]. Should [North Korea] target other U.S. allies in the region, or U.S. installations in Japan or [the Pacific base of] Guam, U.S. forces could be required to assist with postconflict reconstruction in those locations as well.[54]

The United States could instead opt to undertake a more limited military strike, of the kind contemplated at the height of the 1993–94 nuclear crisis. Former officials recount that President Bill Clinton came within hours of authorising surgical air strikes against Pyongyang's known nuclear facilities before the resolution of that crisis.[55] Tensions had initially escalated after inspectors from the United Nations nuclear watchdog, the International Atomic Energy Agency (IAEA), found discrepancies between Pyongyang's declared and actual nuclear activities. The IAEA responded by requesting, for the first time ever, a 'special inspection', which would allow it to visit any site in the country with little or no warning.

North Korea, given its notorious lack of enthusiasm for any form of mandated engagement with the outside world, refused point-blank. It put the military option on the table, threatening dramatically as the crisis deepened to turn Seoul 'into a sea of fire'.[56] In a more unusual episode of American diplomacy, former US president Jimmy Carter travelled to the North (with Clinton's blessing) and brokered an agreement with its leader, Kim Il-sung. The deal was announced on live television without the president's approval, right as Clinton was huddled with advisers in the Oval Office, debating the merits of surgical strikes.[57]

Some commentators have called upon Donald Trump to undertake Clintonesque strikes against North Korea's nuclear-testing and missile-launch sites, especially if Kim Jong-un were ever to make good on his provocative threat to conduct an atmospheric nuclear test over the Pacific Ocean.[58] Within the Trump administration, the favoured limited military option is said to be a 'bloody nose' strike against Pyongyang. This would involve hitting one or more discrete and largely symbolic targets, such as ICBM launchpads. The purpose of bloodying the North's nose in this way would be to demonstrate Washington's resolve and to deter Pyongyang from undertaking further tests, hopefully alleviating the need for a costly and potentially catastrophic full-scale ground invasion.

One shortcoming of a limited strike is that it could not conclusively eliminate North Korea's nuclear and missile capabilities. Many of Pyongyang's most prized military assets – especially those associated with its nuclear program – are hidden underground or beneath the sea. A surgical strike of the kind Clinton contemplated could temporarily thwart some of those capabilities, such as those at the Yongbyon Nuclear Scientific Research Center, North Korea's major nuclear facility, located 100 kilometres north of Pyongyang; but such strikes would not eliminate these programs altogether. Indeed, they may ultimately only deepen Pyongyang's resolve to persist with its nuclear program. Added to this, since the 1993–94 crisis North Korea has developed mobile launch systems, which problematise 'bloody nose' options because these systems are harder to locate.

More worrying still would be Pyongyang's reaction to the 'bloody nose' option. Domestic pressures may force Kim to respond militarily to even a limited strike or risk losing power. As one commentator, Luke O'Brien, has recently argued:

> There's a common misperception in the West that Kim has unlimited power and freedom of action, and so he's the only actor we have to worry about. Yet like all leaders, Kim has constituencies that make up his power base. His actions, therefore, are not purely based upon his perception of the threat from the United States, but also on what is required to keep the support of those elites and remain in power.[59]

Of even greater concern, Kim may simply be unable to work out if the United States is initiating a limited strike or launching a full-scale invasion against him. Faced with such uncertainty and the prospect of his most prized weaponry being severely depleted in a first wave of attacks, he could quite conceivably launch nuclear strikes against American bases in the South, Japan, Guam and Hawaii, in the hope of convincing the United States to pull back.[60]

The longer-term consequences of US military action need to be carefully weighed too. It is no exaggeration to say that a North Korean retaliatory strike against Seoul could spell the end of the US–South Korea alliance and perhaps much of South Korea. Even if Pyongyang chose not to deploy its nuclear and missile capabilities, the bulk of North Korea's approximately 15,000 artillery pieces are located along the border with the South, a mere fifty kilo metres away from Seoul. Embedded in mountains and protected by blast-proof doors, this artillery would be a potent tool in any military clash. Although speculation that the North's combination of cannons and rocket launchers could level Seoul is likely overblown, a significant military attack would inflict considerable physical and psychological damage upon its ten million inhabitants.[61] For that reason, the current liberal government of South Korea – which won power on a pledge to engage with Pyongyang – has stated repeatedly that a military solution to tensions in Korea is 'unacceptable', that the United States should 'under no circumstances' take military action without Seoul's consent and that the current crisis needs to be resolved diplomatically.[62]

Trump's 'America first' mentality could lead him to think that the collateral damage of losing an ally is a price worth paying to defend the US homeland against North Korean ICBMs. Yet this underestimates the substantial costs to America that Korean conflict would entail. On any given day, up to half a million US citizens are in South Korea. Hundreds of thousands more live in nearby Japan. The need for surprise when initiating military action against the North would mean Washington could not give them advanced warning of a strike.

Moreover, the economic reverberations of a North Korean counterattack on Seoul would be felt back in the United States and around the globe. South Korea is the world's eleventh-largest economy and America's sixth-largest trading partner. Were North Korea to target US military bases in Japan, the ramifications would be even more severe, given Japan's position as the world's third-largest economy and America's fourth-largest trading partner.[63] Asian trade and investment could come to a standstill because of the conflict, with dire consequences globally. Widespread capital flight would occur rapidly as investors moved their funds to less risky locales, putting pressure on interest and exchange rates around the world. The insurance costs of moving goods in this central global shipping region would also increase, while fears of potential supply disruptions could lead to surging world energy prices.[64]

Back to the future: failed diplomacy again?

Diplomatic avenues aimed at resolving the Korean crisis have been tried before, many times, but the outcomes have not proved enduring.

During the late 1990s, Seoul embraced a strategy known as the Sunshine Policy towards the North. This approach derived its title from Aesop's famous fable about a battle between the north wind and the sun to determine which was stronger. The contest came down to whether the sun or the wind could succeed in getting a traveller walking below them to remove his cloak. While the wind failed in this quest because its bluster only encouraged the traveller to clutch his cloak ever tighter, the sun prevailed by radiating warmth upon him.

Consistent with this children's story, the Sunshine Policy sought to assuage Pyongyang's fears and insecurities through engagement and cooperation. A signature initiative was the Kaesong Industrial Park, set up not far from the DMZ. Funded by South Korean government and business interests to the tune of almost US$27 million, it provided jobs for 47,000 North Korean workers at the 100-plus South Korean firms based there. A second Sunshine Policy poster child was the Mount Kumgang tourism project, which allowed hundreds of thousands of South Koreans to visit the picturesque, historically significant mountain, located in a special administrative region of North Korea, in the hope they might develop more positive feelings towards the North.[65] In short, the purpose of the Sunshine Policy was to resolve tension on the Korean Peninsula by transforming its underlying hostility into understanding. South Korea's Sunshine Policy came to an abrupt halt following the 2008 election of the hardline conservative leader Lee Myung-bak, who opposed it.

The Clinton administration followed through on Jimmy Carter's efforts to defuse the 1993–94 nuclear crisis by formally negotiating an Agreed Framework with the North: Pyongyang committed to eventually putting an end to all nuclear development in exchange for a series of technological, economic and diplomatic benefits. This deal held for eight years, during which time the North's plutonium-based nuclear activities at the Yongbyon facility remained on hold.

Several years into the Agreed Framework, Washington discovered that North Korea was secretly developing nuclear weapons. But Pyongyang wasn't the only party guilty of flouting their commitments. The United States had lagged in its commitments to provide the North with energy assistance. The framework fell apart.

In another attempt at diplomatic resolution, from 2003 to 2009 the United States, China, Russia, Japan and the two Koreas engaged in the Six-Party Talks. These talks were hosted by China, and delegates met on a total of six occasions. The high point came in September 2005, when, after thirteen days of negotiations, the parties agreed to a 'roadmap' for denuclearising the Korean Peninsula. Under this plan, Pyongyang pledged to abandon nuclear weapons in return for energy assistance. The United States promised that it would not deploy nuclear weapons on the Peninsula and that it would work towards productive ongoing diplomatic relations with the North. Most significantly, the parties also agreed to discuss the provision of 'proliferation resistant' nuclear reactors – which do not produce material suitable for use in nuclear weapons – to Pyongyang when the time was right. Disagreements emerged around this latter idea, however, before the ink had even begun to dry on the agreement. In 2006, Pyongyang fired off a spate of missiles and conducted its first nuclear test. Pyongyang eventually walked away from the talks in April 2009.[66]

A similar document, the Leap Day Agreement, signed on 29 February 2012, committed Pyongyang to a moratorium on nuclear and missile testing, and on its nuclear activities, but it did not last the month.[67] The deal fell over after a mere two weeks, when Kim Jong-un attempted to launch a satellite, in direct contravention of the agreement.[68]

History is repeating. After years in the diplomatic wilderness, North Korea has again become one of the world's most sought-after interlocutors. In late April 2018, Kim Jong-un and South Korean president Moon Jae-in spent twelve hours together in the Truce Village, Panmunjom. They pledged to begin a peaceful chapter of inter-Korean relations and proposed to turn the armistice into a peace treaty.[69] Less than two months later, following his summit with Kim, Trump declared on Twitter, 'There is no longer a Nuclear Threat from North Korea' and that his fellow Americans could 'sleep well tonight!'

Things could be different this time, some foreign-policy commentators say. But past diplomatic failures provide pause. Negotiating agreements with North Korea has always been only half the battle. Ensuring compliance with these agreements has proven more difficult.

Given the secrecy of the North Korean regime, it is tricky for other nations to confirm that Pyongyang is sticking to its side of any bargain. At the April 2018 inter-Korean summit, Kim promised to allow American and South Korean weapons inspectors to witness the demolition of his Punggye-ri nuclear test site, which he did, on 25 May.[70] But there are suggestions that the demolition may not be irreversible, more a spectacle for the cameras than a genuine move towards denuclearisation.[71] And how much further will Kim go? North Korea is an insular nation, after all. In 1993, when the United Nations nuclear watchdog the IAEA requested inspections after discovering discrepancies at the North's nuclear facilities, their demand was rejected, and Pyongyang withdrew immediately from the Treaty on the Non-Proliferation of Nuclear Weapons (NPT), plunging the Korean Peninsula into crisis.[72]

Domestic politics also get in the way. In 1977, during the first year of his presidency, Jimmy Carter tried to withdraw all US forces from South Korea. But he was stymied by opposition from Congress and the military.[73] A key reason for US foot-dragging on its commitments under the Agreed Framework in the late 1990s and early 2000s was opposition from a Republican-led Congress hostile to the deal. The agreement unravelled during President George W. Bush's first year in office. Any attempt to reduce the American presence on the Korean Peninsula could encounter similar domestic opposition.

The history of failed diplomacy has created profound distrust. Having seen Pyongyang cheat on past agreements, Washington now refuses to give the North anything before it abandons its nuclear weapons – completely, verifiably and irreversibly. But those weapons are Pyongyang's last bargaining chip. Without them, Kim leaves himself open to the same fate as Saddam Hussein or Muammar al-Gaddafi. He wants economic rewards and ironclad security assurances provided upfront.

Trump's approach of applying maximum economic pressure against Pyongyang has been credited with bringing the hermit kingdom out of its cave to negotiate with the outside world. North Korea has for decades been the most heavily sanctioned country on earth. But new measures introduced over the past year are among the harshest it has faced. In September 2017, for instance, the United Nations Security Council (UNSC) imposed its strongest-ever sanctions against the North, which included restrictions on its textile exports – a major source of income for Pyongyang – and its oil imports.[74] America supplemented these measures with additional sanctions, including against Chinese companies accused of keeping the North Korean regime afloat.[75]

While international sanctions targeting Pyongyang make great sense in theory, it has never been easy to implement these in a coordinated manner. Political change in South Korea, for instance, has seen Seoul's approach lurch from the Sunshine Policy of the late 1990s to the hard-line posture of the Lee Myung-bak government between 2008 and 2013, and back to diplomacy under the recently elected Moon administration. Chinese and Russian support for sanctions has also proven elusive. The much-touted 'toughest-ever' UN sanctions were allegedly softened to win support from Beijing and Moscow.[76] In December 2017, reports emerged that US spy satellites had caught Chinese vessels illegally transferring oil to North Korean ships on at least thirty occasions, prompting Trump to tweet that he had caught Beijing 'red-handed'.[77]

Pyongyang has also found ways to successfully slip the sanctions noose. From the 1950s, the North

Korean regime has adhered to an ideology of *juche,* which, roughly translated, means self-reliance. Aside from its considerable economic dependence upon China, Pyongyang remains largely removed from the global economy. The transactions it conducts are typically executed illicitly through a sophisticated, shadowy network of front companies, middlemen and money-laundering operations.[78] The regime has also managed to secure income through other illegal means – North Korean hackers, drawing on Pyongyang's expanding cyber capabilities, have targeted banks in Bangladesh and Taiwan, stripping these institutions of tens of millions of dollars.[79]

More narrowly focused 'smart' sanctions, with the potential to target the illicit activities of the North Korean regime, are being developed continually. But sanctions are a notoriously unreliable tool of statecraft. They can serve useful purposes, such as deterring other would-be rogue states from going down the nuclear path. And North Korea has without question been considerably weakened by a decades-long sanctions regime; the now iconic satellite images showing the North shrouded in darkness by night, in stark contrast to the bright lights of Seoul, serve as a powerful reminder of this. Yet one of the biggest shortcomings of sanctions is that they take a very long time to 'bite', or demonstrate their full effect, even in cases where they do ultimately work.

All or none: a Mexican stand-off

The controversial director Quentin Tarantino typically includes a Mexican stand-off scene in his movies. Several characters hold one another at gunpoint, knowing that if one pulls the trigger they will all perish. When relationships like this develop between states, strategists call it deterrence.

If a diplomatic solution does not eventuate, a Mexican stand-off is the default position for the Korean Peninsula. The United States deters the North from attacking the South and forcing it to reunify on Pyongyang's terms; Pyongyang deters Washington from forcibly denuclearising or reunifying the North under the South's rule. US deterrence is underwritten by the presence of military forces at the front line of this flashpoint. North Korea relies increasingly on its nuclear and missile arsenal to deter the United States. Its long history of reckless provocation of South Korea and other nations also leaves little doubt around its willingness to use military force.

This two-way deterrence has until now prevented a coda to the Korean War. But it is important to recognise that this relationship is inherently unstable. The military capabilities of each side, coupled with the geographic proximity of their armed forces, give either the option of launching a debilitating first strike against their opponent. In fact, they create an imperative to do so, especially for Pyongyang. While the North would anticipate a full-scale invasion well in advance, given the troop movements required – and the deterioration in the political and security situation that would likely have occurred by that point – Pyongyang would get only minutes' warning of an incoming US missile strike or aircraft bombing raid. Cruise missiles fired from an American destroyer off the coast of Korea, travelling at speeds of 800 kilometres per hour, would reach their targets in the North within ten to fifteen minutes. Pyongyang's antiquated radars would provide even less warning of air strikes delivered by sophisticated US stealth bombers.[80] Such time pressures put the Korean Peninsula on a perpetual knife-edge.

That dynamic has seen this region come dangerously close to conflict on several occasions. As the Clinton administration considered a limited military strike at the height of the 1993–94 nuclear crisis, North Korean forces were mobilising in preparation to launch pre-emptive military action of their own. In 2003, George W. Bush deployed twenty-four long-range bombers to the Pacific base of Guam, sent four aircraft carriers within range of the Korean Peninsula and conducted high-profile military exercises with South Korea, showing his willingness to use force to coerce Pyongyang into abandoning its nuclear weapons. North Korea's leader at the time, Kim Jong-il, responded by ordering the country's armed forces to a state of 'full combat readiness' and going into hiding along the border with China for fifty days.[81]

Pyongyang is also working on biological, chemical and cyber weaponry, further complicating the deterrence calculus. Washington and Seoul are not standing still in response. In September 2017, the Trump administration agreed to lift the 500-kilogram weight limit in place on the conventional warheads it provides to South Korea. This move could give Seoul much greater capacity to strike against the North in the event of conflict.[82] More importantly, in the same month the United States and South Korea completed the installation of a controversial American missile-defence system known as THAAD (Terminal High Altitude Area Defense).[83] The United States has also been working on developing its own homeland missile defences.

Much work remains to be done on these systems before they are, in the words of former Clinton administration official Robert Gallucci, 'ready for prime time'.[84] Despite President Trump's outlandish claims that US missile defence works 97 per cent of the time, it remains a technically difficult feat to shoot down an incoming missile. Success rates in US national missile defence testing have so far been in the 50 to 60 per cent range, with these tests conducted in highly favourable weather conditions and during daylight.[85] While THAAD has enjoyed considerably better testing success rates, the main weakness of this system is that it is only designed to cope with smaller short-and medium-range missiles, and can easily be overwhelmed should an adversary launch these simultaneously and in large numbers.

Washington's ability to provide Asian allies shelter under its 'nuclear umbrella' is being challenged as Pyongyang develops the capacity to strike the US homeland. Will Washington be willing to defend Seoul or Tokyo if the price is the loss of one or more American cities?

Some commentators believe that Japanese and South Korean concerns over Washington's waning commitment will prompt the two countries to distance themselves from the United States and to develop nuclear weapons, creating their own deterrent relationships with North Korea and sparking an Asian nuclear arms race.[86] Of the two, Japan is the more likely to go down this path, given its technological capacity to do so. Tokyo could build a nuclear bomb within months. It may take longer to overcome domestic opposition to such a move, though, given that Japan is the only country against which nuclear weapons have ever been used in anger.

The long game: predictions for the Korean Peninsula

With the threat of war looming over the Korean Peninsula, the desire for a quick fix is understandable. But this geopolitical flashpoint is not conducive to speedy solutions. The potential for wide-scale conflict will continue to hang, like South Korea's rock drops, over Asia's peace.

President Trump boldly asserted in November 2017 that 'the era of strategic patience is over'.[87] But trust takes time to build. In truth, the period of strategic patience has only just started. It is worth remembering that the Korean War armistice was the product of 1076 meetings held over more than two years.[88] Stanford professor Siegfried Hecker – who once directed the Los Alamos National Laboratory, birthplace of the atomic bomb – estimates that North Korean denuclearisation will take a full decade.[89] Will Trump be willing to wait that long for the complete dismantling of North Korea's weapons program? Kim Jong-un won't give up his treasured nuclear capacity without significant inducements, but will Trump really be willing to play his game short of that absolute standard? Will China continue over time to keep up its all-important economic pressure on Pyongyang, even as its larger strategic competition with America intensifies? None of this seems likely.

A history of failed diplomacy doesn't auger well for the future. It suggests that the longer this diplomatic process plays out, the greater the risk of derailment. Should diplomacy falter, conflict might be the result – especially with President Trump and his hawkish national security adviser, John Bolton, in the White House. But a Mexican stand-off is the more likely scenario for the foreseeable future. This will require America to double-down on its military commitments, rather than pulling back. Washington will want to leave Pyongyang in no doubt that a nuclear strike on an American city would mean the end of North Korea. A doubling down will also be needed to reassure Seoul and Tokyo of America's commitment to their defence.

There is a bigger picture, too. The United States has long underestimated the strategic importance of its alliance with South Korea in terms of the broader Asia-Pacific. Korea is characterised as America's 'forgotten war'. Jimmy Carter and now Donald Trump have toyed with the idea of withdrawing US troops from the Peninsula. Yet they do so at America's peril. The United States could arguably remain a regional player without a connection to South Korea; alliance with Japan is the cornerstone of the American presence in Asia. But this presence would be much less influential without South Korea, and the door would open for Beijing to exert considerably more influence over Asia's crucible. America would be one step away from leaving this region. And that could spell global disaster.

THE EAST CHINA SEA FLASHPOINT

CHAPTER 3

BITTER ENMITY: THE EAST CHINA SEA

The Yasukuni Shrine is located in downtown Tokyo. An impressive example of ornate nineteenth-century architecture, it honours Japan's war dead. Conservative Japanese politicians routinely send ritual offerings or visit the shrine to pay their respects, evoking outrage from their Chinese and South Korean counterparts. That is because the shrine also pays homage to a handful of well-known war criminals.

More contentious than the Yasukuni Shrine is its adjacent military history museum: the Yushukan. This controversial facility offers a highly subjective account of Japan's wartime history. It indicates that American military and economic encirclement 'forced' Japan into World War II. On proud display among its exhibits is a carriage from the infamous Thailand–Burma railway – also known outside Japan as the Death Railway – but the signage neglects to mention the thousands of prisoners of war who perished during its construction. The heinous 1937 raping and pillaging of the Chinese city of Nanjing by Japanese forces is also glossed over.

A short plane ride away, in central Beijing, sits the grandiose National Museum of China. Admission is free, and millions visit each year, making it one of the world's busiest museums. Its historical interpretation of Asia's past is a world apart from the Yushukan's. A permanent exhibition entitled *Road to Revival* recounts the history of the Middle Kingdom's 'century of humiliation' at the hands of external powers, which ended with the Sino–Japanese war of 1937–45. The view of this conflict is very different to that found in the Yushukan: it describes the 'Rape of Nanjing' as the single worst episode of this period, and displays images of half-naked Japanese soldiers leering at Chinese women. And yet, perhaps predictably, no mention is made of China's most infamous massacre, even though it happened right outside the museum's doors, on the austere concrete of the imposing Tiananmen Square.

Due to the animosities of the wartime past, mutual antipathies between China and Japan run deep. An accidental Sino–Japanese clash in the skies above or on the contested waters of the East China Sea risks unleashing nationalist sentiments that have the potential to spiral out of control. As this chapter explains, efforts have been made to reduce the risk of such clashes. Yet these efforts have ultimately been stymied by the same nationalistic pressures they are intended to guard against.

It seems almost paradoxical that the risk of conflict persists between two countries as economically intertwined as China and Japan. Yet the East China Sea flashpoint epitomises Park Geun-hye's 'Asian paradox' of economic cooperation and historic enmity growing in parallel.[1]

Tug of war: a history of contention

At 1.25 million square kilometres, the East China Sea is less than half the size of the South China Sea. Yet this adjacent body of water, which receives much less media coverage, is just as important strategically, and just as hotly contested.

The East China Sea is home to a series of territorial disputes. Some of these are less significant than others. One involves a standoff between two American allies – Japan and South Korea – over a set of islands that Tokyo refers to as 'Takeshima' and Seoul dubs 'Dokdo'. Yet the chance of Washington being forced into making a Solomonesque choice between its key north-east Asian partners because they clash over them is remote.

The same cannot be said for a conflict over a clutch of uninhabited islets that Beijing calls 'the Diaoyu' and Japan refers to as 'the Senkaku'. One historian, Unryu Suganuma, even goes so far as to suggest that 'war might be inevitable between Japan and China if both governments mismanage their diplomatic relations regarding these territorial disputes'.[2] To complicate the situation further, this flashpoint also has a third claimant: Taiwan.

The Senkaku/Diaoyu Islands sit between the three locations, 120 nautical miles off the coast of Taiwan, 200 nautical miles from China and the same distance from the Japanese island of Okinawa. They consist of eight land features, five of which are formally classified as islands and three as barren rocks. In contrast to the high strategic stakes involved, the Senkaku/Diaoyu are small in size, measuring a mere seven square kilometres in total. The largest among them, which the Japanese call Uotsuri and the Chinese, Diaoyu Dao, covers an area of 4.3 kilometres and stands 383 metres from sea level at its highest point. None of the islands would currently be able to sustain human life for any extended period of time – fauna, in the form of feral goats and a rare species of mole, is found there, but there are few if any sources of fresh water. And yet, during those all-too-frequent periods when relations between Beijing and Tokyo have deteriorated, tensions over this seemingly innocuous set of land features have come alive and proved a focal point for those deep-seated antipathies.

China and Japan have endured a troubled history, which has erupted into major conflict several times. In 1894–95, for instance, they fought over the Korean Peninsula, which had traditionally been controlled by the Chinese. This war resulted in China's defeat, and a forced signing of the humiliating Treaty of Shimonoseki, in which it ceded Korea to Japan. The island of Taiwan also became a Japanese colony through this treaty, remaining so until 1945. A decade later, in the Russo–Japanese War of 1904–05, Japan became the first Asian country to inflict military defeat upon a European power. Significantly, during this war Japan seized the Chinese province of Manchuria, which was a Russian colony at the time, deepening its presence and influence in China. From 1937 to 1945, China and Japan fought a devastating war during which an estimated fifteen to thirty-five million perished.[3]

Chinese and Japanese interpretations of the Senkaku/Diaoyu dispute are no different from their highly subjective depictions of wartime history. Beijing makes a claim to the islands on historical grounds: it argues that Chinese fishermen used these land features as navigational aids and for shelter during the fifteenth century, asserting that the islands were named as early as 1403. Beijing points to travel records and maps dating back to the Ming (1368–1644) and Qing (1644–1911) dynasties to support these claims. Indeed, it also has evidence suggesting that Japan has historically acknowledged Chinese ownership of the islands. A map produced by the Japanese military strategist Hayashi Shihei in 1785, for instance, assigns Chinese names to the islands and has them shaded pink – the same colour used for the Chinese mainland. Beijing argues that the islands only fell into Japanese hands when they were 'stolen' from China in the Treaty of Shimonoseki.[4]

Tokyo disputes Beijing's historical claims, contending that it 'discovered' the islands in 1884 and found them to be uninhabited (or *terra nullius,* in legal parlance). Japan conducted a series of surveys of the islands during this period and asserts it found no evidence of Chinese ownership. The islands were subsequently annexed by the Japanese cabinet in January 1895, so Tokyo claims, and became part of the Okinawa prefecture. Japan erected markers at this time. A Japanese businessman, Tatsushiro Koga, was given permission to develop the islands, and he conducted economic activities that included the collection of albatross feathers for export to Europe. Docks, warehouses and reservoirs were also built on the islands. Most significant from Tokyo's perspective is the fact that Japan's 'discovery' of the islands preceded the Treaty of Shimonoseki, which was signed in April 1895 and came into force a month later. This, Tokyo claims, renders the Senkaku/Diaoyu Islands dispute separate from the treaty and the conflict from which it emanated.[5]

Japanese development of the islands continued until the onset of World War II. But the resolution of that bloody conflict six years later served only to muddy the contested waters of the East China Sea. The key wartime conferences held between the Allied nations and, more importantly, the resulting documents – the Cairo Declaration (1943), the Yalta agreements (1945) and the Potsdam Declaration (1945) – said little about the status of the Senkaku/Diaoyu Islands. But as the Allied coalition unravelled in the aftermath of World War II, America began to turn its attention to these islands. With its wartime ally the Soviet Union becoming an adversary in an emerging Cold War, and with China falling to the communists, Washington grew concerned that allowing seemingly inconsequential land features in the East China Sea to fall into enemy hands could increase the vulnerability of US military bases in the Asia-Pacific and, indeed, the United States' entire Cold War strategy in Asia. US policymakers saw a need to maintain control over the Ryukyu island chain, of which they regarded the Senkaku/Diaoyu Islands as part, because they saw it as forming an important link in a larger 'strategic perimeter' designed to prevent the spread of communism further into Asia.

The onset of the Korean War reinforced this line of thinking, with the Ryukyu serving as a launching point for operations into the Asia-Pacific theatre. By this time, America needed to balance its desire to maintain control over the island chain with the need to cultivate an alliance with its former nemesis Japan. Washington saw great potential for Japan to serve as an economic growth engine for Asia, which would improve the stability of this fractious region and create trading opportunities for America. Just as importantly, Japan also served as a valuable location for US military bases. Yet Tokyo was not particularly enamoured with the idea of ceding its surrounding islands to America. To resolve this tension, while the United States decided to maintain sovereign powers over the Ryukyu – giving it administrative, legislative and jurisdictional authority – US secretary of state John Foster Dulles made clear at the Treaty of San Francisco conference of September 1951 that American sovereignty over the Ryukyu would only be 'residual' in nature. By this, Dulles meant that the United States would exercise sovereign powers over the island chain until its international status could be resolved. More significantly, Dulles also stated at this meeting and subsequently that it was not Washington's intention to transfer its sovereign power over the Ryukyu to any nation other than Japan.[6]

A key turning point in tensions over the East China Sea occurred in 1968, when a geological survey conducted under United Nations auspices estimated that substantial oil resources existed beneath the waters surrounding the Senkaku/Diaoyu Islands. By this time, US Cold War geopolitical calculations and machinations also came into play.

The renewal of the Treaty of Mutual Cooperation and Security between the United States and Japan (known as the US–Japan Security Treaty) in 1960 had provoked a strong backlash in Japan, resulting in widespread demonstrations. Protesters saw the potential for the alliance to drag Japan into war with China, North Korea or the Soviet Union. By the late 1960s, violent rallies erupted as Japanese citizens took to the streets in droves to oppose the Vietnam War. Washington grew worried about losing Tokyo as an ally, fearing the possibility of a more independent Japan either developing nuclear weapons or deepening ties with China and the Soviet Union. The Nixon administration, believing that the United States' continuing hold on the Ryukyu would only encourage Japan's drift into the communist camp, announced in November 1969 its intention to consult with Tokyo regarding the islands' reversion.[7] Less than two years later, in June 1971, an agreement was signed, and in May 1972 administrative control of the islands formally reverted to Tokyo.

From its announcement, the prospect of the Ryukyu coming under Japanese sovereignty drew fierce opposition from Taiwan, another American Cold War ally. Beijing's increasing interest in the islands was also important from Washington's perspective, as it occurred against the backdrop of historic efforts by Nixon and his national security adviser, Henry Kissinger, to tilt the Cold War balance by drawing communist China into America's camp. Having to balance Japanese, Taiwanese and Chinese concerns, the Nixon administration announced that the June 1971 treaty would in no way have an impact upon the underlying legal status of the islands, including Taiwan's claims to them. In other words, as one oft-cited analysis of the Senkaku/Diaoyu Islands dispute has observed, 'what the U.S. was giving to Japan with one hand, it was taking away with another'.[8]

Nixon's tilt towards China stunned Japan, prompting Tokyo to quickly normalise its own relations with Beijing in 1972. Beijing continued to assert its claims to the islands, but agreed to put the issue aside. The dispute flared up again in 1978, when more than 140 Chinese fishing vessels – some of them armed and displaying signage asserting China's claims to the islands – sailed within 12 nautical miles of the Senkaku/Diaoyu. Beijing claimed that the incident was an accident, and the two capitals proceeded with two rounds of negotiations, which led to the signing of the Treaty of Peace and Friendship between Japan and the People's Republic of China in August 1978. Chinese leader Deng Xiaoping sagely suggested that the dispute be 'shelved' for a decade, on the basis that the next generation of leaders would be better equipped to break the impasse.[9]

Deng's formula lasted well beyond the decade he envisaged. The relationship between Beijing and Tokyo over the islands had temporary setbacks, such as in November 2005, when a Chinese submarine was detected in waters off Okinawa. But by the late 2000s, the relationship between these two historical rivals was being characterised as a 'warm spring of friendship'.[10] In June 2008, Beijing and Tokyo even managed to agree to pursue joint development opportunities in the East China Sea.

The calm ended abruptly in September 2010, when an allegedly drunk Chinese fishing-boat captain operating close to the Senkaku/Diaoyu Islands plunged his vessel into the side of a Japan Coast Guard ship. Whereas Japan had always arrested Chinese citizens who landed 'illegally' on the islands, it had tended not to charge these individuals. Instead, offenders were swiftly deported back to China, with an eye to defusing tensions that could otherwise have inflamed the broader Sino–Japanese relationship. In the case of the fishing-boat captain, Tokyo broke with tradition and treated the incident as a legal matter, laying charges and holding the captain in custody for more than two weeks. This sparked a diplomatic crisis, with Beijing calling for his immediate release, along with compensation and an apology from the Japanese government.[11]

The fishing-boat collision fed directly into a more serious Sino–Japanese crisis when, in September 2012, the government of Japan announced its intention to 'nationalise' three of the Senkaku/Diaoyu Islands. Uotsuri, Kita and Minami were among four islands purchased by Tatsushiro Koga's son, Zenji Koga, from the Japanese government in the 1930s. The younger Koga had subsequently sold the features to another Japanese family, the Kurihara. In late 2011, Kunioki Kurihara, the private owner of the islands in question, entered into secret negotiations with the notoriously nationalist mayor of Tokyo, Shintaro Ishihara, who planned to use municipal funds to make the purchase. Japan's central government, in a move that it claimed was designed to prevent Ishihara from destabilising Sino–Japanese ties, stepped in and agreed to buy Uotsuri, Kita and Minami from Kurihara for a reported sum of US$25.5 million. Beijing failed to see any altruism in the arrangement, calling the purchase 'a gross violation of Chinese sovereignty' and 'highly offensive to the 1.3 billion Chinese people'.[12] Japan's actions led to the largest anti-Japanese demonstrations in China in almost a decade. Tens of thousands of protesters took to the streets in more than 100 Chinese cities, burning Japanese flags, ransacking Japanese-owned department stores and clashing with riot police, who on occasion used tear gas to control these mostly youthful crowds.

Tensions in the East China Sea intensified over the next two years, taking on a concerning military dimension. In late 2012, a small Chinese maritime surveillance aircraft penetrated Japanese airspace over the islands. Significantly, this was the first such penetration since 1958, prompting Japan to scramble F-15 fighters in response. In early 2013, in two separate incidents, Chinese vessels allegedly locked their fire-control radars – a step usually taken immediately prior to the firing of weapons – upon a Japanese destroyer and a ship-based helicopter. Later that year, Beijing provoked international condemnation when it declared an Air Defence Identification Zone (ADIZ) over part of the East China Sea, including the disputed islands. Beijing announced that any aircraft travelling through this ADIZ would need to notify Chinese authorities and that 'defensive emergency measures' would be taken against non-compliant planes. The United States responded to this move by flying, without notice, two B-52 bombers through the zone. Similar episodes continued during 2014, with reports of Chinese and Japanese aircraft flying dangerously close – on occasion, within metres – of one another.[13]

The friction over the East China Sea began to stabilise in November 2014, when Chinese president Xi Jinping and Japanese prime minister Shinzō Abe met for the first time on the sidelines of the APEC (Asia-Pacific Economic Cooperation) summit in Beijing. The meeting became known for the awkward handshake that occurred between the two leaders before what was reportedly a productive twenty-minute discussion. Beijing and Tokyo were able to arrive at a 'four-point consensus' for improving Sino–Japanese ties. One of these points of consensus was acknowledgement that each side held different perspectives on the disputed islands.[14]

But beneath these diplomatic niceties, East China Sea tensions continued to intensify. As Chinese military aircraft operated further south, near Okinawa and along the Ryukyu, Japanese fighters chased them away in record numbers. In March 2017, Tokyo reported that Japan's air force had conducted 851 scrambles against Chinese intrusions into its airspace over the previous twelve months.[15] The number and duration of Chinese sea patrols around the disputed islands has also increased, as has the size and firepower of the ships and submarines undertaking them.[16]

High stakes: the strategic significance of the islands

Given the two nations' troubled past, it is hardly surprising that many Chinese and Japanese citizens dislike one another. Recent opinion polls suggest that a mere 11 per cent of the Japanese public has a favourable view of China, while an only slightly higher 16 per cent of the Chinese population hold positive impressions of Japan. Significantly, the number of those in each country with a favourable view of the other has shrunk over the past decade. The Chinese and Japanese individuals surveyed routinely describe one another as 'violent', 'arrogant' and 'not honest', according to some polls. A startling 80 per cent of Japanese are concerned that territorial disputes between the two nations could escalate into military conflict, while 59 per cent of Chinese hold the same view.[17] These persistent – and growing – antipathies are a critical driver of hostilities over the East China Sea. Moreover, as the widespread protests following Japan's attempts to nationalise the Senkaku/Diaoyu Islands demonstrate, the nationalist underpinnings of this flashpoint add to its potential for combustion: events could escalate unpredictably and with relatively little warning.

Tensions over the islands are symptomatic of a larger Sino–Japanese power shift. In late 2010, China overtook Japan to become the second-largest economy in the world. This was a position that Japan had occupied for more than four decades. While Japan remains the world's third-largest economy, recent projections produced by the accounting firm PricewaterhouseCoopers (PwC) show it slipping further down this list, to a predicted eighth position by the year 2050. By this time, PwC projects that China's economy will have become the largest in the world, and will be approximately 30 per cent larger than that of the next country on the list, India.[18] China's growing economic and strategic weight is generating insecurities in Japan, due to their geographic proximity and given their troubled history.

The resource potential of the East China Sea is also an important factor. The oil and gas reserves lying beneath these waters are thought to be less than those of the South China Sea, but they are significant. The proximity of East China Sea gas fields to coastal Chinese cities, such as Shanghai, makes them commercially attractive to Beijing. The importance of the area in trade and commercial shipping cannot be underestimated, either. The trans-Pacific trade of both China and South Korea passes through these waters. According to one estimate, approximately one-quarter of all China–US seaborne trade goes through the Osumi Strait, in the northern part of the Ryukyu.[19] Similarly, Chinese trade to Oceania, Central America and South America often passes through the Miyako Strait, which lies between the Japanese islands of Miyako and Okinawa. Most of Japan's seaborne trade to China also passes through the waters of the East China Sea.[20]

Strategically, the East China Sea is highly significant. Chinese strategists view the Ryukyu as a potential barrier, or 'bottleneck', to the Middle Kingdom's ability to project military power more broadly. Beijing is bent on improving its capacity to 'shatter' this bottleneck.[21] It has been developing the means to execute missile strikes and aerial bombardment along the Ryukyu, as well as to swiftly seize islands in this chain should the need arise. Chinese bombers, military aircraft and surface ships now routinely exercise through the Miyako Strait. Highlighting once again the interrelation of Asia's flashpoints, Beijing also sees the Ryukyu as a potential staging point for military operations against Taiwan. The East China Sea's proximity to major Chinese cities, while an economic advantage, is also a strategic vulnerability for China should either Taiwan or the Senkaku/Diaoyu dispute erupt into war.[22]

Last but certainly not least, alliance politics are a compelling factor in the East China Sea. Japan's status as America's closest Asian ally raises the stakes here considerably for Washington. The US– Japan alliance provides America with access to key military bases from which it can project power into Asia. As such, Tokyo and other US allies view Washington's commitment to this alliance as a barometer for American commitment to the region. It is precisely for this reason that Barack Obama, before touring through Asia in April 2014, became the first sitting American president to state publicly that the US–Japan Security Treaty extends to the Senkaku/Diaoyu Islands. Obama reiterated this pledge exactly a year later, as did current US defense secretary James Mattis when he visited Asia in February 2017.[23] Washington has traditionally preferred to take a neutral stance on this and Asia's other territorial disputes; the recent willingness of two US administrations to clarify their commitments in the East China Sea speaks to the intensity of the politics involved.

The Senkaku/Diaoyu dispute: in danger of escalation

As East China Sea tensions sharpened in September 2012, the cover of *The Economist* magazine carried the headline 'Could China and Japan Really Go to War Over These?' above a picture of the disputed islands. The prospect of the world's second-and third-largest economies coming to blows over uninhabited rocks is ostensibly bizarre. And neither Beijing nor Tokyo craves such a conflict. Their historical animosities notwithstanding, the two countries are intertwined economically. China has moved to become Japan's leading trading partner, while Japan is China's second-largest trading partner, behind the United States.[24] According to some estimates, the Sino–Japanese trading relationship is the third-largest in the world.[25] Consistent with this, figures produced in late 2016 estimated that 32,313 Japanese firms were operating in China. Significantly, this is considerably more than the approximately 8422 US firms operating there.[26] Moreover, while Tokyo initially seemed to feel coolly towards recent Chinese economic schemes – such as the Belt and Road Initiative (BRI) and the Asian Infrastructure Investment Bank (AIIB) – it has gradually become more favourably inclined, despite their potential to augment Beijing's regional influence. In a major speech delivered in June 2017, Prime Minister Abe suggested that the BRI 'holds the potential to connect East and West as well as the diverse regions found in between'.[27] And Japan has recently shown some inclination to join the AIIB too.[28]

Yet China and Japan could quite conceivably go to war as a result of an accidental military clash or a miscalculation. The chances of such an occurrence have likely increased since Beijing's November 2013 declaration of an East China Sea ADIZ. Japan too has an ADIZ encompassing the disputed islands, which overlaps with China's. This is one factor that has resulted in Chinese and Japanese military aircraft coming into frequent contact. And the pilots from each nation are not operating according to a common set of rules and procedures. China's reporting requirements for aircraft entering its ADIZ go well beyond what other countries typically require; China seems to be treating its ADIZ essentially as a form of territorial airspace. In response, Tokyo has largely refused to recognise the zone and has instructed its pilots not to comply with Beijing's demands. There is little evidence of pilots on either side displaying what is referred to in the trade as 'good airship', with accusations of aircraft flying dangerously close to one another emanating from both sides. The same problems are replicated below, between ships on the waters of the East China Sea.[29]

The virulent nationalism underpinning this flashpoint also increases the potential for a clash. The sheer scale of Chinese protests following Japan's nationalisation of the Senkaku is a case in point: tens of thousands of protesters in more than 100 Chinese cities shows that levels of animosity and insecurity are running high. So too does the Chinese public's response in late 2014 when Beijing and Tokyo moved to ease tensions. As news of this development emerged, scores of Chinese internet users unleashed their frustrations online. Some bayed for blood, calling for the immediate initiation of hostilities with Japan. Others turned their anger against Beijing, alleging that Chinese diplomats were working for the 'Ministry of Traitors'.[30]

Beijing thus faces a peculiar dilemma. Nationalism is a useful means for rallying support around the Chinese flag and the Chinese Communist Party; at the same time, China's leaders fear such sentiment running rampant and ultimately being turned against them. Almost paradoxically, the intensity of nationalist sentiment around territorial disputes in the East China

Sea is at once both stabilising and destabilising. It serves to limit the likelihood of either Beijing or Tokyo using military force for fear of letting the nationalist genie out of the bottle. And yet were that genie ever to escape, the chances of uncontrollable military escalation occurring, and occurring rapidly, are dangerously high.[31]

It is difficult to anticipate how full-blown conflict in this flashpoint would play out. China certainly has a numerical advantage over Japan in terms of weaponry. It spends three times as much annually on its defence. According to the most recent figures, China has sixty-two submarines in its arsenal, versus Japan's nineteen. The Chinese Navy operates eighty-three surface combatants, whereas Japan operates only forty-seven. China also runs a larger coast guard, with a fleet of 440-plus vessels, versus Japan's estimated 367.[32] It is worth noting that despite a dedicated military modernisation effort over the last two decades, a significant amount of older equipment remains in service in the Chinese military. Questions also continue to be raised around the quality of the equipment that China's indigenous defence industry is producing. Yet the German philosopher Hegel's well-worn maxim that 'quantity has a quality all of its own' is clearly relevant in this case.

However, despite its numerical advantage, Beijing must be far from certain that it would prevail in an East China Sea conflict. If the United States were to come to the aid of its Japanese ally, as it has indicated it would, the odds would tilt considerably in Tokyo's favour. Even if America did not become involved, a Chinese victory would not be assured. During the Sino–Japanese War of 1894–95, Japanese forces scored a swift and relatively easy win against the Qing dynasty's massive military. The professionalism of the Imperial Japanese Navy contributed to their unanticipated victory. Today, the Japanese Navy enjoys a similar reputation for excellence, especially in areas of critical importance to this flashpoint, such as undersea warfare.[33] The risk of China's ongoing military modernisation being derailed by a devastating military defeat – of the kind it experienced during the late nineteenth century – is one clear constraint upon Beijing's willingness to use military force over the Senkaku/Diaoyu Islands.

For much of the period since World War II, Article 9 of the Japanese constitution – the famous 'pacificist clause' – has constrained Tokyo's ability to use force in geographic areas that do not involve direct protection of the Japanese homeland. Although these arrangements largely held during the Cold War, Japanese prime ministers from the early 2000s on, starting with Junichiro Koizumi (who held the office from 2001 to 2006), have moved to stretch and reinterpret Article 9. In September 2015, Japan's parliament passed controversial legislation to loosen these legal constraints still further, while in May 2017 Prime Minister Shinzō Abe made a surprise announcement outlining his intention to revise the constitution to make 'explicit the status' of the Japanese military by 2020.[34] Consistent with this, from 2012 onwards Japan's defence budget has increased by somewhere in the order of 1 to 2 per cent per year, in contrast to its stagnation throughout the previous decade. The Japanese Ministry of Defense's budget request for the 2018 fiscal year (US$48.1 billion) was the largest on record, and marked a 2.5 per cent increase on that approved for the previous year.[35]

In October 2013, Abe gave approval for the military to shoot down foreign drones entering Japan's ADIZ above the Senkaku/Diaoyu Islands, while Tokyo also reportedly has plans in place to base surface-to-ship missiles (with a range of approximately 300 kilometres) on some of the disputed islands. These are the longe-strange missiles ever produced by Japan.[36]

None of this is to suggest that Japan is eager to use its increasingly potent military in this flashpoint. As Michael Green, one of the world's leading authorities on Japanese foreign and security policy, has observed, Tokyo has traditionally been risk-averse when it comes to the use of force.[37] Moreover, Japan's lack of recent experience in combat would likely reinforce that sense of aversion should push really come to shove around the Senkaku/Diaoyu Islands. For as James Holmes, another leading strategic analyst, has noted in reference to the East China Sea, 'Battle, not technical specifications, is the true arbiter of military technology's value. Accurately forecasting how ships, planes, and missiles will perform amid the stresses and chaos of combat verges on the impossible.'[38]

But the vulnerability of modern military technology could also have the perverse effect of making conflict in the East China Sea more likely. Scholars Robert Ayson and Desmond Ball argue that even a limited military clash between Japan and China could quickly escalate into full-blown, very possibly nuclear, war. The reason is simple. Modern militaries rely upon a sophisticated network of systems to track their opponent's movements. Underwater sensors, for instance, are used to detect enemy submarines. But these systems are highly vulnerable to attack and difficult to defend. Should a Sino–Japanese conflict occur, Beijing and Tokyo would face the temptation of escalating the shooting quickly to target their opponent's systems, rather than holding off and risking an attack against their own.[39]

America could also get caught in this technological trap because the systems employed by the United States and Japanese militaries in the area have become increasingly integrated. America and Japan, for instance, have jointly developed a whole string of underwater sensors stretching from the Ryukyu across to Taiwan. These sensors track Chinese submarine movements between the East and the South China Seas, and between the East China Sea and the Pacific Ocean. It is hard to imagine a Chinese attack on those systems not provoking a military response from Washington.[40]

Breaking the circuit: the role of diplomacy

Diplomacy was effective for many decades in reducing the risks of escalation over China's and Japan's claims in the East China Sea. This was due largely to Deng's formula for peace. Whenever the pendulum of Sino–Japanese relations swung significantly to one side, Beijing and Tokyo could fall back on Deng's suggestion to shelve the disputes.

What initially looked like a promising diplomatic initiative in the East China Sea emerged from one of those periods of acrimony. In May 2004, Japan discovered Chinese drilling installations in the Chunxiao gas field. This field lay approximately five kilometres on the Chinese side of a 'median line' that Japan had proposed – and which Beijing had contested – for dividing the East China Sea equidistantly between them. Because of that field's proximity to the median line, Tokyo accused China of siphoning off gas from the Japanese side.[41]

Beijing and Tokyo engaged in eleven rounds of negotiations during the mid-2000s. The result was a June 2008 consensus to establish a 2700-square-kilometre 'joint development zone' in a gas field straddling Japan's proposed median line.

Consistent with Deng's formula, the joint development zone was located away from the disputed islands. Had the zone been closer to the islands, an argument could be made that this would have weakened Japan's case by more formally acknowledging Beijing's claim to them. However, the June 2008 consensus was ultimately not a binding agreement. Its implementation required the signing of a treaty. And to this day, that step has not been taken.[42]

The September 2010 collision between the Chinese fishing boat and the Japanese coast guard ship ultimately delivered a terminal blow to Deng's formula. In the period of heightened animosity that followed, senior Japanese officials denied that the 1978 consensus had ever existed.[43] In response to Japan's arrest of the fishing-boat captain, Beijing suspended elite-and provincial-level contacts with Japan and appeared to place an embargo on the export of rare-earth elements – which are used in the manufacture of mobile phones, flat-screen televisions, wind turbines and guided missiles.[44] The temporary freeze in high-level diplomacy became more permanent following Japan's nationalisation of the Senkaku/Diaoyu Islands two years later.

Multilateral diplomacy has sometimes served as a useful circuit-breaker for Beijing and Tokyo, during such periods when bilateral channels are shut off. For instance, in an unusual episode in the history of Sino–Japanese diplomacy, Chinese foreign minister Li Zhaoxing and his Japanese counterpart, Taro Aso, were reportedly able to carry out 'meaningful discussions' when they ran into each other in the toilets on the sidelines of the July 2006 ASEAN Regional Forum. This encounter occurred during one of the more acrimonious periods in the relationship.[45]

More often, however, multilateral forums have proven arenas where China and Japan have played out, and often deepened, their differences over the East China Sea. Tempers flared infamously at the May 2014 Shangri-La Dialogue in Singapore. In his keynote address, Prime Minister Abe unleashed a barrage of criticism against China, promising a larger Japanese role in regional security to counter Beijing's assertiveness, and pledging to provide additional weaponry to the Philippines and Vietnam. Not to be outdone, the lead Chinese speaker at the event, Lieutenant-General Wang Guanzhong, hit back, characterising Abe's (along with US Defense Secretary Chuck Hagel's) address as 'full of hegemony, full of words of threat and intimidation'.[46]

Deter and prevent: the best hope for the future

In the absence of a viable diplomatic solution, deterrence remains the preferred approach. The United States is key to this approach, adopting a two-dimensional strategy. Despite professing neutrality in relation to the disputed islands, Washington has moved to deter acts of aggression by formally committing to defend Japan should Beijing attempt a forceful resolution. However, Washington has also sought to reassure Beijing that its intentions in the East China Sea are purely defensive and that it will, if required, rein in unduly provocative acts by Japan.[47] Indeed, for much of the history of the US–Japan alliance, Beijing has viewed America as a metaphorical 'bottle cap' keeping the Japanese military genie in check.

Yet as tensions in the East China Sea have intensified, America's carefully calibrated deterrence strategy has come in for increasing scrutiny. Faced with growing Chinese assertiveness, Japanese leaders have become more anxious over Washington's pledge to come to their aid. These fears stem partly from the fact that America's commitment to its Asian allies has traditionally been somewhat ambiguous, especially when compared to more clearly codified US– European alliances. America's Asian alliances tend to be vague in terms of what they cover: while an ally's home territory is generally regarded as within the scope of the relevant treaties, it is often unclear whether US commitments extend beyond this to cover areas subject to territorial dispute.

The tactics that Beijing has employed in the East China Sea – establishing an incremental presence around the Senkaku/Diaoyu Islands through predominantly non-military (coast guard and fishing) vessels, without resorting to the use of military force

– has further worried Japanese policymakers. Tokyo fears that such an approach may, over time, result in Japan losing its hold on the disputed territories without a shot being fired, and therefore without the US–Japan Security Treaty ever being invoked.

Responding to these anxieties, Washington has tried to offer Tokyo a greater level of assurance. The Obama administration's official statements affirming that the alliance extends to the Senkaku/Diaoyu Islands can be read as part of this campaign. So too can the joint military exercises that the United States and Japan now routinely conduct close to the islands.[48]

China certainly has cause to see these steps as more than mere symbolism. Japan sits at the apex of an unstated hierarchy of America's Asian alliances. Maintaining an Asian military presence would be considerably harder, if not impossible, for the United States without Japan, meaning that America has vital interests at stake in this flashpoint. The growing level of integration between American and Japanese forces reflects this, while also serving to reinforce the credibility of Washington's defence commitments to Tokyo. Unlike in the South China Sea, where the United States has wavered in its commitment to its Filipino ally, the integration of US and Japanese forces gives Washington skin in this game.

This is not to suggest that the United States has abandoned the second element of its East China Sea deterrence strategy: reassuring Beijing of its defensive intent and willingness to rein in Tokyo if needed. Indeed, some commentators caution American policymakers against backing Tokyo too unambiguously in the East China Sea, lest it encourage potentially destabilising Japanese assertiveness.[49] Washington has shown some readiness to be critical of its ally: in December 2013, for instance, the US Embassy in Tokyo issued a statement criticising Prime Minister Abe's visit to the Yasukuni Shrine on the grounds that it exacerbated tensions with Japan's neighbours.[50]

During his first, ill-fated term as prime minister of Japan, Abe and his Chinese counterpart, Hu Jintao, agreed to create a 'communication mechanism' designed to avoid unintended clashes between the navies of their two countries.[51] Initially the intent was to establish a 'hotline': a direct telephone link between leaders that could be used in crisis situations. Talks proceeded in fits and starts over the next decade, punctuated by periods of actual Sino–Japanese crisis. Progress towards the hotline stalled, for instance, in the wake of the September 2010 fishing boat collision. Yet Beijing's calculus appears to have been altered by a series of 'near misses' involving Chinese and Japanese aircraft operating over the East China Sea in mid-2014.[52] The hotline concept evolved and was formally renamed in January 2015 as the Japan–China Maritime and Air Communication Mechanism. This re conceived arrangement would still involve a telephone link between senior defence officials, and it would also include other measures aimed at reducing the chances of an accidental clash, such as the implementation of common radio frequencies for Chinese and Japanese ships and aircraft.

A significant 'breakthrough' was finally achieved in Shanghai in December 2017, as both sides reached an in-principle agreement on implementation of the communication mechanism.[53] A follow-up memorandum to begin operation of the mechanism was signed the following May, although it is unclear whether this agreement will cover the disputed islands. As in the ill-fated June 2008 consensus for a joint development zone, Tokyo insisted that no mention of the islands be made for fear of strengthening China's claim. Beijing argued otherwise, and the two sides compromised by simply skirting the issue.[54]

A similar agreement between Japan and Russia, arrived at in 1993, is a useful comparison. While Japanese intercepts of Russian aircraft over the East China Sea are second only to those involving Chinese planes, the seemingly much lower incidence of dangerously 'close calls' can be attributed to the existence of agreed protocols.

Questions do remain over what, if any, role such a mechanism would ultimately play in an actual crisis. In past Sino–American crises, senior US officials and military leaders have often been unable to communicate with their Chinese counterparts or to even identify who the appropriate contact on the Chinese side is. When an American spy plane collided with a Chinese fighter near China's Hainan Island in April 2001, for instance, Washington's calls to China's foreign ministry and to its military headquarters went unanswered.[55] The hope is that communications between China and Japan do not suffer the same fate.

Crowded and contested waters: the need for a plan

When Dean Acheson was US secretary of state during the early years of the Cold War, he spoke of the need for America to create 'situations of strength' – areas around the Soviet periphery where the United States and its allies were so strongly unified that Moscow wouldn't entertain employing aggression there.[56]

The East China Sea is a contemporary situation of strength. This flashpoint's balance of military power is firmly in America and Japan's favour, and will remain so for the foreseeable future. Beijing can be fairly certain that the United States would come to Japan's defence in the event of East China Sea conflict, given that this is America's most important Asian alliance, and without it, an American presence in this part of the world would be next to impossible. That is why US senior officials routinely refer to Japan as the 'cornerstone' of America's Asia policy.

As China's strategic weight increases, it will almost certainly continue to test Japanese and American resolve around the disputed islands. The US–Japan alliance will need to adjust to meet that challenge. This may require a more visible US military presence. America and Japan might need to redeploy military assets from elsewhere in the region and beyond. If Tokyo and Washington make such shifts, China will not mount a serious military challenge, either to seize the disputed islands or to control the East China Sea. Beijing knows it would end up on the losing side of a very costly conflict if it did.

As these waters become more crowded and contested, however, the biggest danger is not a planned military campaign, but a lower-level military clash occurring during a tense time in Sino–Japanese relations. Some might disagree, pointing to the hundreds of Soviet–American maritime incidents that occurred during the Cold War without escalation.[57] What differentiates this situation from almost any other, though, is its strong nationalist underpinnings. What would have happened in January 2013, for instance, if the skipper of that Japanese destroyer had not held his nerve, believing instead that the Chinese frigate that had just locked its weapons-targeting radar on his ship was being steered by a rogue captain about to send a couple of missiles his way? And what if that Japanese skipper had fired first, sinking the Chinese vessel and unleashing a sea of anti-Japanese protests across China? In such a scenario, could China's leaders have sat idle without risking that nationalist sentiment turning against them?

Useful steps have been taken to head off this possibility with the recent breakthrough on a China–Japan communication mechanism. But the fact that it took a decade of negotiations to reach consensus doesn't auger well.

Moreover, the new measures do not go far enough. History tells us that mechanisms intended to avoid crises are far from failsafe. New dangers can also emerge in the midst of crisis and, as when a car goes into a skid, different techniques and approaches are often needed to navigate through these and to prevent further escalation.

At the height of the Cuban Missile Crisis of the 1960s, both sides made mistakes that could have ended in nuclear catastrophe. The commander of a damaged Soviet submarine momentarily believed that war had erupted and ordered the launch of his craft's nuclear torpedo. At Vandenberg Air Force Base in California, an ICBM test-firing scheduled well in advance of the crisis was conducted, which fortunately the Soviets did not detect. And as the crisis drew to a close, American radar operators incorrectly reported that a missile had been launched from Cuba due to a training error.[58]

Accidents of this sort are unavoidable, especially in the heat of crisis. Beijing and Tokyo need, with much greater urgency and ambition than they have shown, to agree in advance upon ways to manage such episodes when they inevitably occur during a major Sino–Japanese crisis.

But nationalism of the most visceral variety pulls them back. The dispute over the Senkaku/Diaoyu Islands is about much more than contested rocks or access to oil and gas resources. It is about America's place in Asia's evolving strategic order, the growth and stability of communist China, and the simmering tensions between two of Asia's oldest and most inextricable rivals. The ghosts of Asia's past continue to haunt the East China Sea.

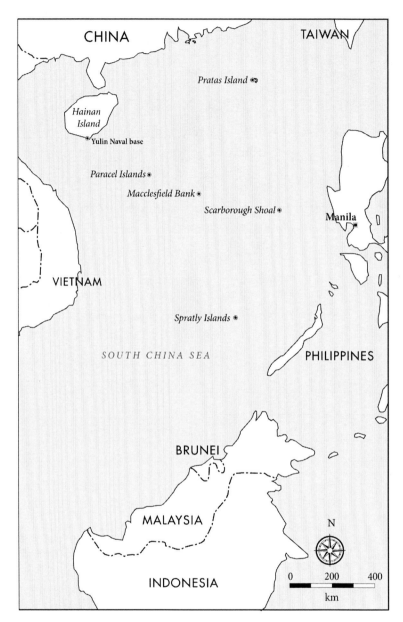

CHINA

TAIWAN

Pratas Island

Hainan
Island

Yulin Naval base

Paracel Islands

Macclesfield Bank

Scarborough Shoal

Manila

VIETNAM

Spratly Islands

SOUTH CHINA SEA

PHILIPPINES

BRUNEI

N

MALAYSIA

0   200   400

INDONESIA

km

THE SOUTH CHINA SEA FLASHPOINT

CHAPTER 4

CHINESE LAKE: THE SOUTH CHINA SEA

The USS *Harnett County* has a harrowing history. During World War II, it served as an American tank landing ship. By 1970, it had become the RVNS *Mỹ Tho* following its donation by Washington to the South Vietnamese Navy. After a brief period traversing the rivers of Vietnam in the country's infamous civil war, this 100-metre-long vessel changed its name and its national affiliation following the fall of Saigon. By 1976, it had moved to the Philippines and was known as the BRP *Sierra Madre.* In 1999, Philippines president Fidel V. Ramos ordered that the *Sierra Madre* be run aground on a submerged reef in the South China Sea. This reef is known as Ayungin in Manila, Ren'ai Jiao in Beijing, and Second Thomas Shoal throughout much of the Western world.

Small numbers of Filipino marines spend six-month rotations on this bastion in the sea. The ship is now in a parlous state, rusted and riddled with holes – including many on its main deck, where a careless misstep could result in an unfortunate marine plunging to their death in the cavernous hull below. Rations are in short supply, meaning that the ship's inhabitants are forced to fish in the surrounding shark-infested waters to supplement their provisions. In 2014, China sought to blockade the *Sierra Madre* to prevent fresh rations reaching the crew. Beijing has long sought the ship's removal. It has even threatened to tow or sink it.[1]

The *Sierra Madre* is an apt metaphor for where the South China Sea is headed. This is Asia's most complex and confusing flashpoint. Yet, for all its complexity, it is also the least combustible. The use of military force is unlikely, as none of Asia's major powers have interests in it vital enough to wage war over. The possible exception is Beijing, whose strategic aspirations of projecting military power into the Pacific require it breaking from the geographical constraints of the South China Sea to operate beyond these waters.

The low risk of imminent conflict also reduces the perceived need for resolution. Diplomacy has been tried, but progress is painstakingly slow.

However, the future of this area is not uncertain. Just as the waters of the South China Sea corrode the *Sierra Madre,* so too will Beijing's creeping assertiveness allow it to increase its influence and ultimately impose its will on this flashpoint.

Dangerous ground: navigating a contentious past

Several countries lay claim to portions of the South China Sea, a 3.7-million square-kilometre body of water with hundreds of islets, rocks, low-tide elevations and reefs. These claims often overlap and have morphed over time. In November 2011, US secretary of state Hillary Clinton, standing on the deck of an American warship docked in Manila Bay, provoked Beijing's ire by referring to this body of water as the 'West Philippine Sea', using the name preferred by the Philippines.[2] If she were speaking at the iconic Vietnamese military port of Cam Ranh Bay, she may have instead played to Hanoi's preferences, describing it as the 'East Sea'. Beijing favours 'South China Sea' because this implies Chinese ownership.

Similar descriptive disputes are rife when it comes to the South China Sea's innumerable land features. What Beijing calls the Xisha Islands, for example, are known in Hanoi as the Hoàng Sa Archipelago. Much of the rest of the world refers to this chain of islets as the Paracel Islands.

Four island groupings are at the crux of disputes over this area. The two most prominent are the Paracels and the Spratly Islands.

The Paracels are located approximately 350 kilometres from China's Hainan Island and 400 kilometres from the Vietnamese coastline. They consist of some 130 small coral islets and reefs that are divided into two groups: the Amphitrite group in the northeast, named for the French frigate *Amphitrite,* which observed the landmasses during a seventeenth-century voyage carrying missionaries to China; and a 'Crescent' group in the west, which form a rough hemisphere enclosing a deep lagoon. Woody Island, which is part of the Amphitrite group, is home to approximately 1000 Chinese residents. The Paracels are currently occupied by China, but Taiwan and Vietnam also lay claim to them.

The Spratlys lie further south, between Vietnam and the Philippines. They comprise 100 islets and reefs scattered over approximately 410,000 square kilometres. China, Taiwan and Vietnam lay claim to all of the group, while Brunei, Malaysia and the Philippines assert ownership over parts of them. Barring Brunei, each of the petitioners occupy parts of the Spratlys.

The Pratas Islands, three land features located 300 kilometres south-east of Hong Kong, is the third contested grouping. Only one of these features (Pratas Island) is above water, and it has been occupied by Taiwan since the late 1940s. But it is also claimed by China. Dominated by a 5000-foot runway, it is home to approximately 200 Taiwanese Coast Guard personnel. A handful of ecologists are also based there, having arrived after Taipei declared the islands a national park in 2007. The area is rich in flora and fauna, home to more than 200 species of plants and birds and over 500 kinds of fish.[3] However, this too is a source of tension, with Taiwan's Coast Guard regularly required to ward off Chinese poachers.[4]

The last disputed grouping includes Macclesfield Bank and the Scarborough Shoal, two submerged features that sit between the Paracels and the coastline of the Philippines. China and Taiwan claim each of these features, while the Scarborough Shoal is also contested by the Philippines.[5] As with the other disputed islands, these areas are valuable partly because they are full of marine resources. Scarborough Shoal, for instance, is surrounded by a 150-square-kilometre lagoon that Chinese and Filipino fishers have exploited for decades.[6]

For hundreds of years the South China Sea was regarded as a danger zone rather than a strategic opportunity. Allegedly, there is evidence of human engagement in these waters dating as far back as the third century BC, but this evidence is scant. The lack of a more comprehensive historical record stems from the fact that many of the mariners who traversed the South China Sea did not live to record their voyages. These waters were renowned for their strong tidal currents, their violent and unpredictable storms, and their complex topography, which in places included hazardous shallows. Reference can be found in third-century AD Chinese literature to the many 'magnetic rocks' located in waters south of China. Several hundred years later, another Chinese writer likened the area to the *wei-lu*: a mythical drain where the world's oceans meet and descend into the underworld.[7] Navigational charts drawn up during the British Empire labelled the islets, rocks and reefs of the South China Sea more simply, although no less ominously, as 'dangerous ground', and advised that the area was best avoided.

By the twelfth century, some of the challenges of navigating the rocks and shoals of the South China Sea had been alleviated. The invention of the maritime compass and watertight hulls allowed vessels to venture out much further from the coastline and into open waters. This encouraged a growth in maritime trade, which from the thirteenth to fifteenth centuries began to burgeon. China established itself as the region's dominant maritime power; the Ming dynasty, which reigned from the mid-1300s through to the mid-1600s, exerted such control that the South China Sea became a veritable 'Chinese lake' through a combination of China's economic influence and naval dominance. Exemplifying this supremacy, the legendary eunuch Admiral Cheng Ho led seven official voyages to Africa in the early fifteenth century, initially to track down Emperor Zhu Di's missing nephew, Zhu Yunwen. Zhu Di had overthrown his relative, whom his forces had reportedly killed when they burned his palace to the ground. But rumours subsequently surfaced that Zhu Yunwen had escaped, disguised as a monk, and was living abroad. Each of Cheng Ho's voyages, which were also designed to demonstrate China's naval prowess, transited through the waters of the South China Sea.[8]

Four centuries of Chinese naval dominance came to an abrupt end in the late fifteenth and early sixteenth centuries. This precipitous decline was due to several factors: internal squabbles in the Ming court, the prohibitive costs associated with building and maintaining a massive naval fleet, burgeoning trade deficits and an unstable currency. These factors combined to force the late Ming and its successor, the Qing dynasty, to downsize.[9] Yet as European interest in the South China Sea began to grow, it provoked Chinese vulnerabilities and sensitivities. This situation finally came to a head in 1884–85, when China waged a disastrous war against the French: China's maritime power was decimated and its naval incompetence exposed. The nation lost its vassal state Vietnam, along with control of the South China Sea. But in the post-war agreement of 1887, France appeared to acknowledge that the Paracels and the Spratlys were part of China.[10]

From 1902 to 1908 China launched three official expeditions intended to consolidate its remaining claims following the humiliating defeat by the French. France, however, swiftly resumed its South China Sea patrols, and in 1889 proposed the construction of a lighthouse on one of the Paracel Islands.[11] Yet Paris ultimately waited until the mid-1920s to make a play for the islands, when it began conducting 'scientific surveys' of the Paracels. In April 1930, with China severely weakened and plunging into civil war, it made its decisive move. The French warship *Malicieuse* took formal possession of Spratly Island and several of its surrounding features. The French seemed oblivious to the fact that the British had also laid claim to Spratly Island and another landmass in the area. According to London, the British whaling ship *Cyrus* had discovered the island in 1843 and named it after its captain.[12] The French and the British quietly continued this dispute, until they put it in abeyance when the two countries found common cause in their concerns over Japan's developing designs on the South China Sea.

By the mid-1930s, Japanese interest in the South China Sea had taken on decidedly strategic dimensions. British and French anxieties were aroused in part by the way Japan had utilised Taiwan – which it had occupied in 1895 – as a staging point for operations in the Sino–Japanese war of 1937. London and Paris were especially concerned that Tokyo might use Hainan Island as a launching pad for challenging European hegemony in the South China Sea. For Paris, the Paracels' proximity to French Indochina served as an additional source of apprehension.

From the late 1930s, these British and French fears were realised. In 1937, Japan occupied Pratas Island and gained a foothold on the two largest islands in the Spratlys: Itu Aba and Spratly Island. In 1938, it established a presence on Woody and Lincoln islands in the Paracels. And by 1939, the worst fears of London and Paris materialised as Japan seized Hainan Island and declared sovereignty over the entire Spratly group. Japan established a submarine base on Itu Aba, and used the Paracels and the Spratlys as listening posts. The former 'Chinese lake' was now essentially under Japanese control.[13]

This period of Japanese occupation turned out to be short-lived: it ended suddenly following Japan's defeat in World War II. The vacuum left by Tokyo's withdrawal from the South China Sea ushered in a new era of complexity and contestation.

The Philippines, which had been granted independence from the United States in July 1946, wasted little time in joining this centuries-long contest. A Filipino businessman named Tomás Cloma, along with his brother and around thirty compatriots, landed on the Spratlys' Thitu Island and Itu Aba. Finding these unoccupied, Cloma named the area 'Kalayaan' (which in Tagalog means 'Freedomland') and issued a declaration entitled 'Notice to the Whole World', announcing that fifty-three land features in the Spratly area collectively constituted an independent state.[14] The Cloma brothers appear to have enjoyed some government backing, including from the then vice-president of the Philippines, Carlos P. Garcia. But it was not until the early 1970s that Manila officially claimed 'Kalayaan' and sent military forces to the Spratlys. Nonetheless, the Cloma brothers' audacious land grab provoked immediate reactions from several other claimants. Taiwan deployed a naval detachment to Itu Aba, China moved to permanently occupy other features in the Spratlys, and South Vietnam claimed ownership of the Spratlys *and* the Paracels.[15]

In the late 1960s, speculation began to mount that the South China Sea was rich in oil. This prompted other littoral states to stake their claim. During the 1980s, for instance, Malaysia and Brunei each declared a 200-nautical-mile exclusive economic zone (EEZ) that extended out to the Spratlys, allowing them to exploit marine resources in that area. As the number of South China Sea claimants increased in the 1970s and 1980s, so too did the temperature around this flashpoint. The Chinese and Vietnamese navies clashed over the area in January 1974, and again in March 1988. Sometime during the second half of 1994, Beijing built structures on the Spratlys' aptly named Mischief Reef, which was claimed but not occupied by the Philippines. Manila only became aware of these developments early the following year. Even then, it was only able to send a small and largely impotent detachment of ageing aircraft, helicopters and ships in response.[16]

The Mischief Reef incident served, somewhat ironically, as a catalyst for an unanticipated period of calm. Much of the heat dissipated from disputes over the South China Sea in the late 1990s and early 2000s, to the extent that many commentators considered the area no longer worthy of the 'flashpoint' moniker. Manila, recognising its limited ability to push back against a rising China, turned to its fellow members of the Association of Southeast Asian Nations (ASEAN) and proposed a code of conduct for regulating international behaviour in these disputed waters. In late 1999, China was brought into the discussions. While the formal and binding code that the Philippines had in mind was a bridge too far for Beijing, in November 2002 an historic, albeit non-binding, Declaration on the Conduct of Parties in the South China Sea (DoC) was signed.

It proved the long calm before a sudden storm.

Tempests of tension: a series of turning points

In March 2009, friction returned to the South China Sea, bringing about an escalation in anxiety in the Asia-Pacific region. Five Chinese vessels antagonised an American surveillance ship, the USNS *Impeccable,* while it was conducting routine operations just south of Hainan. In a series of aggressive manoeuvres, they sailed dangerously close to the ship and dropped pieces of wood in its path. Unarmed, the *Impeccable* could only fire its water cannons upon the Chinese vessels. This did little to deter the crews, who simply stripped to their underwear and continued the harassment.[17]

In April 2012, a more serious crisis erupted, after Manila deployed its largest warship to detain Chinese fishermen in the Scarborough Shoal. A ten-week stand-off ensued between Chinese and Filipino vessels. China's defence minister warned Manila to exercise discretion in words and deeds should it wish for a peaceful resolution.[18] The stand-off was allegedly defused when a senior Obama administration official, Kurt Campbell, brokered a deal with a high-level Chinese counterpart, Fu Ying, in a Virginia hotel room. The terms of this arrangement outlined that Chinese and Filipino vessels were to leave the Shoal simultaneously. However, while Manila kept its side of the bargain, apparently under US pressure, Beijing did not. Within months of the stand-off, it had secured defacto control of the area.[19]

Another crisis broke out in May 2014 – this time involving Chinese and Vietnamese vessels – after Beijing parked an exploratory oil rig within Vietnam's EEZ, near Triton Island in the Paracels. Ships from both sides rammed one another repeatedly over several months, before Beijing withdrew the rig, one month earlier than planned, in July 2014.[20]

Around this time, Beijing's assertiveness took a new turn when it embarked on a huge land reclamation and construction effort on the seven Spratly features it occupies. Most nations with interests in the South China Sea have engaged in land-reclamation activities. What differentiated China's effort was the scale of the operation and the pace with which its dredgers dug up sediment from the seabed, turned it into sand and piled it onto a reef. Vietnam, one of the more active South China Sea land reclaimants, has created 120 new acres – the equivalent of 100 football ovals – at ten of the features it occupies. China, by contrast, has created a massive 3200 acres, or approximately 3000 football ovals.[21] Admiral Harry B. Harris Jnr, the commander of the US Pacific fleet, christened it a 'great wall of sand' in March 2015.[22]

Only months after this, Beijing announced an end to its land-reclamation program and maintained that it had no intention of using the Spratlys for military purposes. Recent photos published in the Philippines press showing largely complete air and naval bases in Chinese outposts on the islands seem to suggest otherwise.[23] So too did revelations in early 2016 that China had installed powerful surface-to-air missiles with the capacity to shoot down aircraft flying at 80,000 feet, as well as incoming ballistic missiles, on Woody Island.[24] Beijing has since deployed similar missiles further south in the Spratlys.[25]

Another key turning point came in July 2016, when the Permanent Court of Arbitration at The Hague, which resolves disputes that arise out of international agreements between nations, ruled on proceedings that the Philippines had initiated against China in January 2013. Manila had asked the tribunal to examine three issues: the veracity of China's historical claims to approximately 90 per cent of the South China Sea, the status of particular maritime features within this body of water and the lawfulness of certain Chinese actions in the area. China had challenged the tribunal's jurisdiction to rule on these matters, refusing to participate in the proceedings. Contrary to widespread expectations, the tribunal found overwhelmingly in favour of the Philippines. Beijing's 'historic rights' were judged invalid and its land-reclamation program found to be illegal, alongside its harassment of Filipino fishers. China was also chastised for the irreparable environmental damage its land reclamation has done to the marine ecosystem.[26]

As expected, Beijing rejected the tribunal's findings. Surprisingly, however, a brief period of tranquillity followed the July 2016 ruling. The Philippines' May 2016 election of Rodrigo Duterte, a populist president with virulent anti-American views, was a critical factor here. Duterte has made good with Beijing, unceremoniously announcing Manila's 'separation' from the United States while speaking before an audience of Chinese businesspeople in October 2016.[27] In late 2017, ASEAN and China agreed restart discussions on the detail of a South China Sea code of conduct.[28] While sceptics saw this development as a Chinese stalling tactic, it nonetheless served to further dampen tensions in the area.

The history of the South China Sea is much like the intrepid waters themselves: periods of calm are inevitably interrupted, almost cyclically, by tempests. And today, history is repeating. To Beijing's outrage, the Trump administration has stepped up its freedom-of-navigation operations – naval patrols that challenge the legality of China's artificial features in the South China Sea. Beijing has responded by upping the tempo of its military drills. In March 2018, it sailed a massive naval flotilla into the area to participate in exercises centred on its aircraft carrier, the *Liaoning.* Beijing has pledged to make these drills a monthly occurrence.[29]

Critical crossroads: where ambition and anxiety meet

Economic factors have long driven interest in this area. The South China Sea is rich in fish, oil and gas. According to some estimates, approximately 12 per cent of the world's total fish catch is taken from these waters. The activity is proceeding at such an alarming rate that stocks look set to halve by as early as 2045, with some local species already considered near extinction.[30] The coastal states of the South China Sea – Brunei, Cambodia, China, Indonesia, Malaysia, the Philippines, Thailand and Vietnam – are among the world's leading consumers and exporters of fish. While some of their catch is sent to key export markets in the United States and Europe, their citizens also eat twice as much seafood per day as individuals in other parts of the world, raising the spectre of malnutrition as fish stocks plummet.[31] The economic gains to be had from lucrative seafood exports, when combined with these food-security issues, mean that dire environmental predictions have done little to curb the plundering of the region's stocks.

It is far from clear how much oil and gas the South China Sea contains. The tensions in this area have hampered seabed exploration and prevented definitive estimates of the extent. One of the more authoritative estimates, produced by the US Energy Information Administration, suggests a figure of eleven billion barrels of oil and 190 trillion cubic feet of natural gas.[32] The Chinese National Offshore Oil Corporation is significantly more bullish, putting this figure at 125 billion barrels of oil and 500 trillion cubic feet of natural gas.[33] Resource extraction at those high levels would present significant challenges, especially given the South China Sea's demanding geology, inclement weather and under developed infrastructure. One respected commentator, BBC News reporter Bill Hayton, estimates that while up to one-third of the South China Sea's oil and gas resources could conceivably be brought to the surface, only around 10 per cent could be extracted on a commercially viable basis.[34]

But it is the South China Sea's strategic location more than these economic attractions that explains the high-stakes game at play in this flashpoint. The sea serves as a maritime gateway between the Pacific and Indian oceans. More than half of the world's commercial shipping passes through these waters, carrying in excess of US$5 trillion of trade each year.

This trade passes through one of four narrow 'choke points': the Malacca, Sunda, Lombok and Makassar straits. The Strait of Malacca, located between the Malay Peninsula and the Indonesian island of Sumatra, is an especially important channel, providing passageway for an estimated 25 per cent of all oil transported by sea. Despite the substantial maritime traffic it carries, the Strait of Malacca is a mere 1.5 nautical miles wide at its narrowest point.[35]

Beijing feels these strategic realities acutely. Approximately 80 per cent of China's oil imports come through these waters on their way from Africa and the Middle East. So too do significant imports of gas. The Chinese leadership calls this their 'Malacca dilemma'. They fear that the United States and its allies could seek to block off these choke points in the event of a conflict, slowly strangling the Middle Kingdom. Beijing is seeking to avoid this potentiality by implementing a massive pipeline construction program; the aim is to move oil and gas overland from places such as Myanmar and Russia. While this may reduce Beijing's dependence upon the South China Sea, critics of the project have raised serious questions about whether these pipelines can be built quickly enough to meet China's growing energy demands and whether they can be protected from sabotage.[36] Wrapping the project into China's massive Belt and Road Initiative of Eurasian infrastructural development could potentially go some way towards pumping the pipeline-construction process along. But even then, the scale of China's growing energy demand is such that pipelines will likely only prevent China's 'Malacca dilemma' from deepening, rather than alleviating it altogether.

Military insecurities also drive Beijing's interest in this flashpoint. In an interesting parallel with Admiral Harris's 'great wall of sand' description, Xi Jinping has called upon China to develop 'an impregnable wall for border and ocean defense'.[37] The South China Sea is central to this goal. Its deep waters provide what strategic analysts call a 'bastion' for China's growing submarine fleet. The largest of China's submarines berth under a mountain in the Yulin Naval Base at the southernmost part of Hainan Island; [38] precisely because the Paracels sit at the approach to Yulin, Beijing has a strong desire to control them. Chinese strategists are also alert to the possibility of American ships and planes using the South China Sea as a staging point in a conflict over Taiwan.

For China to realise another of Xi's aspirations – that of becoming a great 'maritime power' – it will need to exert influence beyond what Beijing terms its 'near seas' (the East China, South China and Yellow seas) into what it calls the 'far seas'. Here, again, the South China Sea is critical. Along with the Miyako Strait in the East China Sea, the Luzon Strait, located between Taiwan and the Philippines, can accommodate China's submarines and larger vessels. Were a Chinese aircraft carrier to deploy to the Indian Ocean, for instance, it would need to do so via one of these two routes. The

Miyako Strait is the riskier proposition, given its proximity to Japan, a longstanding Chinese rival with powerful anti-ship and anti-submarine warfare capabilities. Neither the Philippines nor Taiwan possesses such capabilities, making the 3000-feet-deep waters of the Bashi Channel in the Luzon Strait more appealing. Moreover, the notoriously inclement weather in this area makes anti-submarine warfare difficult, meaning that Chinese submarines can more easily slip out into the open seas undetected.[39]

Underpinning Xi's ambitions is a desire to make China the dominant power in Asia and to right the historical wrongs of its 'century of humiliation' in the process. Beijing started to lose its 500-year grip over the South China Sea during that period; this is one reason why it rails so vociferously today against external involvement in the area. The United States and Japan are frequent targets of such criticism. When Tokyo announced in March 2017 that it would be sending the largest vessel in its navy, the helicopter carrier JS *Izumo,* on a three-month tour through the South China Sea, Beijing's response was strident. In a direct reference to Japan's militaristic past, Chinese foreign ministry spokesperson Hua Chunying urged Tokyo 'to remember history and mind its words and steps'. And, 'If the Japanese side still refuses to realize its error and plays up regional tensions,' she added, 'China will definitely respond to any action that harms China's sovereignty and security.'[40]

Like China, the United States' primary interest in the South China Sea is strategic. Addressing the June 2017 Shangri-La Dialogue in Singapore, US Defense Secretary James Mattis asserted: 'We will continue to fly, sail and operate wherever international law allows, and demonstrate resolve through [an] operational presence in the South China Sea and beyond.'[41] Access to Asia's waterways has been a constant theme in US grand strategy, going back to July 1853, when Commodore Matthew C. Perry's Black Ships steamed into Tokyo Bay and forced a feudal Japanese state to open trade with America. Washington regards military and economic access to Asia as one and the same. Right of entry to the South China Sea also goes to the heart of America's identity as a military superpower, with global interests and an ability to shape developments anywhere in the world. Without admittance to these waters, the US Navy would not be able to move as quickly, or as cost-effectively, between the Pacific and the Indian oceans.

Keeping the South China Sea 'free and open' is one reason why the US Navy spends an average of 700 'ship days' per year operating in these waters. This means that at least one to two US Navy vessels are in the South China Sea at any given time, conducting operations ranging from military exercises to routine patrols, their presence designed to reassure American allies and partners.

Access to the South China Sea also enables the United States to conduct surveillance operations within China's

EEZ. Such activities are arguably not illegal under the United Nations Convention on the Law of the Sea, which permits any state the right to freedom of navigation and overflight through these zones. Yet they remain a source of considerable tension in relations between China and America. There is some debate in Washington as to whether the intelligence gained through close-in surveillance is worth the diplomatic damage.[42] Persisting with these operations not only raises the risk of a clash between American and Chinese ships and aircraft operating close to the Chinese coast, but also the likelihood of Beijing mimicking this approach elsewhere in the world – as it did in July 2017, when it sent a surveillance vessel to monitor a US– Australia military exercise conducted inside Australia's EEZ.[43]

The South China Sea also matters to Washington because of the alliance politics involved. Despite Rodrigo Duterte's public attempts to divorce the United States, the Philippines remains a formal US treaty ally. This means that Washington's level of commitment to Manila in the South China Sea potentially influences its reputation as an alliance partner. Some Japanese observers, for instance, grew anxious over Washington's unwillingness to take a much stronger line against Beijing during the Scarborough Shoal stand-off of 2012. They feared that this could be a harbinger of an American unwillingness to side with Japan and to stave off the Chinese challenge to Asia's US-led security order.[44]

With US leadership in the Asia-Pacific being called into question, Tokyo's renewed interest in the South China Sea is unsurprising. Japan's nightmare scenario is a complete American withdrawal from the region that leaves Japan to suffer under Chinese hegemony. Tokyo is therefore at pains to encourage a continued US military presence in Asia. This includes support for Washington's South China Sea engagements. When the *Izumo* sailed into these waters in June 2017, for instance, it did so alongside the American super-carrier USS *Ronald Reagan.*[45] Beyond its existential fears, Tokyo also sees this flashpoint through the lens of the East China Sea. It is concerned that any aggressive manoeuvres Beijing employs in the South China Sea will set a precedent for what in time transpires closer to Japanese shores.

As a hedge against possible US withdrawal from the region, Tokyo is also helping to beef up the military capabilities of several claimants of land features in the South China Sea. In August 2016, the Philippines took delivery of the first of ten maritime patrol vessels funded by a Japanese loan worth approximately US$200 million.[46] Likewise, in January 2017 Japanese prime minister Shinzō Abe promised Vietnam six new patrol boats to replace the second-hand vessels Tokyo had previously provided Hanoi.[47] Tokyo's aim here has not been to take sides in the South China Sea disputes; like the United States, Japan has largely maintained a neutral position on the validity of arguments put forward by the various claimants. Nor is such assistance purely designed to help these nations resist Chinese coercion. Rather, its underlying objective is to dissuade Manila and Hanoi from cutting separate South China Sea deals with Beijing that could potentially undermine international maritime law. Freedom of navigation in the area is critically important to Japan, given that much of its energy trade passes through these waters.

The rules-based international order is also important to many of the region's smaller and middle-sized nations that, in the words of Australian former diplomat Peter Varghese, 'can neither bully nor buy [their] way in the world'.[48] In keeping with this theme, during a keynote address at the 2017 Shangri-La Dialogue, Australian prime minister Malcolm Turnbull outlined a vision for an Asian region 'where might is not right, where transparent rules apply to all – the big fish, the little fish and the shrimps'.[49] If anything, though, the gulf between that aspiration and the reality of the strategic manoeuvring and power plays in this area appears to be widening.

Inevitable war? The rhetoric versus the reality

The prospects for military conflict in the South China Sea are being talked up across the world. The nationalistic Chinese newspaper *Global Times* has been at the forefront of this conjecture, suggesting that US–China conflict over the sea is 'inevitable' unless

Washington is willing to back down.[50] Another controversial editorial in this state-owned outlet cautioned Australian military aircraft against flying too close to China's artificial islands. 'It would be a shame,' read the editorial, 'if one day a plane fell from the sky and it happened to be Australian.'[51] And it hasn't been just the Chinese beating the South China Sea war drums; in 2017 Donald Trump's ill-fated secretary of state, Rex Tillerson, threatened to deny China access to its artificial islands. Making good on that threat would almost certainly have required the use of armed force. Only months before joining the Trump team, another of that administration's once-central figures, Steve Bannon, claimed 'there's no doubt' that China and the United States will fight a war over the South China Sea within the decade.[52]

Conflict between these key powers in the South China Sea would have catastrophic consequences. The disruption to trade that would occur in one of the world's busiest maritime regions would result, according to some expert estimates, in a '$5 trillion meltdown'.[53] Commercial shipping would be significantly reduced, and, if history is a guide, would soon come to be controlled by governments and directed towards national war efforts. Such shipping would also be costly, and significantly more dangerous than during peacetime. Vessels would be vulnerable to the region's burgeoning submarine fleets, which can attack with little warning. The costs of redirecting shipping via less treacherous routes, which would add significant time to any cargo deliveries, would also be substantial. According to some estimates, the act of rerouting oil tankers alone would cost Japan US$600 million and South Korea US$270 million each year. Australia could be forced to reroute up to US$20 billion worth of cargo each year in the event of a South China Sea conflict.[54]

As Beijing's strategic weight increases, South-East Asian states' ability to hold their own in armed conflict with China is diminishing rapidly. Vietnamese forces were defeated in the Paracel Islands in 1974 by a ramshackle flotilla of Chinese naval ships still weakened by the travails of the Cultural Revolution.[55] The Chinese military today is a considerably more powerful proposition. The deterrent effect of this military power is already in evidence: in July 2017, Beijing reportedly threatened to attack Vietnamese-occupied features in the Spratlys if Hanoi did not cease oil-exploration activities within its EEZ; Hanoi acceded swiftly to these demands.[56] While the Philippines and Vietnam have embarked on programs to modernise their militaries, and while their proximity to the South China Sea gives them some geographical advantages, Beijing has had a substantial head start over these nations. Moreover, China has not had to endure the same level of economic volatility and political instability that some South-East Asian governments, such as Indonesia and the Philippines, have faced over the past two decades.

But China faces its own constraints. Its capacity to project military power across the entire South China Sea remains limited. China currently has only two aircraft carriers in its arsenal – one bought second-hand from the Ukraine, the other domestically built. This puts it well behind America's fleet of ten nuclear-powered carriers, which can each accommodate more than twice as many aircraft as their Chinese counterparts. A key motivation behind Beijing's construction of artificial islands may well be to compensate for this shortcoming; these islands enable Chinese military aircraft to operate further away from the mainland than they otherwise could. However, this strategy has limitations: even if the islands were to survive the waves of air and missile strikes sent their way during a major conflict, there would not be sufficient space on these small outposts to sustain the requisite levels of troops, missiles, basic rations and electricity. That is why the defence analyst Kyle Mizokami concludes that 'China would be wise to consider the islands only as a temporary solution, until the People's Liberation Army has enough hulls to maintain a permanent presence in the region'.[57]

Despite Steve Bannon's incendiary comments, the United States also has little appetite for conflict in the South China Sea. Washington's interests in this area are significant, but they are not 'vital' – those interests core to America's continued independence, and over which the nation would be willing to go to war. The United States' strategic relations with the Philippines and Vietnam are in a very different category from its alliance with Japan. When asked during an April 2014 tour through Asia whether the US–Philippines Mutual Defense Treaty would apply in a South China Sea conflict, President Obama tellingly side-stepped the question.[58]

The most likely trigger for conflict in the South China Sea would be an 'accidental' clash. There have certainly been several near misses in recent years, both in the air and on the water. In May 2016, for instance, the Pentagon accused a Chinese fighter plane of undertaking an 'unsafe' intercept after it flew within 15 metres of an American EP-3 surveillance aircraft.[59] The number of claimants and external actors with a stake in this flashpoint heightens the risk of such clashes occurring. For example, Chinese and Vietnamese ships collided – both intentionally and unintentionally – during the oil rig crisis in May 2014, resulting in the sinking of at least one Vietnamese fishing vessel.[60] In June 2009, a Chinese submarine collided with anti-submarine sonar equipment being towed by a US destroyer off the coast of the Philippines.[61]

Not since World War II has the South China Sea played host to major hostilities. The largest loss of life seen in the area in recent decades occurred at the 1974 battle in the Paracels. Tragic though that episode was for those who died, this naval skirmish lasted mere hours and resulted in the deaths of just over 100 personnel.

What explains the absence of escalation in a sea where military clashes have not been in short supply? One factor is the maritime geography. History tells us that adversaries have often found themselves unwilling or unable to wage war across large bodies of water. The hardline American professor John Mearsheimer calls this phenomenon the 'stopping power of water'.[62] According to his thinking, when clashes occur in maritime environments, escalation occurs much more slowly, giving diplomats time to negotiate solutions. Another leading American academic, Robert Ross, explains that in such instances, unlike in cases where countries share a land border, 'neither side has to fear that the other's provocative diplomacy or movement of troops is a prelude to attack and immediately escalate to heightened military readiness. Tension can be slower to develop, allowing the protagonists time to manage and avoid unnecessary escalation.'[63] That is why conflict is much less likely in the vast maritime expanses of the South China Sea, compared with the much shorter warning times at play in the confined strategic spaces of the Korean Peninsula.

Duplicitous diplomacy: tipping the scales to China

Commentators and experts have suggested several diplomatic angles for addressing South China Sea disputes. One route is to cement the current order by implementing the principle of international law *uti possidetis, ita possideatis* – a concept first employed in Ancient Rome, meaning 'what you have, you may continue to hold'. Applying this archaic idea today would, for example, allow Vietnam to maintain possession of the twenty-five features it currently occupies in the Spratlys. A more modest version of the formula calls for stake holder nations to halt all 'provocative' acts, such as land reclamation and the militarisation of islands.[64] But Beijing has rejected such proposals outright.

As in the East China Sea, joint resource development has also been attempted. In 1990, Chinese premier Li Peng – better known as the 'Butcher of Beijing' for his central role in the June 1989 Tiananmen Square massacre – called for disputes between China and other nations to be shelved in favour of joint development. The problem with his proposal was that Beijing would only partake if other parties first acknowledged its claims to sovereignty. In 2005, China, the Philippines and Vietnam agreed to conduct a joint seismic survey in one portion of the South China Sea, as a precursor to a larger development project. That initiative also made little headway.[65] Manila tried once more in 2011, proposing that joint resource development take place within a newly created Zone of Peace, Freedom, Friendship and Cooperation. Under this scheme, claimants could still unilaterally extract resources within their own EEZs.

Beijing swiftly vetoed this proposal, arguing that the areas claimed by Manila belonged to China.[66]

The most high-profile example of diplomacy is the proposed code of conduct for regulating behaviour in the South China Sea. Building on the earlier, non-binding Declaration on the Conduct of Parties in the South China Sea, its aim is to establish agreed behaviours that avoid claimants using force to advance their interests. The code is therefore more a risk-reduction measure than a means to resolve tensions in the area. Even with that less ambitious aim, negotiations have proceeded fitfully for nearly two decades, often progressing at a glacial pace when they do take place. They have encompassed frequent disagreements, including over whether the code should be legally binding and precisely which parts of the South China Sea it applies to.[67]

Diplomacy in this arena has encountered three obstacles. First, because there is only a remote chance of conflict in this flashpoint, there is little urgency around diplomatic solutions. Unless and until there is a major South China Sea crisis, this sense of complacency will prevail. As two longstanding experts versed in this flashpoint, Leszek Buszynski and Christopher B. Roberts, have observed:

> The shock effect of a crisis often releases blockages in immobilised decision-making systems, making political leaders aware of the dangers of continuing with familiar behaviour, and demanding

of them a major change of policy and attitude ... at the present moment, it seems that only crisis will trigger the necessary change of attitude over the South China Sea, particularly within China.[68]

Second, Beijing is guilty of dragging its heels. There are several reasons for this. As the military balance in the South China Sea tilts in its favour, Beijing is reluctant to commit to an arrangement, such as the implementation of *uti possidetis, ita possideatis,* when its negotiating position may be stronger in the future. China's capabilities in resource extraction already far outstrip those of the other claimants in the area, and this gap will only continue to grow. But Beijing also has diplomatic insecurities: it has long harboured suspicions that Asia's multilateral groupings could become forums for 'ganging up' diplomatically against it. These worst fears were realised at the November 2011 East Asia Summit, the first attended by an American president. With Barack Obama at their back, South-East Asian leaders exerted pressure to convince China's reticent premier, Wen Jiabao, to sit down with them to discuss the South China Sea.[69]

Third, ASEAN – the most prominent multilateral organisation in this drama – has struggled to come to an agreed position on the South China Sea. Some commentators suggest that its failure to do so is a sign of ASEAN's demise. Cracks started to appear in Phnom Penh in July 2012, when ASEAN, for the first time in its forty-year history, failed to produce a joint statement at the end of its annual summit, due to internal squabbling over whether to mention the Scarborough Shoal stand-off. Such scenes have been witnessed repeatedly in the period since, such as at a July 2016 'Special ASEAN–China Foreign Ministers' Meeting' that was held in the Chinese city of Yuxi. On this occasion ASEAN did issue a statement expressing concern over developments in the South China Sea. However, the statement was withdrawn only hours later for 'urgent amendments'.[70]

Chinese pressure has allegedly been behind ASEAN's splintering. Following the ill-fated 2012 summit, for instance, many commentators claimed that Beijing had leaned heavily upon the Cambodian hosts, pressuring them to adopt an uncompromising stance about any public mention of Beijing's South China Sea activities. China's status as Cambodia's leading source of foreign investment certainly would have given it sufficient leverage.[71] Similarly, the bizarre retraction of ASEAN's statement in 2016 was reportedly due to opposition from Cambodia and Laos, the latter another state strongly reliant on Chinese investment.[72]

The new Chinese lake: why China will prevail

Some commentators argue that the best way to counter Chinese coercion over the South China Sea is for the United States to back South-East Asian countries with claims in the area. This would require a significantly greater US presence in the region, and more cooperation between the United States and its Asian allies. Larger numbers of US ships, submarines and aircraft, some of which may even be stationed in the area permanently, would entail greater US access to the military bases of South-East Asian allies. The US military would exercise more frequently with its Asian partners. To help claimant states resist China, the United States would also need to provide them with more-potent capabilities – drones, mines, missiles and air defence systems. Ely Ratner, who was an adviser to former US vice-president Joe Biden, goes so far as to suggest that Washington should be ready to assist South-East Asian allies with their land-reclamation efforts and by fortifying the features they occupy.[73]

Such commentaries contend that it will be fatal for Asia's strategic order, and for America's place in it, if Washington is unwilling to stand up to China in this way. A 2016 report by a leading American think tank, for instance, predicts that without such measures the South China Sea will belong to Beijing by 2030. They envisage a beefed-up Chinese Navy with multiple aircraft carriers at its disposal. At least one of these carriers would be floating in the South China Sea at all times, demonstrating Beijing's dominance and intimidating rival claimants. The South China Sea would become a 'Chinese lake' again, the report argues – much like the Caribbean and the Gulf of Mexico have become American lakes today.[74]

There is one major problem with these proposals. The only way America can successfully stare China down is to convince Beijing that it is willing to go to war should Beijing refuse to change course. This would be a difficult convincing act – America's unwillingness to take a tougher stance during the Scarborough Shoal stand-off in 2012 was telling. So too was US Defense Secretary James Mattis's refusal, at the June 2018 Shangri-La Dialogue, to confirm whether the US–Philippines Mutual Security Treaty extends to Filipino-occupied land features and vessels operating in the South China Sea.[75] As one of Singapore's leading strategic intellectuals, Bilahari Kausikan, concludes:

> The US has made clear that the US–Japan alliance covers the [Senkaku/Diaoyu] islands; it has been ambiguous about the US – Philippines alliance, and hence in effect made clear that it does not cover the disputed areas in the South China Sea. War in support of the principal East Asian ally is credible, if unlikely. War over rocks, shoals and reefs would be absurd.[76]

Other commentators argue that, rather than competing with Beijing directly, Washington would be better to step back its presence in the region to accommodate China's growing power and ambition. Such proposals have so far tended to be vague on detail, with advocates unwilling to specify in precisely which areas America should retreat.[77]

What would happen if Washington gave Beijing the strategic space it craves? Such an accommodation would not mean complete US withdrawal from the region. The US Navy could continue to operate in these waters, but America would cease its high-profile yet largely ineffectual freedom-of-navigation operations challenging the legality of China's artificial islands. It would also cease its provocative surveillance flights within China's EEZ, employing alternative techniques for gathering the intelligence these obtain.

This strategy would not be without risk. It could be perceived as a sign of American weakness in the Asia-Pacific, encouraging Chinese expansion elsewhere in the region. It might cause America's Asian allies to further lose confidence in Washington's commitment to them.

Yet these risks could be managed. If the United States decreased its presence in this area, it could re-assign some of its South China Sea military deployments. Conceivably, these could be shifted to locations where America enjoys 'situations of strength' and where US vital interests *are* at stake, such as on the Korean Peninsula or in the East China Sea. That would help to reassure its more anxious allies, especially Japan. Most importantly, such redeployments would dissuade Beijing from aggressive or expansionary behaviour in those two flashpoints by reinforcing the military superiority that America and its allies enjoy – China would be foolish to enter a conflict in which it would be so outgunned.

In late May 2018, Admiral Philip S. Davidson succeeded Harry B. Harris as commander of the rebranded 'U.S. Indo-Pacific Command'. During his April 2018 confirmation hearing, Davidson created headlines by asserting that 'China is now capable of controlling the South China Sea in all scenarios short of war with the United States'.[78]

That is an exaggeration, and perhaps reflects the fact that this rising star of the US Navy has little experience in Asia.[79] Davidson's analysis underestimates the constraints Beijing confronts in the South China Sea. For instance, China has a limited capacity for anti-submarine and amphibious warfare – two critical capabilities, given the terrain of this flashpoint. Many of Beijing's military aircraft are based on 1950s-era technology. Moreover, the last time China fought a major conflict in the area was in the late 1970s, against Vietnam.

Davidson's overblown conclusion about conflict in the South China Sea is simply hyperbole. War is not inconceivable, but it is highly unlikely. Maritime disputes rarely escalate across such vast expanses of water. More importantly, America has no vital interests at stake in the South China Sea. But his remarks nonetheless offer a useful insight into how this flashpoint will evolve. Just as the waters of the South China Sea wear away incessantly at the corroding hull of the *Sierra Madre,* China's growing weight – evident already in its unprecedented land reclamations and the militarisation of its occupied land features – will slowly but surely shift the power balance in this area decisively in its favour. Although the transition won't happen quickly, these waters will gradually become a Chinese lake once more – just as they were for hundreds of years prior to the late nineteenth century.

Is that such a bad thing? Contrary to breathless analyses cautioning against this future, Beijing needs the South China Sea to remain free and open just as much as any other country, including the United States. China's survival depends upon it. In Australia, much commentary focuses on the fact that up to 60 per cent of the country's seaborne trade passes through these waters. Less noted is that three-quarters of this trade travels to and from China, most of it energy exports critical to the Middle Kingdom's continued growth.[80] What interest would Beijing have in threatening such passage?

But President Donald Trump clearly believes otherwise. Rather than stepping back the US presence in the South China Sea, he seems bent upon making it a focal point in a deepening Sino–American rivalry. After a period of pause, his administration has upped the tempo of its provocative freedom-of-navigation operations, and has vowed to 'compete vigorously' with Beijing over this flashpoint.[81] That is a serious misstep. At some point in the coming two or three decades, Beijing will feel sufficiently confident to push back hard against Washington in the South China Sea and call its bluff. The US government will then be faced with two choices. It could either up the ante and potentially find itself in a conflict with China it has no interest in fighting. Or it will be forced to yield to China in a humiliating way. Neither is a good outcome for US standing in Asia, or for this region's strategic future, which depends on safe and open access to the South China Sea. The United States would be much better served by stepping back now.

Anything is possible under this president, of course, and the South China Sea could conceivably fall off Trump's radar just as quickly as it appeared on it. But what little evidence there is to go on suggests otherwise. While on the campaign trail in 2016, for instance, Trump linked Beijing's militarisation of the South China Sea to its lack of respect for the United States and the US presidency – subjects close to this 'America first' candidate's heart.[82] Following his election, Trump's first of two tweets on the South China Sea was paired with virulent criticism of Beijing's trade and monetary policies – again, topics of immense importance to him.[83]

Trump's relative silence on the South China Sea in the period since is due to his need for Beijing's support in squeezing North Korea. But with Pyongyang and Washington now walking back from the brink of war, and with US–China rivalry intensifying, the chances of Trump pursuing the most sensible course of action over the South China Sea are slim. And the further he wades into these historically troubled waters, the harder it will become for future American presidents to pull back.

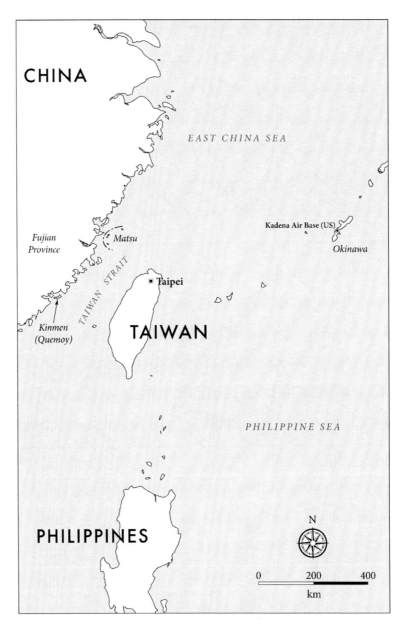

THE TAIWAN FLASHPOINT

CHAPTER 5

A COMING CATACLYSM: TAIWAN

Xi Jinping has a dream: a dream to make China wealthy and formidable again. The 'great rejuvenation of the Chinese nation',[1] as Xi likes to call it, has powerful domestic drivers. If Xi accomplishes the historically unprecedented feat of pulling more than a billion people from poverty, it will deliver a huge boost: both to his legitimacy as China's 'leader for life', following China's abolition of presidential terms, and to that of the Chinese Communist Party. But Xi's 'Chinese Dream' also has external motives. The 'century of humiliation', which saw the once formidable Middle Kingdom carved up by foreign powers, remains deeply etched in the Chinese psyche. To Xi's way of thinking, only a strong China will stamp out the possibility of such ignominy occurring ever again.

Central to Xi's Chinese Dream is regaining the lost island of Taiwan. Whereas his predecessors Mao Tse Tung and Deng Xiaoping thought that resolving this perceived blight on China's past could wait a hundred or even a thousand years, Xi is not displaying similar patience. A man in a hurry, Xi is on record asserting that the Taiwan problem 'cannot be passed from generation to generation'.[2] In a three-and-a-half-hour address to China's National Party Congress in October 2017 – an address in which Xi was already expected to take a hard line on Taiwan – he went even harder than most commentators anticipated: 'We will resolutely safeguard the national sovereignty and territorial integrity and will absolutely not tolerate the tragedy of the country's split ... We will have a firm will, sufficient faith, and adequate capacity to defeat any intention of "Taiwan independence" in any form.'[3] In a March 2018 speech Xi went further still, promising that Taiwanese separatism 'will be condemned by the Chinese people and punished by history'.[4]

The tensions around Taiwan have typically lain dormant for decades at a time. Yet sooner or later, each period of stability erupts into one of intense crisis. The current dormancy has lasted for more than two decades. This has led some commentators to conclude that this dispute should no longer even be considered a geopolitical hotspot, a flashpoint.[5] This chapter begs to differ. Against the backdrop of Xi's Chinese Dream, Taiwan is on the cusp of a new crisis. Political and demographic shifts on the island, Beijing's growing impatience with the dispute's irresolution, and mounting uncertainties around Washington's willingness and ability to come to the island's defence are converging to send this area in a very dangerous direction.

Game of thrones: from colonisation to crisis point

The island of Taiwan is approximately 36,000 square kilometres. It is separated geographically from China by the 180-kilometre-wide Taiwan Strait. Throughout its history, numerous actors have laid claim to its shores. The Dutch East India Company was the first entity to formally administer the island, for a brief period from 1624 to 1662. Ironically, this was at China's suggestion. Dutch administration was ended by the Chinese warlord Zheng Chenggong, whose force of 25,000 to 30,000 troops seized control of the island. Zheng used Taiwan as a base for rebellion against China's ruling Qing dynasty. The Qing subsequently took the island by force in 1683, ushering in more than two centuries under its rule. During this period, the British, American, French, Japanese and Prussian governments all entertained thoughts of acquiring Taiwan – either through buying it or by seizing it from the Qing. Ultimately, the Qing's defeat in the Sino–Japanese war of 1894–95 resulted in their ceding of Taiwan to Tokyo under the Treaty of Shimonoseki.

Regardless of which nation has controlled Taiwan, conflict has been a constant feature of the island's history. As early as the late 1500s, Japan sent troops to conquer Taiwan, only to be beaten back by warriors from the island's indigenous communities. Likewise,

French forces held a portion of Taiwan for a year, from 1884 to 1885, before Qing resistance, coupled with bouts of cholera and typhoid among the troops, forced their withdrawal. Local uprisings continued throughout the periods of Dutch, Chinese and Japanese rule. More than 150 sizeable rebellions occurred under Qing rule alone. The Japanese responded brutally in quashing similar opposition to their rule. In May 1902, in a sequence resembling a scene from the television drama *Game of Thrones,* Japanese authorities invited rebels to surrender; 360 accepted the invitation, and when they arrived at the banquet ostensibly in their honour, the doors were locked and they were slaughtered in the dining hall. Later, the Japanese allegedly used chemical and biological weapons to staunch an indigenous uprising.[6]

The political consequences of World War II had a profound impact on Taiwan. Because China had fought on the Allied side, the victors initially supported the idea that Taiwan be returned to the Chinese mainland. Yet the ruling nationalist party in China, the Kuomintang (KMT), was soon at civil war with the Chinese Communist Party, led by Mao Zedong. General Chiang Kai-shek's KMT forces succumbed to their communist counterparts in the ensuing Chinese Civil War (1945–49). Those who survived retreated to Taiwan, where Chiang established a Chinese government in exile. The stated intention of the severely depleted KMT was to one day regain control of the mainland. So was born the Taiwan flashpoint as we currently know it.

It did not take long for tensions between the 'two Chinas', located on either side of the Taiwan Strait, to flare. The first of three cross-strait crises erupted in August 1954 when Chiang – who was by then negotiating with Washington to join its fledging network of Asian alliances – moved 70,000 troops to two small island groupings off China's coast, Quemoy and Matsu. These offshore islands were among several controlled by the KMT, which saw them as an important foothold in the grand plan to retake the mainland. In September 1954, China responded by bombarding Quemoy with up to 5000 artillery shells, prompting the United States to deploy three aircraft carriers to the area.

The connections between the four flashpoints are crucial here. Four years earlier, in 1950, the Truman administration's failure to make its commitment to defending Korea clear had encouraged North Korea's surprise attack against the South. To avoid repeating this error, Truman's successor, Dwight Eisenhower, inked a formal alliance agreement with Taiwan in November 1954. China condemned the pact and, warning of unspecified 'grave consequences' if the United States did not withdraw its military support for Taiwan, resumed bombardment of Quemoy and Matsu. Of greater concern to Washington, reports emerged that Beijing was planning to invade these offshore islands. The Eisenhower administration responded by threatening to use tactical nuclear weapons to quash any invasion. This threat seemed to have the desired effect, prompting China to back down and indicate its openness to negotiations aimed at defusing the crisis.[7]

Those negotiations commenced in August 1955, but they ultimately ended in stalemate. This led to a second Taiwan Strait crisis, in 1958. It was again sparked by Chiang deploying troops – this time 100,000 – to Quemoy and Matsu. The troops collected intelligence on China, interrupted Chinese military communications and sowed general discord on the mainland, prompting China to deploy aircraft opposite Taiwan. A series of aerial dogfights between Chinese and Taiwanese fighter planes ensued, and Washington again sent aircraft carriers to the region. What followed was largely a repeat of 1954: Beijing resumed shelling the offshore islands and threatened to 'liquidate' Taiwan; Washington threatened force (which this time prompted Moscow to assert that an attack on China was an attack on the Soviet Union); Beijing signalled its willingness to negotiate. In one of the more unusual episodes of crisis management, China indicated in the negotiations that it would limit its shelling of the islands to odd days of the week, while Taiwan pledged to return fire only on even days. This bizarre arrangement ran right through to the late 1970s.[8]

Nixon's historic visit to communist China in February 1972 – the first by an American president – has been described as 'the week that changed the world'.[9] It was a bold geopolitical play, designed to tilt the Cold War balance of power between the United States and the Soviet Union in America's favour. It also had significant implications for Taiwan. Nixon and Mao were unable to reach a resolution on what to do with Taiwan once US–China diplomatic 'normalisation' was complete. Nixon's national security adviser, the consummate geopolitician Henry Kissinger, presented a somewhat ambiguous formulation that became the basis of a *modus vivendi.* The United States would 'acknowledge that all Chinese on either side of the Taiwan Strait maintain there is but one China' and would not do anything to 'challenge that position'.[10] From that point on strategic ambiguity was a deliberate and, indeed, defining feature of Washington's approach to Taiwan.

As Nixon and Kissinger had hoped, the normalisation of US– China relations fundamentally altered the global balance of power in America's favour. The price Washington had to pay for this significant Cold War victory was an end to its alliance with Taiwan. Taipei was given only hours' notice before US president Jimmy Carter announced this development in December 1978. Taiwan's supporters in Congress were enraged because they had not been consulted. In response, they drafted legislation for the ongoing provision of American support to Taiwan, which ultimately became the 1979 *Taiwan Relations Act.* This legislation obligated the United States to supply the island with the 'defensive' weaponry required 'to enable Taiwan to maintain a sufficient self-defense capability'. The clause remains a point of severe contention in US–China relations. In addition, the distinction between 'offensive' and 'defensive' weaponry has never been clear. A case in point is submarines, which can be employed for both defensive and offensive operations. Added to this, the *Taiwan Relations Act* included an ambiguous American commitment to regard military action or economic sanctions targeting Taiwan as 'a threat to peace in the Western Pacific and of grave concern to the United States'.[11]

The son of Chiang Kai-shek, Chiang Ching-kuo, was by this time the president of Taiwan. He pleaded with the Americans to reconsider, arguing that Washington was on the wrong side of history and that Taiwan would one day retake the mainland.[12] Over time, reality set in and Taipei gradually relinquished this aspiration. It instead began to think about Taiwan's future as an independent political actor. Chiang Ching-kuo put in motion a series of political reforms in the mid-1980s that set Taiwan on a path to become a democracy. In part, this decision was made to shore up the legitimacy of the KMT, which had committed authoritarian abuses during the almost four decades of its rule under martial law. More importantly, political reform improved the prospects for continued American support to the island. Chiang's deputy, Lee Teng-hui, succeeded him as president and in March 1996 became the island's first democratically elected leader.

Taiwan's inaugural presidential election provided the trigger for the third crisis in the Taiwan Strait, which occurred in 1995–96. Beijing could see the game that Taipei was playing in hoping to curry favour with the Americans and did not feel sufficiently reassured by the US response to Taiwan's entreaties. China's leaders were especially displeased that both houses of the US Congress voted overwhelmingly in favour of granting a visa to Lee Teng-hui to attend a reunion at his alma mater, Cornell University. Beijing regarded this as a shift in US policy towards formal recognition of the island.

In 1995, China launched several rounds of missile tests and conducted military exercises off the Taiwanese coast, actions that grew in intensity in the lead-up to the election. For two weeks prior to Taiwan's first democratic vote, China conducted large-scale wargames off the coast of its Fujian province – directly opposite Taiwan – which involved 260 aircraft, forty ships and an estimated 150,000 troops.[13] The purpose of these drills was to intimidate Taiwanese voters and remind them of the costs of independence. The Clinton administration, worried that this show of force might call American credibility as the region's 'security guarantor' into question, responded by deploying two aircraft carrier groups to the Taiwan Strait. This was the largest US naval deployment to Asia since the Vietnam War. It had the desired effect of defusing the crisis. Taiwan's first democratic election proceeded smoothly, with Lee Teng-hui and the KMT clinging to power.

The KMT lost the presidency four years later, however, to the Democratic Progressive Party (DPP) candidate Chen Shui-bian. Chen was Beijing's least preferred candidate given his party's pro-independence posture. Despite Chen's initial efforts to reassure China that Taiwan would not formally declare independence as long as it wasn't attacked, Beijing remained sceptical. It refused to engage with Chen until Taiwan pledged its commitment to the One China policy: a statement that there is only one Chinese government, despite both sides disagreeing over who that government should be. For Chen to make such a commitment would have been political suicide – no leader in his position would have done it.

Guardian angels and great dragons: US and Chinese relations with Taiwan

Beijing's concerns intensified following the election of George W. Bush as US president. Only months after taking office, in April 2001 Bush pledged in a live television interview to do 'whatever it took to help Taiwan defend herself'. The following day he announced that he was approving the sale of more than US$6.4 billion in weaponry to Taiwan. In dollar value, this was the largest American arms-sale package to Taiwan since Bush's father had, controversially – in the run-up to the 1992 presidential election, when he was trailing Democrat candidate Bill Clinton in the polls – approved the sale of 150 F-16 aircraft to the island. The April 2001 package included four naval destroyers, twelve anti-submarine aircraft and eight submarines.[14] Reports emerged alleging US officials had conveyed to Chen that Bush Jnr was Taiwan's 'secret guardian angel'.[15]

Beijing's response to these developments was to largely ignore the DPP and Taiwan's new president and continue to cultivate ties with the KMT, which was much more inclined to maintain the cross-strait status quo. In September 2001, for instance, China allowed the KMT to open an office in Beijing.[16] Famously, in May 2005 it gifted Taiwan's then premier and the chairman of the KMT, Lien Chan, two giant pandas as a goodwill gesture when he visited the Chinese mainland.[17]

Beijing's efforts were rewarded in 2008 when KMT candidate Ma Ying-jeou – a former mayor of Taipei, once described as the 'most handsome leader in the world' – won the presidency by securing almost 60 per cent of the popular vote.[18] Cross-strait ties deepened considerably under Ma's eight years as president. In November 2015, Ma and Xi became the first leaders of China and Taiwan to meet in person. The warmth of their handshake at the start of that Singapore meeting was in stark contrast to Xi's frosty first encounter with Japanese prime minister Shinzō Abe exactly twelve months earlier. And yet, consistent with China's 'missile diplomacy' on the eve of Taiwan's first presidential election, the historic November 2015 meeting was clearly intended to send a message to Taiwanese voters about the merits of sticking with the KMT in the upcoming presidential and legislative elections, to be held in January 2016.[19]

Taiwanese voters decided otherwise, returning the DPP to power in a landslide victory. Taiwan's first female president, Tsai Ing-wen, won 56 per cent of the vote. Her nearest rival trailed her by more than 25 per cent, making it the largest winning margin in the island's short democratic history. For the first time, the DPP also took control of the legislature, winning 68 out of a total of 113 seats.

While the 2016 election result was largely a result of dissatisfaction with domestic economic developments in Taiwan – including the island's stagnating economy, rising labour prices and a growing gap between rich and poor – Ma's closeness to China unquestionably played a part. Popular discontent with his approach had already been on display through the Sunflower Student Movement, in which crowds of Taiwanese students and civic groups occupied Taiwan's legislature between 18 March and 10 April 2014. They were protesting the island's growing dependence upon China and its susceptibility to political coercion from Beijing.

As with her DPP predecessor Chen Shui-bian, Tsai set out by seeking to reassure Beijing. Yet Beijing's reaction to her entreaties was predictably cool. Some might even say it was cold: in the Chinese city of

Xiamen, opposite Taiwan, China conducted extensive live-fire military exercises and landing drills, which saw amphibious armoured vehicles ploughing through the waters, aircraft firing missiles, and troops parachuting from choppers.[20] Chinese internet users moved in droves to post derogatory messages on Tsai's Facebook profile.[21] Beijing was adamant that Tsai needed to embrace the One China policy – a step as politically unsustainable for her as it had been for Chen, given the DPP's voter base. Beijing therefore suspended all talks with Taiwan. The numbers of tourists travelling from China to Taiwan also dropped significantly, halving from 1.14 million during the first quarter of 2016 to 659,575 for the same period in 2017.[22]

Trump's election and his generally erratic behaviour on Taiwan since has added much fuel to this already combustible situation. In December 2016, Trump broke with past protocol to become the first US president-elect to speak with Taiwan's leader, when he took a congratulatory call from Tsai. Only a month later, even more controversially, Trump suggested that the One China policy, which has been a cornerstone of Sino–American relations since normalisation in the 1970s, was open for negotiation. By February 2017, however, Trump had agreed, at Xi's request, to honour the policy.[23] Consistent with this, in April 2017 he rebuffed Tsai's suggestion of another call between the two, indicating that he would speak to Xi before doing so again.[24] Yet by June 2017 Trump had again raised Beijing's ire by approving the sale of US$1.4 billion worth of weaponry to Taipei, including powerful weapons for Taiwan's air force.[25] Most significantly, in his biggest pro-Taiwan move to date, in March 2018 he signed into law the *Taiwan Travel Act,* permitting two-way exchanges between American and Taiwanese officials at all levels of government.[26]

As with so many other areas of his presidency, much uncertainty surrounds Trump's motives here. There is speculation that pro-Taiwan elements within his administration have simply taken advantage of the new president's ignorance of foreign policy. Another line of thinking suggests that Trump is savvier and is using Taiwan as a bargaining chip to moderate Beijing's behaviour on the Korean Peninsula and in the South China Sea.

Vital interests: why conflict could occur over Taiwan

Of the three key players with vital interests in this flashpoint, Taiwan's are arguably the clearest. At stake is the fate of the island's twenty-three million inhabitants and their ability to determine their political destiny freely, with no outside coercion.

Taiwanese public opinion on the island's relationship with China has gradually shifted since the KMT retreated to Taiwan in the late 1940s. As recently as the early 1990s, when formal polling on these matters began, almost half the population saw themselves as both Chinese and Taiwanese. At that time, only a quarter identified as being exclusively Taiwanese. Today, almost 60 per cent of the population see themselves as exclusively Taiwanese and a mere 3 per cent identify as exclusively Chinese. Clearly, a much stronger sense of distinctly Taiwanese identity has emerged over the past quarter-century. Significantly, this sentiment is strongest among younger Taiwanese, most of whom were born and raised on the island. According to recent polling, 100 per cent of those in the under-29 age bracket identify as exclusively Taiwanese.[27]

Public opinion has remained relatively stable on the question of whether the island should become independent from or unify with the mainland. For over a decade now, polling data suggests that approximately half the population would like to see the status quo maintained. When asked what the status quo is, approximately three-quarters of the population regard Taiwan as an 'independent country', in direct opposition to the One China policy and Beijing's insistence that Taiwan is a province of China. Once again, these trends are even more pronounced among Taiwan's younger generation, with 86 per cent of the population under the age of forty supporting formal separation from China and a startling 43 per cent maintaining this position even if would mean Taiwan coming under military attack.[28]

A Chinese military attack against the island is conceivable. Beijing is unswerving in its characterisation of Taiwan as a 'core Chinese interest'. Its use of this terminology is significant: Chinese officials have traditionally maintained that military force can and will be used whenever the country's 'core interests' are threatened. Since the term first entered the Chinese foreign policy lexicon in the early 2000s, it has generally only been applied in relation to Taiwan, Tibet and Xinjiang.[29] In Taiwan's case, the risk is amplified: due to China's Anti-Secession Law, which was passed in 2005, in the event of Taiwanese independence or the exhaustion of possibilities for peaceful reunification, 'the state shall employ non-peaceful means and other necessary measures to protect China's sovereignty and territorial integrity'.[30] Beijing is legally obliged to use force.

Taiwan's military value to Beijing also cannot be underestimated. As with the Miyako Strait in the East China Sea and the Luzon Strait in the South China Sea, Taiwan is critical to China's ambitions to project military power further afield. One Chinese strategist has even gone so far as to describe the island as 'a lock around the neck of a great dragon'.[31] Beijing is also concerned that its lack of direct control over Taiwan impedes China's three main naval fleets – the North Sea Fleet, the East Sea Fleet and the South Sea Fleet – in their ability to work together. For instance, in the 1974 Battle of the Paracels, Mao Zedong took a significant gamble when he sent warships from the East Sea Fleet through the Taiwan Strait to reinforce the South Sea Fleet, given the risk that they could have been ambushed by Taiwanese forces. These forces were formidable: the United States had provided Taiwan with access to advanced weapons systems, as well as the opportunity to train and exercise their troops alongside the US military. Therefore, while this episode occurred more than four decades ago, and at a time when Chinese military forces were considerably weaker, it reportedly continues to influence Beijing's strategic thinking today.[32]

The United States has considerable interests at stake in this flashpoint, too. In 2017, Taiwan ranked as the United States' tenth-leading trading partner. The US Department of Commerce recently estimated that exports to Taiwan support approximately 217,000 American jobs. Arms sales to Taiwan – the best-known example of which was President H.W. Bush's authorisation of the sale of 150 F-16 fighters – have been especially lucrative for US defence contractors. This one sale, in a deal worth over US$6 billion, provided 6000 new jobs to the state of Texas, which Bush hoped would translate into votes. (They didn't.)[33] The Obama administration sold more than double that dollar value in arms to Taiwan during its first term alone.[34]

A degree of sentimentalism is also at play. Some analysts have also observed that the island serves as a beacon for democracy in a region where a growing number of states, such as Thailand and the Philippines, are travelling in more authoritarian directions. As a scholar versed in Taiwan, Denny Roy, has observed, 'The spectre of a large "communist" country bullying a small and admirable democracy pulls at American heartstrings.'[35]

Taiwan's supporters in the United States can point to the fact that China would be able to deploy its air and naval forces deeper into Asia if it gained control of the island. If Beijing were to establish military bases on Taiwan, this would basically extend the Chinese coastline up to 400 kilometres eastward. Further, if Beijing focused less of its military energies on the prospect of retaking Taiwan by force, this would free up considerable Chinese resources for redeployment elsewhere – including to the other three flashpoints examined in this book.

As with those flashpoints, complete American abandonment of Taiwan might cause other Asian allies of the United States to question Washington's commitment. US calls for an abandonment have been voiced for some time: Taipei's detractors have labelled the relationship a strategic and economic liability for the United States, one that not only prevents China and America from developing a bond but also risks dragging them to war. Yet such arguments are stymied by the assertion that selling Taiwan down the river could unravel America's Asian alliances.[36]

An abandonment might also lead Taiwan down the nuclear path, a prospect it actively considered from the late 1960s to the late 1980s. Such a move would have obvious consequences for stability in Asia.

Taipei's early efforts in developing nuclear techology were a direct response to China's first nuclear test in 1964. The Taiwanese nuclear program, which began three years later, in 1967, was conducted under the cover of a military-run research institute. Attempts at secrecy were not always effective: its covert activities were detected by UN weapons inspectors on numerous occasions. The program was finally closed in 1988 under heavy pressure from Washington, after the institute's director – Colonel Chang Hsien-yi, who was also a long-time CIA intelligence asset – confirmed the existence of Taiwan's nuclear program following his 1987 defection to the United States. By this stage, Taipei was an estimated one to two years away from having an indigenous nuclear bomb.[37] A Taiwan armed with nuclear weapons is not in the interests of China or of the United States.

Reflecting these various strategic considerations, the US National Security Strategy of December 2017 made history when it became the first document of its kind to explicitly note America's commitment to the island: 'We will maintain our strong ties with Taiwan in accordance with our "One China" policy, including our commitments under the *Taiwan Relations Act* to provide for Taiwan's legitimate defense needs and deter coercion.'[38]

A war like no other: could China take Taiwan by force?

The National Security Strategy did not go down at all well in Zhongnanhai, the headquarters of the Chinese Communist Party. Beijing's response to this document was to accuse Washington of adopting a 'Cold War' mentality.[39] Yet unlike that longstanding struggle, where competition between superpowers never resulted in bloody military conflict, the United States and China could quite conceivably come to blows over Taiwan.

A decade ago, two respected American analysts, Richard C. Bush and Michael O'Hanlon, wrote a book suggesting that America and China were dangerously close to stumbling into a war over what they termed the 'Taiwan tinderbox'. Their book, *A War Like No Other,* posited that such a war would directly affect 1.5 billion people, would very likely involve the use of nuclear weapons and would bring about 'fundamental change in the international order'.[40]

Beijing has several options should it opt to retake Taiwan by force. The simplest would be to strangle the island into submission through a blockade. Taiwan imports 80 to 90 per cent of its food and close to 100 per cent of its oil. Cutting off these imports could generate major economic and psychological shock in Taiwan.

To achieve this, Beijing would first need to gain control of the airspace around the island. Drawing inspiration from the East China Sea, it might attempt to do this by establishing an Air Defence Identification Zone, or a 'no-fly zone', which its fighter planes could enforce. China could then move to establish a more traditional naval blockade around the island. This could consist of several layers, including an inner ring of sea mines to prevent cargo ships entering or leaving Taiwanese ports, a second ring of surface warships and submarines, and an outer ring of maritime patrol aircraft. In tandem with such measures, Beijing could seek to cut the island off from the outside world by waging cyberwarfare. Taiwan is one of the most interconnected societies on earth, meaning that a blackout of its internet and communications networks could lead to widespread panic and confusion.[41]

Second, and more severe, Beijing could launch massive missile attacks against Taiwan. It has the firepower to do so: China has up to 1500 short-and medium-range ballistic missiles stationed directly opposite Taiwan, in the Fujian province. Among these is one of its newest missiles, the Dongfeng 16 (DF-16). The DF-16 can consistently hit within ten metres of its assigned target, which is a marked improvement upon the estimated 500-metre margin of error of its predecessors, the older DF-11 and DF-15 missiles. With a range of 800 to 1000 kilometres, the DF-16 can also hit targets beyond Taiwan, including US bases in Okinawa.[42]

Beijing could use missile strikes against Taiwan for a variety of purposes. As with a blockade, a primary objective could be to break the resolve of the Taiwanese people or cause them to lose confidence in their leadership. Alternatively, by taking out Taiwan's air defence system, radar facilities, missiles (some of which can now strike China) and the air bases from which Taiwanese fighters would launch, such strikes could also serve as a prelude to a larger-scale amphibious assault of the island.[43]

Third, and most terrifying, China might choose to launch a sudden and full-scale invasion of Taiwan. Such an operation would need to start with Taiwan's numerous offshore islands; bypassing these and heading straight for the main island would run the risk that these land features could be used to target Chinese military airbases and naval ports. With the offshore islands secured, Beijing would send a flotilla of largely civilian vessels loaded with troops, under the cover of Chinese jet fighters, towards Taiwan. Upon reaching the island, these forces would disembark and seek to establish a foothold in Taiwanese harbours and docks, before unleashing China's battle tanks to begin an unrelenting drive inland. Chinese forces would employ deceptive tactics along the way, such as releasing false radio chatter, to confuse their enemy. The tanks would move to surround major Taiwanese cities – especially the island's capital, Taipei – and, with support from forces in the air and at sea, would commence bombing the population into submission. Those tanks and Chinese troops would then be sent into the cities to root out those who refused to submit under the weight of this bombardment.[44] The casualties, both civilian and military, would be horrifying.

But Taiwanese need not yet panic with this nightmarish scenario. A full-scale invasion would be the most challenging of the three military options. Taiwan's geography is not conducive to an amphibious attack. The island's west coast is lined with mudflats, with few suitable areas to land troops. Taiwan's east coast is characterised by steep, high cliffs that rise straight out of the sea. The weather in this part of the world is unpredictable and highly inclement. The tides of the waters surrounding the island are strong and uncertain. The Taiwan Strait is often blanketed in thick fog.

Despite the great leaps forward that China's military has made in recent decades, its navy still lacks enough specialist military transport ships and aircraft to deliver large numbers of troops across the strait. Beijing would need to rely upon a flotilla of commercial vessels to assist with this task. The captains and pilots of such craft would have little, if any, experience in military operations. Communications across this makeshift armada would be fraught, and the vessels would not be able to move as quickly as ships and aircrafts designed specifically for the task, making them more vulnerable to attack. Beyond these and other logistical challenges, it would be difficult for the flotilla to gather reliable intelligence on the unfolding conflict – particularly about the location and movements of Taiwanese forces. Given the operation's complexity and a potential lack of coordination across the invasion force, China's leadership could equally be faced with the challenge of information overload, especially if surrounding countries seized this moment to advance their own claims – over the East China Sea or the South China Sea, for instance – while Beijing was distracted.[45]

Taiwanese forces, who would be fighting for the survival of their society and way of life, could be expected to put up fierce resistance. Taiwan is thought to have an elaborate defensive system in place that includes large rows of sea mines ('belts of death', as one analyst has described them) and 'seawalls of fire' (underwater pipes that would spray oil and gas onto advancing Chinese troops, who would quickly catch alight amid heavy gunfire).[46] Having had decades to prepare for an invasion, Taiwan also has hardened facilities, where its most prized military assets can be sheltered in the early stages of conflict. Many of its advanced fighter jets, for instance, can be housed in nuclear-proof bunkers located beneath mountains. And even if Taiwanese troops found themselves on the losing side as a battle progressed, they could destroy critical infrastructure and literally 'head for the hills', from where they could conceivably continue to wage a guerrilla-style campaign. In such a worst-case scenario, Taiwan's leaders would also have the option of unleashing hastily constructed weapons of mass destruction – containing biological agents, poison gas and possibly even nuclear material – on advancing Chinese forces.[47]

According to most estimates, in the event of a full-scale Chinese invasion, Taiwan would likely be able to hold off advancing Chinese forces for at least two to four weeks. While it is not impossible that Taiwanese forces could hold off an attack for longer than that, and even come out as victors should things go badly awry for the attackers, the odds of such an outcome are slim, and are becoming slimmer as China's military modernisation continues.

Taipei has also allowed the island's military to languish, spending only US$10 billion on defence in 2017, compared to China's US$144 billion defence budget. Taiwan's mounting debt, rising unemployment, an ageing population and a growing gap between rich and poor have all put pressure on the island's underperforming economy, diverting funds away from defence. Some in Taipei also believe that Washington is taking advantage of its status as Taiwan's key military supplier, grossly overcharging the island for the systems it is willing to sell. Accordingly, Taiwan now has only four sub marines in its arsenal. Two of those entered service in the 1940s and reportedly can no longer fire torpedos. This stands in contrast to the sixty-two submarines – up to thirteen of which are nuclear-powered – that Beijing has at its disposal.[48] Given this, Taiwan would almost certainly need US forces to come to its assistance within two to four weeks.

Even then, beating back a Chinese invasion would not be as straightforward as it would have been a couple of decades ago. According to one recent study, at the time of the Third Taiwan Strait Crisis, in 1995–96, the Sino–American balance of military power was so tipped in the United States' favour that it could have gained air superiority within seven days of entering a Taiwan conflict, using only a single 'air wing', consisting of seventy-two aircraft. By 2017, this figure had risen to three to four air wings, while the time needed to gain air superiority had increased to twenty-one days. Significantly, this number of planes is the equivalent of the existing US air capacity based in Japan.

Moreover, whereas in the mid-1990s China did not have the ability to strike US bases in Asia, it does now because of the improved accuracy of its ballistic missiles.[49] The same is true at sea, as China's increasing satellite and anti-shipping missile capabilities heighten the risk to US Navy ships in the region. China's Dongfeng 21D (DF-21D) missiles, for instance, give Beijing the capacity to sink aircraft carriers out to a range of 1550 kilometres.[50]

This is not to suggest that Beijing would prevail against the United States in a Taiwan Strait conflict. America would certainly sustain more casualties than was the case two decades ago. US forces would also need to operate at a greater distance, beyond the range of China's increasingly capable missiles. They may, for instance, seek to exert military and economic pressure against Beijing as part of a 'distant blockade', stopping or seizing shipping bound for China, especially oil tankers. And US military capabilities have also improved markedly since the Third Taiwan Strait Crisis. America's ability to strike targets on the Chinese mainland, for example, is much greater today than it was two decades ago.[51]

Beijing could also opt to employ elements of all three approaches – blockade, bombardment and invasion – in tandem. Yet there are problems associated with each of them that even their use in combination would not likely resolve. If missiles were to come raining down upon the small democratic island, causing large-scale death and destruction, it would attract widespread international opprobrium and increase the chances that other countries – such as the United States, Japan and Australia – might come to Taiwan's defence. A sustained blockade could have the same effect, particularly if there was evidence of Taiwan's residents starving as food supplies were compromised.

So despite China's considerable geographic advantage over the United States, given its proximity to Taiwan, and the impressive military advances that it has made over the past twenty years, the outcomes of a conflict over Taiwan are uncertain and are likely to remain so for up to a decade. As with the East China Sea, this uncertainty is liable to dissuade Beijing from using force against Taiwan – unless, of course, Taipei issues a formal declaration of independence.

Deep freeze: a diplomatic impasse

There are limited diplomatic avenues for addressing the dispute over Taiwan. Beijing does not recognise Taiwan as an independent state and refuses to negotiate with it on that basis. When Xi and Ma held their historic meeting in 2015, they addressed each other simply as 'Mister' to avoid any diplomatic controversy or ambiguity around this point.[52] Likewise, when negotiations between China and Taiwan take place, they do so under the auspices of two semi-official organisations known as the Straits Exchange Foundation (SEF) of Taiwan and the Association for Relations Across the Taiwan Straits (ARATS) of China. These bodies have managed to make modest progress in the past, such as the 1992 Consensus, in which both sides agreed that there was only one China, even if their interpretations differed. But such talks frequently stall – in one case, for almost a decade, from 1999 to 2008.[53]

Diplomatic constraints notwithstanding, Beijing has been open to negotiating some form of peace treaty with Taiwan. China officially endorsed the idea in 2005, and it has occasionally made an appearance in major statements by Chinese and Taiwanese leaders. Chinese president Hu Jintao confirmed Beijing's willingness to reach a peace agreement in his remarks to the

October 2007 National Party Congress.[54] Both candidates in Taiwan's 2008 presidential election – KMT's Ma Ying-jeou and his DPP rival, Frank Hsieh – called for such a treaty to be negotiated. Yet as grand as this proposal sounds, a treaty of this sort would essentially be an interim measure in which Taipei would pledge not to declare independence in return for Beijing's commitment not to use force against the island.

Following his election, Ma indicated that he would not seek to negotiate such an arrangement during his first term but would do so if elected for a second term. While Ma ultimately reneged on that electoral promise, the idea remained on the KMT's party platform until August 2017, when it was removed as part of an attempt to lure back voters lost to the DPP.[55]

Beijing has also proposed applying a 'one country, two systems' formula, like that used to facilitate Hong Kong's handover from Britain to China in 1997. In fact, when Deng Xiaoping first articulated this concept in 1979, he referenced Taiwan, not Hong Kong. In Deng's terms, 'so long as Taiwan returns to the embrace of the motherland, we will respect the realities and the existing system there'.[56] Successive Chinese leaders have reiterated this proposal, indicating that Taiwan would be able to retain its capitalist economic system, appoint its own local leaders and even keep its armed forces, provided it recognises Beijing as the central government of China and allows it to have jurisdiction over foreign affairs.[57]

However, Taiwanese have never been particularly taken by the 'one country, two systems' approach. They have reportedly become even less enamoured in recent years, having seen China's dwindling commitment to the concept with Hong Kong, as evidenced by Beijing's recent arrests of pro-democracy activists, its violent breaking up of protests and its increasingly overt attempts to manipulate election outcomes. In 2017, *The Economist* observed about Hong Kong, 'confidence in "one country, two systems" has been replaced by the fear of it becoming "one country, 1.5 systems"'.[58] Those fears are felt every bit as acutely, if not more so, in Taiwan.

Beyond these cross-strait proposals, China's approach to Taiwan has involved reducing the island's freedom of diplomatic manoeuvre by limiting its interactions with the rest of the world. China has attempted this in two ways. First, it has sought to prevent Taiwanese membership of multilateral organisations. Taiwan was forced to withdraw from the United Nations in 1971, marking the beginning of China's curtailment of what is referred to as the island's 'international space'. In one of the more dramatic examples of this curtailment, Australian foreign affairs minister Julie Bishop was shouted down by Chinese delegates during a May 2017 meeting of the Kimberley Process; Chinese representatives demanded the expulsion of a Taiwanese delegation, who were subsequently removed.

Given that the Kimberley Process is a group established to stop the trade in 'conflict diamonds', which are mined from warzones and sold illicitly to finance insurgencies, invasions or warlords, the action might seem churlish, but such is the strain on relations and the deep-rooted anti-secessionist sentiment from China.[59]

When Taiwanese participation in multilateral processes does occur, Beijing insists that it happens under highly circumscribed conditions. Taiwan's membership of the Asia-Pacific Economic Cooperation (APEC) process is as the economy of 'Chinese Taipei', not as a fully-fledged nation-state. Likewise, when Taiwanese representatives participate in international gatherings such as the Shangri-La Dialogue, they must do so merely as individuals, not as members of a foreign delegation.

Beijing has also made a point of picking off the small number of diplomatic allies that Taiwan has left, largely by using economic inducements. During the early to mid 2000s, this led to a bidding war between Beijing and Taipei for the affections of small Pacific Island nations. Both sides engaged in chequebook diplomacy, providing fragile and often impoverished Pacific governments with loans and other forms of assistance in return for political allegiance. It led to one especially bizarre episode in 1999, when Papua New Guinea switched its allegiance from China to Taiwan and back to China within the space of a week. A decade on, Taiwan's foreign minister was forced to resign after spending US$30 million as part of a failed attempt to win back Port Moresby. Around the same time, China and Taiwan agreed to a freeze on such activities. This truce began to unravel in 2016, however, as Beijing established ties with two countries outside the Pacific region – Gambia, and São Tomé and Príncipe – who had formerly recognised Taiwan.[60] In June 2017, longstanding ally Panama severed ties with Taiwan to establish diplomatic relations with China, while in May 2018 the Dominican Republic followed suit.[61]

During Ma's time in office, Taiwan and China arrived at a range of commercial agreements. These opened Taiwan to tourists from China, allowed for limited Chinese investment on the island and reduced trade barriers. The crowning achievement of this suite of deals was the June 2010 China–Taiwan Economic Cooperation Framework Agreement (ECFA), which provided a roadmap for even deeper integration and an eventual free-trade agreement.

Yet more sinister motives arguably underpinned this warming in China's relations with the island. What the American analyst Denny Roy has termed the 'patient school' of thought within China – prevalent in foreign-ministry and think-tank circles – argues that Taiwan can be absorbed back into the mainland over time through such means. According to this line of argument, deeper economic integration will ultimately lead to greater political integration. Time is on Beijing's side. This view is juxtaposed against a more 'impatient school' of thought, most popular in the higher echelons of the Chinese military, which contends that Beijing should not be allowing Taiwan to enjoy the benefits of closer economic ties with China while also letting the island distance itself politically. Roy argues that the 'impatient school' tends to predominate during periods when Taiwan's appetite for independence is on the rise.[62]

Taiwanese voters' fears that they were falling victim to the approach championed by the 'patient school' was a key factor in the DPP's landslide election victory of January 2016. This, in turn, has seen the 'impatient' camp regain the ascendency in China's domestic debate, as reflected in Xi's increasingly strident comments on Taiwan.

While cross-strait relations remain at this impasse, the prospects for diplomacy look bleak.

New uncertainties: discarding the old playbook

Until very recently, the United States has held a clear military advantage over China, while the prospect of provoking a Chinese military response has served as a constraint on Taiwan. Taipei has made moves towards greater independence since the mid-1990s, but has remained unwilling to formally separate from China. Beijing has made clear that Taiwan's *de jure* independence is a red line, the crossing of which would be met with military force. Failure to make good on that threat would almost certainly provoke a crisis of legitimacy for China's leadership.

Washington's position on Taiwan, which stops short of supporting formal independence, has also served as an important moderating influence on Taipei's behaviour. Successive US governments since the 1970s have quite intentionally maintained an ambiguous stance on whether they would side with Taiwan in a cross-strait conflict. As James Baker, secretary of state under Ronald Reagan, observed:

> If we said we would come to the defense of Taiwan under any and all circumstances, she would declare independence and China would move – no doubt about that in my mind. If we said we wouldn't, China would move. And so we shouldn't say under what circumstances and to what extent we will aid Taiwan, but we should make it clear that we would view with the gravest concern any resort to the use of force.[63]

While a policy of strategic ambiguity has helped to keep this dispute peaceful, as the power balance between China, Taiwan and the United States shifts, new uncertainties are emerging, and these uncertainties are beginning to challenge the Beijing–Taipei–Washington triangle of deterrence. As China's military power continues to grow, so too do doubts that Washington has either the willingness or the ability to come to Taiwan's assistance in a cross-strait contingency. Pessimists point to the failures of former US president Barack Obama's rebalancing strategy, along with President Trump's inward-looking 'America first' policies, as evidence of Washington's waning commitment. But it is America's shrinking ability to come to Taiwan's defence physically, much more so than the will of its leaders, that is the single biggest factor in Washington's capacity to shape the course of this flashpoint.

Similar doubts are emerging over the level of resistance the Taiwanese populace would put up in the event of a Chinese attack. Taiwan's armed forces – which number approximately 215,000 active military personnel – have a formidable reputation, having been indoctrinated throughout their careers to prepare for war with China. But what about the resilience of the reservists, who would also be required to stave off a Chinese invasion? Many of Taiwan's younger generation, despite their robust views on independence from the mainland, may not have the stomach for conflict. This demographic is often described disparagingly as the Strawberry Generation, a reference to an outwardly attractive appearance but a highly fragile and easily bruised character. As Denny Roy has observed, 'Critics have said these youth tend to be soft, selfish, lazy and apolitical, and that a high percentage or even a majority of Taiwan's young men would not fight in a war against China.'[64] Taiwan has also become an affluent society: would the population at large be willing to forgo its current standard of living in the face of a blockade or sustained military strikes? While Taiwanese society has demonstrated tremendous resilience in the past, the fortitude of the island's current inhabitants has never been tested.

The use of force or a dialling up of other coercive measures against Taiwan would not come without cost for China. Since the early 1990s, Taiwan has risen to become China's fifth-largest trading partner. Taiwan is also by far the largest source of foreign direct investment (FDI) in China. Much of this investment is in the high-technology sector, where Taiwanese know-how and funding has been key to the success of innumerable Chinese start-ups.[65] The economic costs of conflict with Taiwan could potentially extend beyond these cross-strait commercial ties, particularly if the United States and even Japan were to enter the hostilities. If Beijing were seen to have acted egregiously against the island, other governments may seek to impose economic sanctions against China.

Some commentators argue that now is the time for the United States to double down on deterring Beijing.[66] They call for America to be clearer in its commitment to defend Taiwan in the event of conflict. They suggest that Washington should be willing to sell Taipei more sophisticated forms of weaponry – such as the F-35 joint strike fighter and attack submarines – which have until now been off the table because such sales would infuriate Beijing. And they advocate a more visible US military presence in and around Taiwan through US Navy ships making regular port visits – a step that senior Chinese diplomat Li Kexin says would violate the 2005 Anti-Secession Law and trigger a military response.[67]

Critics of this approach argue that to deter China, Washington needs to be able to convince Beijing it is willing to climb the ladder of military escalation all the way to a full-scale nuclear war, which is where a conflict over Taiwan could end up. Beijing would have to believe that Washington was willing to use nuclear weapons in Taiwan's defence and to suffer the costs of Chinese retaliation – even if that meant losing American cities. With an avowedly 'America first' president in the White House, the chances of the United States sacrificing San Francisco for Taipei seem remote. But Australian commentator Hugh White argues that unless Washington is willing to take things that far, it should not mislead Taipei into thinking it can rely upon US support. Instead, White argues, the United States needs to think much harder about the extent to which it is willing to accommodate Beijing's ambitions regarding Taiwan.[68]

Accommodation along these lines is also not without risk. Should China be given its way on Taiwan, it is possible that China's expansionary ambitions might not stop there. After all, appetite often comes with eating. And the consequences of the United States not standing up to China over Taiwan could potentially be catastrophic for Asia's strategic order. Other powerful states may adopt a similarly aggressive approach. Smaller and medium-sized countries, such as Australia, South Korea and Vietnam, could be encouraged to pursue the development of nuclear weapons to avoid falling to a similar fate, leading to a dangerous arms race. As the Taiwan-based analyst J. Michael Cole concludes – somewhat dramatically, but not erroneously – giving in to Beijing over Taiwan 'would unleash upon the world a beast of unmitigated evil'.[69]

Short of a formal Taiwanese declaration of independence, it seems unlikely that China will use force to resolve this flashpoint. The costs involved and the uncertainty of the outcome would be important factors in Beijing's calculations. And Beijing has other methods. For example, in January 2018 China Eastern Airlines and Xiamen Air announced four new commercial flight routes. One of these routes is a mere 7.8 kilometres from the median line of the Taiwan Strait and adjacent to an area where the Taiwanese Air Force trains. Two others run close to the Taiwan-controlled islands of Kinmen (formerly known as Quemoy) and Matsu. While the official line from Beijing is that the flight paths were developed solely to relieve pressure on the busy Hong Kong–Shanghai route, some commentators have observed that it was more likely intended to undercut Taiwan's claims of sovereignty and embarrass the Tsai administration.[70]

As in the East China Sea, a conflict over Taiwan is most liable to be sparked by an act of misadventure or miscalculation. China's air force circumnavigated the island on fifteen occasions during 2017. Increasingly, these flights are being made by intimidating, nuclear-capable bomber aircraft.[71] The number of Chinese naval vessels operating close to the island has also increased.[72] In this more crowded environment, the risk of an inadvertent clash is growing. On 1 July 2016, the ninety-fifth anniversary of the Chinese Communist Party, a Taiwanese Navy vessel accidentally fired an anti-shipping missile in China's direction. Fortunately (except for the captain, who died) the missile struck a Taiwanese fishing boat and not a Chinese vessel.[73]

Unlike in the East China Sea, there are currently no mechanisms in place to avoid such clashes. During their November 2015 meeting, Xi and Ma agreed to establish a cross-strait hotline to deal with such scenarios. While this hotline began operation in December 2015, it is reportedly no longer in use due to the diplomatic freeze that followed Tsai's 2016 election.[74]

Taiwan: a ticking time bomb

Logic suggests that China, Taiwan or the United States would prefer not to wage a catastrophic war. The costs are too great. But history tells us that states don't always go to war for rational reasons. Throughout history, emotional factors, such as fear and honour, have provided sparks for conflict. So the next decade is set to be a dangerous one.

America's military ability to defend Taiwan is already at its limit. The US advantage will likely be gone in a decade, as Chinese military advances and favourable geography combine, allowing Beijing to deny America access to this theatre. In an era of deepening Sino–American rivalry, Washington's instinct will be to use whatever remaining influence it has over this flashpoint while it still can. The *Taiwan Travel Act* suggests as much.

Panic could set in on the island as its affinity with the mainland weakens further and as it watches America's grip on this area slipping. Taiwan's incentive to push for formal independence sooner rather than later could grow.

Time is on China's side. It will not yet seek to resolve this dispute with force unless provoked into doing so. But the temptation for Beijing to use its increasingly powerful military and other coercive measures will intensify. For a leadership seeking to cement its legitimacy and that of the Chinese Communist Party, weakness on such a core interest is not an option.

Rather than poking the Chinese panda, a better course for Washington would be to gradually ease off on its commitment to defend Taiwan, to the point where Taipei is responsible for its own defence a decade from now.

Taiwan's supporters will regard as unconscionable any suggestion of a small democratic Asian society being subsumed into Xi's Chinese Dream. Their influence is strong, particularly within the US Congress, meaning that any American drawdown from this flashpoint would not happen quickly.

If such a drawdown were to occur, Taiwan's fate is not sealed. Should current trends continue, Beijing could be in the position to forcibly take the island ten years from now; but Taipei has been quietly readying itself for a David-versus-Goliath-type struggle for at least a decade, investing in some weapons – such as powerful precision-guided missiles – that might still make Beijing think twice about the costs of military action. Yet it will need to spend considerably more if it is to maintain its military capability over time.

America could continue to sell these arms to Taiwan, even as it backed away from any commitment to defend the island. In April 2018, for instance, the US State Department gave American defence companies the green light to market sensitive technology to Taiwan, to help the island with its efforts to build submarines.[75] The option of Taiwan 'going nuclear' can also not be discounted, although, on a rare point of agreement, both Beijing and Washington would strongly object to this path.

American general Douglas MacArthur once described Taiwan as an 'unsinkable aircraft carrier'.[76] He saw the island as a giant military base from which America could project power along China's coast to support its Cold War containment strategy. But his metaphor has come full circle. Without question, China's ability to project its military power into the Western Pacific would improve if it gained control of Taiwan. But the costs of preventing that outcome are increasingly prohibitive, and they are rising. America risks its own future in Asia, along with the prospects for stable regional order, should it recklessly step up to meet them.

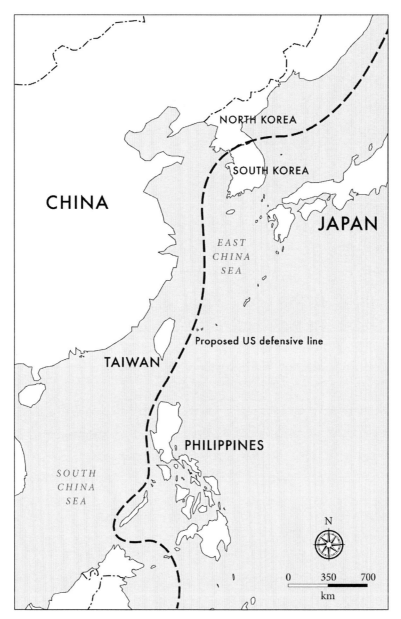

A NEW ASIAN BALANCE OF POWER

CHAPTER 6

CAN ASIA AVOID CATASTROPHE?

On the morning of 1 April 2001, an American EP-3 reconnaissance plane took off from Kadena Air Base in Okinawa to conduct routine surveillance over international waters off China's coast. Two Chinese J-8 fighters deployed from Lingshui Air Base on Hainan Island with orders to tail the US plane. One of the J-8 pilots was 33-year-old Wang Wei, a maverick who revelled in pulling off risky aerial manoeuvres. He slowed his aircraft down to match the speed of the spy plane and came within metres of it. Suddenly, at 9.07am and just over 104 kilometres south-east of Hainan, the Chinese fighter stalled and collided with the American plane. Firing his booster engines in an attempt to recover, Wang took the nose off the EP-3 and plummeted towards the waters of the South China Sea. He ejected, but was never seen again. The EP-3 also spiralled, falling 8000 feet in a matter of minutes. Its crew of twenty-four began destroying the highly sensitive equipment and information on board as its American pilot readied to make an emergency landing at the same airbase from where, minutes earlier, Wang had taken off. After realising that the American mayday was not an April Fools' Day prank, ground control granted permission to land.

The incident was indeed no laughing matter. A highly acrimonious crisis in relations between the United States and China ensued.[1]

What if this collision had instead involved Chinese and Japanese military aircraft, unleashing waves of virulent nationalism in both countries? Such a scenario is far from the stuff of fiction. As detailed in Chapter 3, Chinese and Japanese planes regularly engage in dangerous aerial encounters over the East China Sea. Or what would happen if, during the erratic Donald Trump presidency, Pyongyang believed Washington was readying its forces for preemptive military action, as it did during the 1993–94 North Korean nuclear crisis? Would Kim Jong-un be able to hold his nerve and not initiate an anticipatory strike? Or what if the Taiwanese Navy vessel that accidently fired an anti-shipping missile in the direction of the mainland in July 2016 had struck a Chinese rather than a Taiwanese craft? And rather than this incident occurring on the ninety-fifth anniversary of the Chinese Communist Party, what if it were to occur in the nationalistic atmosphere of the Party's centenary in 2021?

The risk of major war in Asia is much greater today than most individuals assume. All it would take is an accidental clash between the wrong two militaries, at the wrong place or the wrong time, and a highly dangerous escalation could occur. Asia has been lucky so far that it hasn't.

Serendipity has often played a critical role throughout history when leaders have walked back from the brink of war. In the documentary *The Fog of War,* Robert McNamara, who served as US defense secretary during the Kennedy and Johnson administrations, reflects on the part providence played in avoiding nuclear armageddon during the Cuban Missile Crisis: 'At the end we lucked out. It was luck that prevented war. We came that close to nuclear war at the end. Rational individuals: Kennedy was rational; Khrushchev was rational; Castro was rational. Rational individuals came that close to total destruction of their societies. And that danger exists today.'

We should learn from McNamara's wisdom. It would be imprudent to assume that Asia's luck will hold indefinitely.

Crisis slide: repercussions and reverberations

It is not only the danger of localised conflict in Asia that confronts us. The danger of 'wide war' in Asia is growing too, because this region is experiencing what the eminent Australian strategist Coral Bell once described as a 'crisis slide'. As Bell wrote in the early 1970s:

There are periods in history when individual crises remain distinct, like isolated boulders rolling down a mountainside. Each may do some damage, and present some dangers, but they are events discrete in themselves ... There are other periods when the boulders, or the crises, not only come thick and fast, but seem, as it were, to repercuss off each other until the whole mountainside, or the whole society of states, begins to crumble.[2]

Bell pointed to two previous instances when such 'crisis slides' ended in catastrophic conflict. The first was in the lead-up to World War I, which was preceded by a series of international crises – the First Moroccan Crisis (1905–06), the First Balkan Crisis (1908–09), the Second Moroccan Crisis (1911) and the culminating crisis of July 1914, which was sparked by the assassination of Austrian archduke Franz Ferdinand. Bell believed that this pattern of recurring crises backed Europe's leaders into a corner from where they could see no way out other than conflict. She contended that a similar series of events – Hitler's remilitarisation of the Rhineland (1936), his annexation of Austria and his occupation of the Sudetenland under the terms of the Munich Agreement (1938), the signing of the Pact of Steel between Germany and Italy, and Hitler's invasion of Czechoslovakia and Poland (1939) – also constituted a 'crisis slide' and left Britain and France with no option other than to declare war against Germany in September 1939, thus formally starting World War II.[3]

Crisis slides of the kind that preceded the world wars are dangerous for three reasons. First, they make international relations more volatile. Governments become more antagonistic towards, and distrustful of, one another. As with the colliding boulders in Bell's metaphor, these animosities intensify and begin to roll over into other areas. Second, governments increasingly harden their positions and become less inclined to cooperate or compromise with each passing crisis. Every crisis inevitably generates 'winners and losers', and the lessons most losing governments take is that firmer diplomatic and strategic postures are needed to avoid losing face in future. Third, repeated crises have the seemingly paradoxical effect of generating an unhealthy level of complacency. As more crises are resolved short of war – even if their underlying causes are not – governments begin to disbelieve the possibility that they could end up waging full-blown conflict against one another.[4]

This book shows that the features of a crisis slide are evident in Asia today. After a period of relative calm that stretched from the mid-1990s through the 2000s, crises around the four flashpoints have been coming thick and fast. The sinking of the ROKS *Cheonan* and North Korea's bombing of Yeonpyeong Island took the Korean Peninsula to the brink of war in 2010. Tokyo's nationalisation of the Senkaku/Diaoyu Islands and Beijing's provocative reactions had respected commentators talking up the prospects of Sino–Japanese conflict between 2012 and 2014. Similar claims were made about the South China Sea following the Scarborough Shoal and China–Vietnam oil rig crises of 2012 and 2014. This speculation has intensified following Beijing's land-reclamation campaign, which has seen the development of military facilities on many of this area's disputed land features. Today, after two decades of calm, tensions over Taiwan are resurfacing following the election of an independence-leaning president on the island. The clouds of danger also hang over the Korean Peninsula, despite Trump tweeting that this crisis has passed due to his summit with Kim Jong-un and that his fellow Americans can now sleep easy.

The connections between the four flashpoints have also been intensifying. Japan's increasing involvement in the South China Sea reflects Tokyo's concern that what Beijing gets away with there will set the terms for what the international community will accept in future in the East China Sea. Likewise, Trump's harder line on Taiwan has been seen as a reflection of his frustration at Beijing's unwillingness to deal more decisively with Pyongyang or to de-escalate in the South China Sea. These connections are in some ways unsurprising. The four flashpoints, at least in their modern guises, each have their origins in World War II and its aftermath. This commonality renders them even more susceptible to a crisis slide.

The positions of the key players are also hardening. Washington continues to insist upon Pyongyang's denuclearisation as a nonnegotiable element of its diplomacy. Beijing has frozen all ties with Taiwan and refuses to even answer a crisis hotline, although Xi and Ma agreed to this hotline at their historic 2015 meeting in Singapore. China's leaders remain concerned about appearing weak to a virulently anti-Japanese populace, while the same is true in reverse. The United States is concerned that seeming soft in response to growing Chinese assertiveness will further erode regional confidence in American resolve, particularly in the eyes of US allies and partners.

At the same time, there seems a strange complacency about the prospects for conflict in Asia – even as the key players understand how devastating a major war would be. The leaders of China and ASEAN have spent almost two decades discussing the development of a South China Sea code of conduct, intended to avoid the use of military force to resolve disputes in this area. Despite their recent agreement to resume negotiations, they seem no closer to realising that goal than they were in the late 1990s. Washington, too, has spent much of the past quarter-century kicking the North Korean can down the road, leading to the dangerous drift towards war in 2017. Under his policy of 'strategic patience', Obama ignored this threat in the hope it would simply go away. Yet for all the criticism of his predecessor, in June 2018 Trump secured significantly less than in previous deals with North Korea, such as the 1994 Agreed Framework and the 2005 'roadmap plan', showing a disturbing lack of urgency. Similarly, Chinese and Japanese officials have spent a decade haggling over a hotline to avoid accidental air and naval clashes. In May 2018, they finally committed to begin operating this mechanism, although it remains unclear whether it will cover the disputed Senkaku/Diaoyu Islands. Given the glacial pace at which each of these initiatives has progressed, one could be excused for thinking that Asia's leaders are daydreaming about the prospects for peace rather than sleepwalking towards war – to borrow author Christopher Clark's famous metaphor. Such complacency is dangerous, and badly misplaced.

Hierarchy of hazard: which flashpoint is the most explosive?

Several commentators suggest that the most viable way to avoid catastrophic conflict in Asia is for America and China to strike a 'grand bargain', where one side gives up something strategically significant in exchange for something of equal or greater value.[5] Some have even speculated that Donald Trump, given his background in business, might be well disposed towards such a deal.[6] This speculation has generated concern in Taiwan and among some countries that lay claim in the South China Sea that Trump may be willing to trade away American support in these flashpoints in exchange for Beijing's help with resolving the North Korean nuclear issue. There is certainly some historical basis to their concerns: when Nixon and Kissinger famously brought about the diplomatic normalisation of US–China relations in the 1970s, this came at Taiwan's expense, while also catching another American ally, Japan, by surprise.

Even if Trump and Xi were to agree to trade North Korea for Taiwan, there is no guarantee that this would arrest Asia's crisis slide. The North Korean regime would struggle to survive if China cut off its considerable support, but it is difficult to envisage Kim Jong-un giving up without a fight. Instead, he would likely look for succour from other patrons, such as Russia, and through illicit channels. He could, for instance, seek to transfer nuclear weapons materials and technology to non-state actors. In a worst-case scenario, he might engage in nuclear blackmail, holding the world to ransom with his atomic arsenal. Troublingly, declining powers throughout history have shown a tendency to lash out.

Similarly, while Taiwan would struggle to defend itself from Chinese military attack without US backing, even in the absence of such support the outcome of a cross-strait conflict would not be assured. Taiwan's military is small but potent, while China's remains untested in modern conflict. Faced with American abandonment, Taiwan might even develop nuclear weapons, as it sought to do as recently as the late 1980s.

Given the limitations of an essentially top-down 'grand bargain' in a region as diverse as this, a more promising route might be to adopt a 'bottom-up' approach that attempts to arrest Asia's crisis slide by tackling the flashpoints themselves, especially those with the greatest potential to escalate into wide war. But which are Asia's largest and fast-moving boulders, to borrow Bell's metaphor?

Although the four flashpoints are interconnected, each has its own trajectory. Taiwan is by far Asia's most worrying flashpoint. Beijing's growing frustration with leaving this dispute unresolved, Taiwan's changing political and demographic profile, and uncertainties over Washington's willingness and ability to come to the island's defence combine to form a potentially deadly mix.

While Beijing, Taipei or Washington should not logically opt for war, the prospects for an escalation of tensions are growing, given this confluence of factors. China regards Taiwan as a 'core interest'. It is legally required to take the island by force in the event of a formal Taiwanese declaration of independence. The survival of Taiwanese society, and its population of twenty-three million, would be at stake. While Taiwanese opposition could melt away in the event of a Chinese attack, it could equally prove a dogged military opponent.

Some in the United States see Taiwan's strategic value rising exponentially in an era of deepening Sino–American competition. They fear that abandoning the island at this juncture will send the wrong message and do lasting damage to America's other

Asian alliances and strategic partnerships. For others, however, this game is no longer worth the candle for America, fuelling uncertainties regarding US commitment to Taiwan and to the region more generally.

The risk of escalation remains on the Korean Peninsula too, despite the heat that recent summits at Panmunjom and in Singapore have taken out of this nuclear conundrum. Should these ongoing diplomatic efforts falter, there could certainly come a point when Kim Jong-un reads too much into aggressive American rhetoric and mistakenly believes US military preparations are a prelude to attack, prompting him to order an anticipatory strike. Alternatively, Trump could take his 'America first' logic to its extreme and risk sacrificing Seoul and cities in Japan in order to eliminate the threat North Korean intercontinental ballistic missiles pose to the US homeland. Or Kim, feeling invulnerable due to his burgeoning nuclear and missile arsenal, and buoyed by the prospect of a faltering US–South Korea alliance, could launch a surprise conventional strike against Seoul with a view to reunifying Korea by force.

As conceivable as any of these scenarios are, the substantial human and financial costs of such violent conflict render them unlikely – unless the strategic situation changes. Instead, as has been the case throughout much of the history of the Korean Peninsula, deterrence remains the most viable approach for keeping it from firing.

The East China Sea shares similarities with Korea. Conflict here could be truly catastrophic. It is a war that none of the key players in this flashpoint – China, Japan and the United States – should opt for. Yet the possibility of an inadvertent Sino–Japanese military clash, unleashing uncontrollable nationalist fervour in China and Japan, is all too conceivable. If such a situation escalated into military conflict between China and Japan, it is hard to envisage the United States not enlisting on the side of its closest Asian ally, Japan. To stand on the sidelines in such circumstances would risk an unravelling of America's entire Asian alliance network, essentially putting an end to the longstanding US presence in this part of the world. A more likely outcome is the continuation of an uneasy equilibrium around this flashpoint, an equilibrium that continues to be underwritten by American deterrence.

Of the four flashpoints, the South China Sea is the least likely to erupt into a major war. The large number of players with a stake in this sea reflects its economic and strategic significance, but the interests of Asia's major powers are not sufficiently vital to provoke war. The possible exception is Beijing, but its ability to dominate this large body of water militarily is questionable. While China's militarisation of its artificial islands is an attempt to compensate for that shortcoming, those islands would last minutes in the event of large-scale military conflict. Moreover, the very vastness of the South China Sea further limits its potential for escalation. Unlike in geopolitical hotspots across land borders – such as the Korean Peninsula – history shows that tensions tend to develop much more slowly in vast maritime expanses, thereby allowing more time for crisis management and de-escalation.

Diplomacy faces significant obstacles across all four flashpoints. Asia is home to antipathies and animosities that run very deep. The legitimacy of its leaders – even and arguably especially those of non-democratic countries – depends heavily upon their attentiveness to these sentiments. Showing weakness towards a long-time adversary can amount to political suicide. Added to this, the four flashpoints have over the past quarter-century left behind them a long trail of agreements that either collapsed or were never implemented – the 1994 Agreed Framework, the proposed Taiwan peace treaty of the mid-2000s, the Sino–Japanese joint resource development consensus of 2008 and the Leap Day Agreement of 2012, to name just a few.

This is not to suggest that finding a lasting solution to any of the four flashpoints is impossible. As peace processes past – in such far-flung locales as Aceh, Cambodia, Northern Ireland and Sri Lanka – have shown, solutions can spring suddenly from the most seemingly intractable of disputes. Many hope that the Korean Peninsula will prove a case in point. But hope is never a strategy.

In the wake of the Cuban Missile Crisis, Robert McNamara asserted that 'there is no longer any such thing as strategy, only crisis management'.[7] With the risk rising of a major war that nobody wants, and with few credible diplomatic options on offer, McNamara's observation resonates in Asia today. Management through deterrence offers the most likely means for keeping the peace on the Korean Peninsula and in the East China Sea. The recent introduction of measures designed to reduce the risk of miscommunications and accidental clashes will also help. But these measures do not go far enough. We urgently need much more ambitious approaches, agreed to in advance, for managing major crises.

That need is currently greatest in relation to Taiwan. America's ability to deter a Chinese attack against the island is dissipating. It will be gone in a decade. As the waters and skies around Taiwan become more crowded and contested, the risk of an accidental military clash is rising. But with cross-strait relations in a deep freeze, there are no measures to head off this possibility or its resulting escalation of tensions. While some cross-strait communication likely continues through diplomatic back channels, such methods are risky and unreliable. Messages too easily get lost or distorted in the heat of a crisis.

A new power balance: Asia's most viable future

Debate over Asia's future is deeply divided. On one side are those who contend that China will very soon emerge as the region's dominant power, as its inexorable economic and military rise marginalises US influence and eventually evicts America from this part of the world. Some would argue that we have already reached that point. Australia's first ambassador to China, Stephan Fitzgerald, boldly declared in a March 2017 address that 'we are living in a Chinese world'.[8] Whether the transition to Chinese hegemony ultimately happens sooner or later, commentators of this persuasion see it as inevitable. As Hugh White observes starkly in *Without America*: 'How the contest will proceed – whether peacefully or violently, quickly or slowly – is still uncertain, but the most likely outcome is now becoming clear. America will lose, and China will win. America will cease to play a major strategic role in Asia, and China will take its place as the dominant power.'[9] Fitzgerald, White and others who share their view point to China's growing military might, to major Chinese-led economic arrangements such as the Asian Infrastructure Investment Bank and Xi's ambitious Belt and Road Initiative (BRI), and to a decline in America's willingness and ability to continue playing a leadership role in Asia to make their case.

On the other side of this debate are those commentators who argue that the US-led Asian order that has been in place since the end of World War II can still be preserved, provided America and other 'like-minded' countries, such as Australia, India and Japan, are prepared to stand together to stare down the Chinese challenge.

These analysts argue that for this effort to succeed, at least three things need to occur. First, America needs to reverse the defence budget cuts of the Obama era and rebuild its military, thereby maintaining its capacity to stay ahead of China's military advances. Channelling Ronald Reagan, Donald Trump characterises this approach as seeking 'peace through strength'.[10]

Second, like-minded US partners and allies need to stop free-riding on Washington and to assume greater costs and risks in support of the US-led order.[11] Canberra, for instance, should stop prevaricating and send military ships and aircraft within twelve nautical miles of China's artificial islands in the South China Sea.

Third, like-minded countries need to collectively provide viable alternatives to Chinese-led economic arrangements. In a clear attempt to respond to the BRI, Australia, India, Japan and the United States have reportedly included joint regional infrastructure development in discussions to revive the ill-fated Quadrilateral Security Dialogue of the mid-2000s.[12]

Provided this three-pronged approach is pursued, advocates argue, a 'favourable' balance of power can be maintained, and with it the incumbent US-led Asian order.

Asia's most viable future lies somewhere between these opposing camps.

When the United States and its allies think about the Asian balance of power, balance in any genuine sense is hardly what they have in mind. Instead, the 'balance' they are accustomed to is one where their side enjoys a significant margin of strength over its adversaries. This keeps the peace and preserves the international order, because those opponents are in no position to mount a serious military challenge. Condoleezza Rice, when she was George W. Bush's national security adviser, termed this type of arrangement 'a balance of power that favours freedom'.[13]

This kind of lopsided balance cannot last. Indeed, it is already toppling. As China's economic and military strength grow, America's ability to intervene in the Taiwan Strait is receding, while an attempt to re-engage carries the risk of sparking 'a war like no other'. Similarly, Washington will find it increasingly difficult to stare down Beijing in the South China Sea; geography favours China too strongly.

But this does not mean that a Chinese-dominated Asia is inevitable. America and its allies hold the upper hand in the East China Sea and on the Korean

Peninsula. For the foreseeable future, Beijing cannot prevail militarily over America in either of these areas or force its retreat. If Washington withdraws, it will be of its own volition.

These situations of strength can form the basis for a new Asian balance of power – which is why Trump's impulse to withdraw US troops from the Korean Peninsula is so ill-advised. This balance will be less lopsided, but that is in keeping with the original metaphor of balance in international politics. When Italian city statesmen of the fifteenth and sixteenth centuries came up with this concept, what they had in mind was an even distribution of power among the major players, an equilibrium where no sole power could become so strong as to endanger the others.[14]

These situations of strength will not be preserved without effort. As with a set of scales, America will need to adjust continually to the tests to its resolve that China will inevitably make. But with the future of its role in the region on the line, Washington should respond. The re deployment of assets towards these challenges and away from flashpoints where the United States is at a disadvantage will help. This will include a more focused Tokyo, no longer distracted by the South China Sea, putting its shoulder to America's wheel, closer to Japanese shores.

China will be unable to dominate Asia in its entirety. America will continue to meet its longest-standing objective – the prevention of regional dominance by a great power rival. But it will be able to do so credibly and with considerably lower risk than through an ill-advised attempt at preserving the incumbent order. Pulling back from Taiwan and the South China Sea does not represent a radical departure in strategic focus for America. It will not break any treaty commitments to US Asia-Pacific allies: Australia, Japan, the Philippines and South Korea. At the same time, China should be reasonably content because it will have the strategic space it craves to assuage its deep insecurities.

The suggestion that the United States draw back from the South China Sea and Taiwan is bound to be met with three key counterarguments. First, the Munich Analogy, which charges that such a step would be akin to the appeasement of Adolf Hitler in the period preceding World War II. According to this line of thinking, Xi's China, like Nazi Germany, is an expansionist power that will stop at nothing short of Asian dominance. A modern-day equivalent of the Munich Agreement – which allowed Germany to occupy the Sudetenland region of Czechoslovakia in the hope this would avoid war – should be avoided at all costs.

Second, that a pulling back might encourage Chinese opportunism, in much the same way as the infamous January 1950 speech by then US secretary of state Dean Acheson prompted Stalin to give Kim Il-sung the go-ahead to launch an invasion of South Korea.

Third, that Washington has successfully drawn its defensive line forward in the past when threatened by hegemonic aspirants. As Michael Green concludes in his magisterial account of US grand strategy in the Asia-Pacific, 'the American people have learned much since 1935 about the importance of keeping threats as far west across the Pacific as possible'.[15]

These counterarguments are flawed. The Munich Analogy is frequently invoked, but it is not convincing when transplanted to contemporary Asia. There are clear similarities between the behaviour of China today and Germany in the 1930s, but these are similarities that can be found in the behaviours of most great powers on the rise.[16] More important are the considerable differences between Xi's China and Hitler's Germany: nothing in Xi's behaviour to date points to a China so hell-bent on hegemony that it is willing to risk its interests in the way that Hitler so evidently was. All the evidence so far appears to suggest that Xi is more interested in furthering Chinese influence in ways that avoid major conflict. This is most apparent in Beijing's 'salami-slicing' tactics in the South and East China Seas, which seem more in keeping with the sophisticated thinking of the famous Chinese strategist Sun Tzu than with the reckless abandon of the notorious German dictator.

The same is true of the Korea analogy. There is little, if any, evidence to suggest that China would opportunistically move to claim Taiwan with force, even if it became apparent that the United States was no longer committed to defending it. This is also true of China's presence in the South China Sea. Despite Xi's stated impatience on Taiwan, unless Beijing is directly provoked the most likely future for these two areas is incremental drift into China's orbit. Indeed, if there is a contemporary lesson to be drawn from the Korea analogy, it is the importance of states correctly identifying their vital interests to begin with and making clear to potential opponents their willingness and ability to defend these – including with military force – should they come under challenge.

This need for a careful calculation and clarification of vital interests also calls into question the idea that the United States should extend its defensive line in Asia during periods of strategic challenge. In truth, that line has moved back and forth throughout US history, with varying results. At times it has been drawn back as far as Hawaii and, with an avowedly 'America first' president in the White House, a return to that approach is not beyond the realm of possibility. During other periods it has extended onto the Asian continent itself, sometimes with disastrous results. The classic example here is the Vietnam War, which, within a relatively short period of time, absorbed Washington's political attention and saw it devote substantial military assets to a country of questionable strategic relevance in the larger Cold War contest. Rather than Munich or Korea, it is perhaps this historical analogy that the Trump administration should have foremost in mind as it contemplates deeper ties with Taipei and more active involvement in the South China Sea.

Yet in the final analysis, all this discussion of power balances, situations of strengths and defensive lines will be largely meaningless if Asia's worsening crisis slide is not arrested. The good news is that it can be, and catastrophic conflict, sparked by mistake or miscalculation and fuelled by the mounting pressure of repeated strategic crises, can be avoided. But this will not be easy. It will require careful management of Asia's increasingly interconnected flashpoints, which each require subtly different methods of control.

More importantly, it will demand of Asia's leaders a much greater sense of urgency than has so far been shown. Because time is running short. The doomsday clock is ticking, and midnight is almost upon us.

ACKNOWLEDGEMENTS

The ideas in this book have been percolating over a long period. They are the product of almost two decades of travel in the Asia-Pacific, talking with scholars, practitioners, think-tankers and journalists. I thank all those concerned for the many stimulating discussions. I am particularly indebted to Robert Ayson, the late Des Ball, Chris Barrie, Paul Dibb, Tim Huxley, Richard Rigby and Bill Tow for the many doors they have opened to allow me these opportunities and for their input into this book.

I am especially grateful to Michael Wesley and Hugh White, two inspirational mentors who introduced me to the Black Inc. stable and encouraged me to write this book. It has been a joy working with Chris Feik and Julia Carlomagno from Black Inc. The book has benefited immensely from their editorial advice.

Many friends and colleagues have endured countless conversations about this book. Among those, I am particularly grateful for the counsel and support of Joan Beaumont, Nick Bisley, Andrew Carr, Mathew Davies, Peter Dean, Ralf Emmers, David Envall, Bates Gill, Evelyn Goh and Amy King. The administrative support provided by Deanne Drummond and Kian Kuemmel was also invaluable.

I was fortunate to be able to test some of the ideas in this book with receptive audiences. In April 2017,

I gave several talks in the United States, including presentations at the Center for Strategic and International Studies, the East–West Center, Georgetown University, and the Center for Strategic and Budgetary Assessments. In June 2017, I was privileged to share some tentative conclusions with participants in the Southeast Asian Young Leaders' Programme at the 2017 Shangri-La Dialogue. In September 2017, I gave seminars at the S. Rajaratnam School of International Studies and the ISEAS-Yusof Ishak Institute in Singapore. And in October 2017 I shared my emerging thinking in a talk to scholars from China's Sun Yat-sen University.

I am most appreciative of the encouragement and support offered by my mother, Marie Taylor, throughout this project and in all my academic endeavours. Similar thanks are due to my sister, Rebecca, and her husband, Cameron.

Words cannot express the debt of gratitude I owe to my wonderful wife, Jenny. She gave birth to our second daughter, Siobhan, as I was in the final stages of writing the manuscript, and she selflessly took on a disproportionate share of Siobhan's care to allow me to see it through to completion. This book is dedicated to her.

Siobhan was born in January 2018, the same month the Doomsday Clock showed two minutes to midnight. I hope that this book makes some small contribution to turning that clock back and to making the region that I have been so fortunate to grow up in as peaceful and as prosperous for her and her big sister, Sinead.

NOTES

Introduction: Ticking Towards Midnight

[1] Lindsey Bever, 'The Making of the Doomsday Clock: Art, Science and the Atomic Apocalypse', *The Washington Post,* 25 January 2018.

[2] Eugene Rabinowitch, 'The Narrowing Way', *Bulletin of the Atomic Scientists,* vol.9, no.8, 1953, p.294.

[3] John Meclin, ed., 'It is 2 Minutes to Midnight: 2018 Doomsday Clock Statement', *Bulletin of the Atomic Scientists,* Science and Security Board, 25 January 2018.

[4] Jesse Johnson, '80% of Japanese Fear Military Clash Around Senkakus, Poll Finds', *The Japan Times,* 14 September 2016.

[5] Tom O'Connor, 'Only "War" Could Stop China from Controlling the South China Sea, US Military Commander Says', *Newsweek,* 20 April 2018.

[6] J. Michael Cole, 'For Taiwanese, Democracy is the Only Game in Town – And They Would Fight to Defend It', *Taiwan Sentinel,* 20 April 2018.

[7] Bernard Brodie, *War and Politics,* The MacMillan Company, New York, 1973, p.342.

[8] Cited in Robert Jervis, 'Unpacking a US Decision to Use Force Against North Korea: Issues, Options and Consequences', *38 North Special Report,* January 2018.

Chapter 1: Ripe for Rivalry

[1] Aaron L. Friedberg, 'Ripe for Rivalry: Prospects for Peace in a Multipolar Asia', *International Security,* vol.18, no.3, Winter 1993–94, p.7.

[2] Desmond Ball, 'Arms and Affluence: Military Acquisitions in the Asia-Pacific region', *International Security,* vol.18, no.3, Winter 1993–94, p.87.

[3] George Friedman and Meredith LeBard, *The Coming War with Japan,* St Martin's Press, New York, 1991.

[4] Zbigniew Brzezinski, 'The Group of Two That Could Change the World', *Financial Times,* 14 January 2009.

[5] See for example Richard A. Bitzinger and Barry Desker, 'Why East Asian War Is Unlikely', *Survival,* vol.50, no.6, December 2008–January 2009, pp.105–28.

[6] Kevin Rudd, 'It's Time to Build an Asia Pacific Community', Address to the Asia Society Australasia Centre, Sydney, 4 June 2008.

[7]   Robert S. Ross, 'The Geography of the Peace: East Asia in the Twenty-First Century', *International Security,* vol.23, no.4, Spring 1999, pp.81–18.

[8]   See for example Mikael Weissmann, *The East Asian Peace: Conflict Prevention and Informal Peacebuilding,* Palgrave Macmillan, New York, 2012.

[9]   Graham Allison, *Destined for War: Can America and China Escape Thucydides's Trap?,* Houghton Mifflin Harcourt, Boston and New York, 2017.

[10]   Christopher Coker, *The Improbable War: China, the United States and the Logic of Great Power Conflict,* Hurst & Company, London, 2015, p.5.

[11]   Richard McGregor, *Asia's Reckoning: China, Japan and the Fate of US Power in the Pacific Century,* Viking, New York, 2017.

[12]   Malcolm Turnbull, 'Keynote Address at the 16th IISS Asia Security Summit, Shangri-La Dialogue', Singapore, 2 June 2017.

[13]   Chen Weihua, 'Proposal for New Type of Power Relations Still a Win-Win Proposition', *China Daily,* 24 March 2017.

[14]   Timothy D. Hoyt, 'Politics, Proximity and Paranoia: The Evolution of Kashmir as a Nuclear Flashpoint', *India Review,* vol.2, no.3, 2003, p.119.

[15]   Graham Allison, *Destined for War,* p. xiv.

[16]   Hugh White, *Without America: Australia in the New Asia,* Quarterly Essay, no.68, 2017, p.1.

[17]   Graham Allison and Philip Zelikow, *Essence of Decision: Explaining the Cuban Missile Crisis,* 2nd edn, Longman, New York, 1999.

[18]   Joseph S. Nye Jr., 'Inevitability and War', in Richard N. Rosecrance and Steven E. Miller, *The Next Great War?: The Roots of World War I and the Risk of U.S.–China Conflict,* Belfer Center for Science and International Affairs, Cambridge, 2015, p.186.

[19]   Geoffrey Blainey, *The Causes of War,* The Free Press, New York, 1973, pp.228–42.

[20]   For further reading see Victor D. Cha, *Powerplay: The Origins of the American Alliance System in Asia,* Princeton University Press, Princeton and Oxford, 2016.

[21]   For further reading see G. John Ikenberry, 'American Hegemony and East Asian Order', *Australian Journal of International Affairs,* vol.58, no.3, September 2004, pp.353–67.

[22]   For further reading see Kimie Hara, *Cold War Frontiers in the Asia-Pacific,* Routledge, London and New York, 2007.

[23] PricewaterhouseCoopers, 'The Long View: How Will the Global Economic Order Change by 2050?', February 2017.

[24] David E. Sanger and William J. Broad, 'A "Cuban Missile Crisis in Slow Motion" in North Korea', *The New York Times,* 16 April 2017.

Chapter 2: Asia's Crucible

[1] Jon Rabiroff, 'S. Korea's Overpasses to Nowhere Remain Part of Defense Strategy', *Stars and Stripes,* 12 June 2010.

[2] Park Geun-hye, 'A Plan for Peace in North Asia', *The Wall Street Journal,* 12 November 2012.

[3] Tom O'Neill, 'Korea's Dangerous Divide', *National Geographic,* vol.204, no.1, July 2003, p.2.

[4] John Lewis Gaddis, *The Cold War,* Allen Lane, London, 2005, pp.40–1.

[5] ibid, p.42.

[6] David Halberstam, *The Coldest Winter: America and the Korean War,* Hyperion, New York, 2007, p.4.

[7] Korea Foundation, *The DMZ: Dividing the Two Koreas,* Seoul Selection, Seoul, 2010, pp.53–4.

[8] James Pearson and Christine Kim, 'North Korea Replaces Soldiers, South Korea Awards Medals

After Defector's Border Dash', *Reuters,* 24 November 2017.

[9]   David Broder, 'Clinton Warns Summit; U.S. to Press G-7 Leaders to Aid Recovery', *The Washington Post,* 3 July 1993.

[10]   Van Jackson, *Rival Reputations: Coercion and Credibility in US– North Korea Relations,* Cambridge University Press, Cambridge, 2016, pp.100–37.

[11]   Korea Foundation, *The DMZ,* pp.85–6.

[12]   Duyeon Kim, 'The Inter-Korean Deal: Defusing Recent Tensions', *Carnegie Endowment for International Peace,* 31 August 2015.

[13]   Victor Cha, 'What to Do About N. Korean Aggression?', *The Chosun Ilbo,* 6 December 2010.

[14]   Michael J. Mazarr, *North Korea and the Bomb: A Case Study in Nonproliferation,* St. Martin's Press, New York, 1995, p.79.

[15]   AFP, '200 Feared Killed Amid North Korean Nuke Test', *The Australian,* 1 November 2017.

[16]   Michael Elleman, 'From Under the Sea: North Korea's Latest Missile Test', *38 North,* 3 June 2015.

[17]   Michael Elleman, 'North Korea's Third ICBM Launch', *38 North,* 29 November 2017.

[18]   Choe Sang-Hun, 'North Koreans Rely on Smuggled Cellphones to Connect to the Outside World', *The New York Times,* 26 March 2016.

[19]   Daniel Byman and Jennifer Lind, 'Pyongyang's Survival Strategy: Tools of Authoritarian Control in North Korea', *International Security,* vol.35, no.1, Summer 2010, p.63.

[20]   Anna Fifield, 'North Korea Wants Military "Equilibrium" with the U.S., Kim Jong Un Says', *The Washington Post,* 15 September 2017.

[21]   Timothy W. Martin and Thomas Grove, 'Kim Jong Un Defends Nuclear Program as North Korea's "Treasured Sword"', *The Wall Street Journal,* 8 October 2017.

[22]   Jesse Johnson, 'In an Announcement to All Koreans, Pyongyang Calls for Unification and End to U.S. Military Exercises', *The Japan Times,* 25 January 2018.

[23]   Tan Dawn Wei, 'Withdrawal of US Troops in South Korea 'Not on the Table' at Trump-Kim Summit: Mattis', *The Straits Times,* 2 June 2018.

[24]   Jonathan Cheng and Andrew Jeong, 'U.S. Troops in South Korea Emerge as Potential Bargaining Chip', *The Wall Street Journal,* 6 May 2018.

[25]   For further reading see Robert E. Kelly, 'The Real North Korea Threat: A Forced Unification?', *The National Interest,* 16 January 2018.

[26]   U.S. Congress, Senate, Hearing before the Committee on Armed Services, 'Security Implications of the Nuclear Non-Proliferation Agreement with North Korea', 104th Congress, 1st session, 26 January 1995, p.22.

[27]   The Asan Institute for Policy Studies, 'South Koreans and Their Neighbors 2016', *Asan Public Opinion Survey,* 3 May 2016, p.18.

[28]   For further reading see Emma Campbell, *South Korea's New Nationalism: The End of "One Korea"?* Lynne Reinner Publishers, Boulder, 2016.

[29]   The White House, 'President Donald J. Trump's State of the Union Address', Washington, DC, 30 January 2018.

[30]   Maggie Haberman and David E. Sanger, '"It Won't Happen," Donald Trump Says of North Korean Missile Test', *The New York Times,* 2 January 2017.

[31]   Noah Bierman, 'Trump Warns North Korea of "Fire and Fury"', *Los Angeles Times,* 8 August 2017.

[32]   Adam Nagourney, David E. Sanger and Johanna Barr, 'Hawaii Panics After Alert About Incoming

Missile Is Sent in Error', *The New York Times,* 13 January 2018.

[33]   See 'Text of President Bush's 2002 State of the Union Address', *The Washington Post,* 29 January 2002.

[34]   Benjamin Schreer and Brendan Taylor, 'The Korean Crises and Sino-American Rivalry', *Survival,* vol.53, no.1, February–March 2011, pp.13–19.

[35]   Jonathan Cheng and Kwanwoo Jun, 'North Korea Executes Five Senior Officials with Antiaircraft Guns', *The Wall Street Journal,* 27 February 2017.

[36]   Peter Walker, 'North Korea Human Rights Abuses Resemble Those of the Nazis, Says UN Inquiry', *The Guardian,* 18 February 2014.

[37]   Shi Jiangtao, 'North Korea's Kim Jong-un "Snubs" China in Failure to Repay Diplomatic Favour', *South China Morning Post,* 21 November 2017.

[38]   Bates Gill, 'China's North Korea Policy: Assessing Interests and Influences', United States Institute of Peace, Special Report 283, July 2011, p.2.

[39]   Mark Landler and Javier C. Hernandez, 'Trump Warns China He Is Willing to Pressure North

Korea on His Own', *The New York Times,* 3 July 2017.

[40]   For further reading see Brendan Taylor, 'US–China Cooperation on North Korea Remains Critical', *East Asia Forum,* 25 July 2017.

[41]   Sheryl WuDunn, 'North Korea Fires Missile Over Japanese Territory', *The New York Times,* 1 September 1998.

[42]   Jesse Johnson, 'North Korea Says Missile Launches Were Training for Striking U.S. Bases in Japan', *The Japan Times,* 7 March 2017.

[43]   Anna Fifield, 'Japan Warns Citizens They Might Have Only 10 Minutes to Prepare for North Korean Missile', *The Washington Post,* 25 April 2017.

[44]   Anthony H. Cordesman with the assistance of Charles Ayers, *The Military Balance in the Koreas and Northeast Asia,* Center for Strategic and International Studies, Washington, DC, 2017, pp.74–7.

[45]   Amanda Erickson, 'Russia Warns Against "Intimidating" North Korea After Its Latest Missile Launch', *The Washington Post,* 15 May 2017.

[46]   Sofia Lotto Persio, 'Will the U.S. Go to War with North Korea?: Expert Estimates 50/50

214

Chance of Conflict in 2018', *Newsweek,* 9 November 2017.

[47] Evan Osnos, 'Is the Political Class Drifting Toward War with North Korea?', *The New Yorker,* 8 November 2017; Kevin Rudd, 'Chance of Second Korean War Between 20 and 25 Per Cent', *The Sydney Morning Herald,* 6 September 2017.

[48] Peter Baker and David E. Sanger, 'Trump Says Tillerson is "Wasting His Time" on North Korea', *The New York Times,* 1 October 2017.

[49] For further reading see Mira Rapp-Hooper, 'The Cataclysm That Would Follow a "Bloody Nose" Strike on North Korea', *The Atlantic,* 31 January 2018.

[50] Hiroyuki Akita, 'Trump's Military Options in Spotlight After Korean Ambassador Spat', *Nikkei Asian Review,* 3 February 2018.

[51] Michael Birnbaum, Anna Fifield and Loveday Morris, 'The Return of John Bolton, a Hawk on North Korea and Iran, Sparks Concerns Around the World', *The Washington Post,* 23 March 2018.

[52] Dan Lamothe and Carol Morello, 'Securing North Korean Nuclear Sites Would Require a Ground Invasion, Pentagon Says', *The Washington Post,* 4 November 2017.

[53]   David Barno and Nora Bensahel, 'Why Americans Aren't Really Worried About War with North Korea', *War on the Rocks,* 16 January 2018.

[54]   Kathleen J. McInnis, et. al., 'The North Korean Nuclear Challenge: Military Options and Issues for Congress', CRS Report prepared for Members and Committees of Congress, Congressional Research Service, 6 November 2017, p.34.

[55]   Joel S. Wit, Daniel B. Poneman and Robert L. Gallucci, *Going Critical: The First North Korean Nuclear Crisis,* Brookings Institution Press, Washington, DC, 2004, pp.226–7.

[56]   Leon Sigal, *Disarming Strangers: Nuclear Diplomacy with North Korea,* Princeton University Press, Princeton, 1998, p.215.

[57]   Joel S. Wit, Daniel B. Poneman and Robert L. Gallucci, *Going Critical,* p. 227.

[58]   Admiral Dennis Blair, 'Trump's Trip to Asia and Fundamentals to Consider in a High Stakes Environment', Chairman's Message, Sasakawa Peace Foundation USA, 3 November 2017.

[59]   Luke O'Brien, 'Limited Strikes on North Korea Would Be an Unlimited Disaster', *Foreign Policy,* 22 January 2018.

[60] For further reading see Van Jackson, 'Want to Strike North Korea?: It's Not Going to Go the Way You Think', *Politico,* 12 January 2018.

[61] See 'How North Korea Would Retaliate', *Stratfor,* 5 January 2017.

[62] See for example Soyoung Kim, 'South Korea Minister Says Military Option "Unacceptable" on North Korea Crisis', *Reuters,* 25 January 2018; Reuters, 'Seoul Warns Trump: US Must Not Strike North Korea Without Our Consent', *The Guardian,* 16 November 2017.

[63] Abraham M. Denmark, 'The Myth of the Limited Strike on North Korea', *Foreign Affairs,* 9 January 2018.

[64] World Bank Group, 'Balancing Act', World Bank East Asia and Pacific Economic Update, October 2017, p.36.

[65] Victor Cha, *The Impossible State: North Korea, Past and Future,* Harper Collins, New York, 2012, pp.386–93.

[66] For further reading on the Six Party Talks see Leszek Buszynski, *Negotiating with North Korea: The Six Party Talks and the Nuclear Issue,* Routledge, Abingdon, 2013.

[67] Ankit Panda, 'A Great Leap to Nowhere: Remembering the US–North Korea "Leap Day" Deal', *The Diplomat,* 29 February 2016.

[68]   ibid.

[69]   Chung-in Moon, 'A Real Path to Peace on the Korean Peninsula: The Progress and Promise of the Moon-Kim Summit', *Foreign Affairs,* 30 April 2018.

[70]   Kang Jin-kyu, 'Kim Jong-un Promised to Invite Inspectors to Shutting Down of Nuclear Test Site', *Korea Joongang Daily,* 29 April 2018.

[71]   Frank V. Pabian, 'The Punggye-ri Nuclear Test Site: A Test Tunnel Tutorial', *38 North,* 23 May 2018.

[72]   International Atomic Energy Agency, 'IAEA and DPRK: Chronology of Key Events', 2017.

[73]   Clint Work, 'U.S. Soldiers Might Be Stuck in Korea Forever', *Foreign Policy,* 1 May 2018.

[74]   Carol Morello, Michelle Ye Hee Lee and Emily Rauhala, 'U.N. Agrees to Toughest-Ever Sanctions Against North Korea', *The Washington Post,* 11 September 2017.

[75]   Demetri Sevastopulo, 'US Imposes More Sanctions on Chinese and North Korea Companies', *Financial Times,* 25 January 2018.

[76]   Morello et al., 'U.N. Agrees to Toughest-Ever Sanctions Against North Korea'.

[77]   David Brunnstrom and Susan Heavey, 'Donald Trump Says He Caught China "Red-Handed"

Selling Oil into North Korea', *Australian Financial Review,* 29 December 2017.

[78] Kate O'Keefe, 'How North Korea's Global Financing Web Works Around Sanctions', *The Wall Street Journal,* 12 December 2017.

[79] Peter Harrell and Juan Zarate, 'How to Successfully Sanction North Korea', *Foreign Affairs,* 30 January 2018.

[80] Terence Roehrig, 'The Abilities – and Limits – of North Korean Early Warning', *Bulletin of the Atomic Scientists,* 27 November 2017.

[81] Robert S. Ross, 'Comparative Deterrence: The Taiwan Strait and the Korean Peninsula', in Alastair Iain Johnston and Robert S. Ross (eds), *New Directions in the Study of China's Foreign Policy,* Stanford University Press, Stanford, 2006, pp.33–4.

[82] Franz-Stefan Gady, 'US, ROK Agree to Scrap Warhead Weight Limit for Ballistic Missiles', *The Diplomat,* 6 September 2017.

[83] THAAD is a relatively new system, having only entered production in 2008. THAAD is designed to intercept missiles in the downward, so-called 'terminal' stage of their trajectory. For further reading see Ankit Panda, 'What Is THAAD, What Does It Do, and Why Is China Mad About It?', *The Diplomat,* 25 February 2016.

[84] Robert L. Gallucci, 'The North Korean Threat: War, Deterrence and Diplomacy', *The National Interest,* 31 October 2017.

[85] Fred Kaplan, 'The Worst Defense', *Slate,* 17 October 2017.

[86] Hugh White, 'The Prospect of a North Korean ICBM', *The Interpreter,* 17 December 2012.

[87] Andrew Restuccia, 'Trump on North Korea: "The Era of Strategic Patience Is Over"', *Politico,* 6 November 2017.

[88] Korea Foundation, *The DMZ,* p.51.

[89] William J. Broad and David E. Sanger, 'North Korea Nuclear Disarmament Could Take 15 Years, Expert Warns', *The New York Times,* 28 May 2018.

Chapter 3: Bitter Enmity

[1] Park Geun-hye, 'A Plan for Peace in North Asia'.

[2] Unryu Suganuma, 'Japan and China: Senkaku/Diaoyu and the Okinawa/Liuqiu Problems', in Kimie Hara (ed.), *The San Francisco System and Its Legacies: Continuation, Transformation and Historical Reconciliation in the Asia-Pacific,* Routledge, London and New York, 2015, p.56.

[3]   For further reading on the history of Sino-Japanese conflict see Rana Mitter, *China's War with Japan 1937–1945: The Struggle for Survival,* Allen Lane, London, 2013, pp.17–33.

[4]   For further reading on the Chinese claim to the islands see William Choong, *The Ties That Divide: History, Honour and Territory in Sino-Japanese Relations,* Routledge for the International Institute for Strategic Studies, Abingdon, 2014, pp.71–3.

[5]   For a useful summary of Japanese claims to the islands see ibid., pp.73–5.

[6]   For further reading see Jean Marc F. Blanchard, 'The U.S. Role in the Sino-Japanese Dispute over the Diaoyu (Senkaku) Islands', *The China Quarterly,* no.161, March 2000, pp.102–17.

[7]   Michael J. Green, *By More Than Providence: Grand Strategy and American Power in the Asia Pacific Since 1783,* Columbia University Press, New York, 2017, p.342.

[8]   Jean Marc F. Blanchard, 'The U.S. Role in the Sino-Japanese Dispute over the Diaoyu (Senkaku) Islands', p.120.

[9]   Cited in Sheila A. Smith, *Intimate Rivals: Japanese Domestic Politics and a Rising China,* Columbia University Press, New York, 2015, p.103.

[10] Ralf Emmers, *Geopolitics and Maritime Territorial Disputes in East Asia,* Routledge, London and New York, 2010, p.54.

[11] Michael Green, Kathleen Hicks, Zack Cooper, John Schaus and Jake Douglas, *Countering Coercion in Maritime Asia: The Theory and Practice of Gray Zone Deterrence,* Rowman & Littlefield for the Center for Strategic and International Studies, Lanham, Boulder, New York and London, 2017, pp.66–94.

[12] Cited in ibid., p.142.

[13] Nick Bisley and Brendan Taylor, *Conflict in the East China Sea: Would ANZUS Apply?,* Australia–China Relations Institute, University of Technology Sydney, Sydney, November 2014, pp.12–13.

[14] Shannon Tiezzi, 'A China–Japan Breakthrough: A Primer on Their 4 Point Consensus', *The Diplomat,* 7 November 2014.

[15] Jesse Johnson, 'Japan's Fighter Jet Scrambles Set New Record in 2016 Amid Surging Chinese Military Activity', *The Japan Times,* 14 April 2017.

[16] 'Playing Chicken in the East China Sea', Asia Maritime Transparency Initiative, 28 April 2017.

[17]   Bruce Stokes, 'Hostile Neighbors: China vs. Japan', Pew Research Center, 13 September 2016.

[18]   PricewaterhouseCoopers, 'The Long View', February 2017.

[19]   Toshi Yoshihara, 'Chinese Maritime Geography', in Thomas G. Mahnken and Dan Blumenthal (eds), *Strategy in Asia: The Past, Present, and Future of Regional Security,* Stanford University Press, Stanford, 2014, p.52.

[20]   Michael Auslin, 'Don't Forget About the East China Sea', *East and South China Seas Bulletin,* no.2, Center for a New American Security, 3 May 2012, p.2.

[21]   Cited in Toshi Yoshihara, 'Chinese Maritime Geography', p.52.

[22]   ibid., pp.52–3.

[23]   Ankit Panda, 'Obama: Senkakus Covered Under US–Japan Security Treaty', *The Diplomat,* 24 April 2014; Ayako Mie, 'Mattis Clarifies U.S. Defense Pledge, Stays Mum on Host-Nation Support', *The Japan Times,* 4 February 2017.

[24]   Chietigj Bajpaee, 'Japan and China: The Geo-Economic Dimension', *The Diplomat,* 28 March 2016.

[25]   Peter Drysdale, 'The Geo-Economic Potential of the China–Japan Relationship', *East Asia Forum,* 28 September 2015.

[26]   Rumi Aoyama, 'Getting Down to Business on Japan–China Relations', *East Asia Forum,* 21 August 2017.

[27]   Editors, 'Japan Opens the Way to Cooperation on China's Belt and Road Initiative', *East Asia Forum,* 10 July 2017.

[28]   See J. Berkshire Miller, 'Japan Warms to China', *Foreign Affairs,* 17 July 2017.

[29]   For further reading see International Crisis Group, 'East China Sea: Preventing Clashes from Becoming Crises', *Asia Report,* no.280, 20 June 2016, pp.4–6.

[30]   William Choong, *The Ties That Divide,* p.111.

[31]   For further elaboration of this argument see Allen R. Carlson, 'Why Chinese Nationalism Could Impact the East and South China Seas VERY Differently', *The National Interest,* 24 September 2015.

[32]   International Institute for Strategic Studies, *The Military Balance,* vol.118, no.1, 2018, pp.249–74.

[33]   James Holmes, 'The Sino–Japanese Naval War of 2012', *Foreign Policy,* 20 August 2012.

[34]   Motoko Rich, 'Shinzo Abe Announces Plan to Revise Japan's Pacifist Constitution', *The New York Times,* 3 May 2017.

[35]   Mina Pollman, 'What's in Japan's Record 2018 Defense Budget Request', *The Diplomat,* 28 August 2017.

[36]   Leo Lewis and Kana Inagaki, 'Japan Plans Missile to Test Chinese Strategy in East China Sea', *Financial Times,* 17 August 2016.

[37]   Michael J. Green, *Japan's Reluctant Realism: Foreign Policy Challenges in an Era of Uncertain Power,* Palgrave, New York, 2001.

[38]   James Holmes, 'The Sino–Japanese Naval War of 2012'.

[39]   Robert Ayson and Desmond Ball, 'Can a Sino–Japanese War Be Controlled?', *Survival,* vol.56, no.6, December 2014–January 2015, pp.135–66.

[40]   For further reading see Desmond Ball and Richard Tanter, *The Tools of Owatatsumi: Japan's Ocean Surveillance and Coastal Defence Capabilities,* ANU Press, Canberra, 2015.

[41]   James Manicom, *Bridging Troubled Waters: China, Japan, and Maritime Order in the East China Sea,* Georgetown University Press, Washington, DC, 2014, p.139.

[42]   ibid, pp.148–51.

[43]   ibid, p.59.

[44]   James Reilly, 'China's Unilateral Sanctions', *The Washington Quarterly,* vol.35, no.4, Fall 2012, pp.121–33.

[45]   John Aglionby, 'The Art of Toilet Diplomacy', *The Guardian,* 28 July 2006.

[46]   Banyan, 'Dust-up at the Shangri-La', *The Economist,* 1 June 2014.

[47]   For an excellent discussion of America's traditional deterrence approach to East Asia's territorial disputes see Mira Rapp-Hooper, 'Uncharted Waters: Extended Deterrence and Maritime Disputes', *The Washington Quarterly,* vol.38, no.1, Spring 2015, pp.127–46.

[48]   See for instance Franz-Stefan Gady, 'US, Japan Conduct Military Exercise Near Senkakus', *The Diplomat,* 17 August 2017.

[49]   See for example Mira Rapp-Hooper, 'Uncharted Waters', pp.138–9.

[50]   'Statement on Prime Minister Abe's December 26 Visit to Yasukuni Shrine', U.S. Embassy & Consulates in Japan, 26 December 2013.

[51]   Abe was initially elected prime minister by the Japanese parliament (Diet) in September 2006, but was forced to resign twelve months later on health grounds. He subsequently made a political comeback, successfully winning back

the leadership of the Liberal Democratic Party (LDP) in September 2012. The LDP, under Abe's leadership, went on to secure a landslide victory in Japan's 2012 general election.

[52] International Crisis Group, 'East China Sea', p.8.

[53] Ankit Panda, 'Japan, China Agree to Implement East China Sea Crisis Management Hotline', *The Diplomat,* 7 December 2017.

[54] Zhou Bo, 'Crisis Management Pact Will Soothe Choppy Relations: Zhou Bo Says the Long-awaited Agreement Between China and Japan Comes as a Huge Relief', *South China Morning Post,* 15 May 2018.

[55] Dennis C. Blair and David B. Bonfili, 'The April 2001 EP-3 Incident: The U.S. Point of View', in Michael D. Swaine and Zhang Tuosheng (eds), *Managing Sino–American Crises: Case Studies and Analysis,* Carnegie Endowment for International Peace, Washington, DC, 2006, p.380.

[56] Coral Bell, *Negotiation from Strength: A Study in the Politics of Power,* Alfred A. Knopf, New York, 1963, pp.6–7.

[57] See for example Steven Stashwick, 'South China Sea: Conflict Escalation and "Miscalculation" Myths', *The Diplomat,* 25 September 2015.

[58] David A. Welch, 'Crisis Management Mechanisms: Pathologies and Pitfalls', CIGI Papers, no.40, September 2014, p.8.

Chapter 4: Chinese Lake

[1] For further reading see Jeff Himmelman, 'A Game of Shark and Minnow', *The New York Times,* 27 October 2013.

[2] Floyd Whaley, 'Clinton Reaffirms Military Ties with the Philippines', *The New York Times,* 16 November 2011.

[3] Robert D. Kaplan, *Asia's Cauldron: The South China Sea and the End of a Stable Pacific,* Random House, New York, 2014, pp.139–41.

[4] See for example 'Chinese Poachers Caught with Coral Haul Near Taiwan-Controlled Pratas Islands in South China Sea', *The Straits Times,* 28 March 2016.

[5] For a detailed overview of the geography of these four island groupings see Dieter Heinzig, *Disputed Islands in the South China Sea,* Otto Harrassowitz, Wiesbaden, 1976.

[6] Robert Beckman, 'Scarborough Shoal: Flashpoint for Confrontation or Opportunity for Cooperation?', *RSIS Commentaries,* no.072/2012, 24 April 2012.

[7]   Marwyn S. Samuels, *Contest for the South China Sea,* Methuen, New York and London, 1982, pp.10, 16.

[8]   ibid, pp.20–1.

[9]   ibid, p.24.

[10]   ibid, p.53.

[11]   ibid.

[12]   Stein Tonnesson, 'The South China Sea in the Age of European Decline', *Modern Asian Studies,* vol.40, no.1, February 2006, pp.4–6.

[13]   ibid, pp.9–16.

[14]   Sarah Raine and Christian Le Miere, *Regional Disorder: The South China Sea Disputes,* Routledge for the International Institute for Strategic Studies, London, 2013, p.40.

[15]   Stein Tonnesson, 'The South China Sea in the Age of European Decline', pp.50–1.

[16]   Michael Richardson, 'Chinese Gambit: Seizing Spratly Reef Without a Fight', *The New York Times,* 17 February 1995.

[17]   For further reading see Mark Valencia, 'The Impeccable Incident: Truth and Consequences', *China Security,* vol.5, no.2, 2009, pp.26–32.

[18]   Michael Green et al., *Countering Coercion in Maritime Asia,* pp.116–17.

[19] ibid, p.118. 20 ibid, p.202.

[21] See 'Land Reclamation by Country', Center for Strategic and International Studies, Asia Maritime Transparency Initiative.

[22] Admiral Harry B. Harris, Address to Australian Strategic Policy Institute, Canberra, Australia, 31 March 2015.

[23] Asia Maritime Transparency Initiative, 'Comparing Aerial and Satellite Images of China's Spratly Outposts', 16 February 2018.

[24] Michael Forsythe, 'Missiles Deployed on Disputed South China Sea Island, Officials Say', *The New York Times,* 17 February 2016.

[25] Amanda Macias, 'China Quietly Installed Defensive Missile Systems on Strategic Spratly Islands in Hotly Contested South China Sea', *CNBC,* 2 May 2018.

[26] For further reading see Clive Schofield, 'A Landmark Decision in the South China Sea: The Scope and Implications of the Arbitral Tribunal's Award', *Contemporary Southeast Asia,* vol.38, no.3, December 2016, pp.339–47.

[27] Richard C. Paddock, 'Rodrigo Duterte, Pushing Split with U.S., Counters Philippines' Deep Ties', *The New York Times,* 26 October 2016.

[28]   Lee YingHui, 'A South China Sea Code of Conduct: Is Real Progress Possible?', *The Diplomat,* 18 November 2017.

[29]   Jamie Seidel, 'Beijing Launches "Monthly" South China Sea Combat Exercises', news.com.au, 27 March 2018.

[30]   For further reading see Marina Tsirbas, 'Saving the South China Sea Fishery: Time to Internationalise', National Security College Policy Options Paper No.3, Australian National University, June 2017.

[31]   United States Office of the Director of National Intelligence, 'The Future of the Indian Ocean and South China Sea Fisheries: Implications for the United States', National Intelligence Council Report, 30 July 2013, p. i.

[32]   U.S. Energy Information Administration, 'The South China Sea is an Important World Energy Trade Route', 4 April 2013.

[33]   Cited in Frank Umbach, 'The South China Sea Disputes: The Energy Dimensions', *RSIS Commentaries,* no. CO17085, 4 May 2017.

[34]   Bill Hayton, *The South China Sea: The Struggle for Power in Asia,* Yale University Press, New Haven and London, 2014, p.149.

[35]   See Asia Maritime Transparency Initiative, '18 Maps That Explain Maritime Security in Asia', 2015.

[36]   International Institute for Strategic Studies, *Asia-Pacific Regional Security Assessment: Key Developments and Trends,* International Institute for Strategic Studies, London, 2017, p.38.

[37]   Cited in Bill Hayton, 'What Does China Really Want in the South China Sea?', *Nikkei Asian Review,* 29 March 2017.

[38]   Damen Cook, 'China's Most Important South China Sea Military Base', *The Diplomat,* 9 March 2017.

[39]   Toshi Yoshihara, 'Chinese Maritime Geography', pp.52–3.

[40]   'China Urges Japan Not to Stir up Troubles on South China Sea Issue',*Xinhua,* 16 March 2017.

[41]   Jim Mattis and John Chipman, 'Remarks by Secretary Mattis at Shangri-La Dialogue', U.S. Department of Defense, 3 June 2017.

[42]   For further reading see Denny Roy, 'The United States and the South China Sea: Front Line of Hegemonic Tension?', in Ian Storey and Lin Cheng-yi (eds), *The South China Sea Dispute: Navigating Diplomatic and Strategic Tensions,*

Yusof Ishak Institute of Southeast Asian Studies, Singapore, 2016, pp.235–6.

[43] Mark J. Valencia, 'The US-China Maritime Surveillance Debate', *The Diplomat,* 4 August 2017.

[44] See for example Patrick M. Cronin (ed.), *Cooperation from Strength: U.S. Strategy and the South China Sea,* Center for a New American Security, Washington, DC, 2012.

[45] Jesse Johnson, 'U.S., Japan Conclude Joint Drills in Disputed South China Sea', *The Japan Times,* 16 June 2017.

[46] Kyodo, 'Philippines Accepts First of 10 Japan-Funded Patrol Vessels to Beef up Coast Guard', *The Japan Times,* 18 August 2016.

[47] Mai Nguyen and My Pham, 'South China Sea: Japan to Supply New Patrol Boats to Vietnam', *The Sydney Morning Herald,* 17 January 2017.

[48] Peter Varghese, 'An Australian World View: A Practitioner's Perspective', Address to the Lowy Institute for International Policy, 20 August 2015.

[49] Malcolm Turnbull, 'Keynote Address at the 16th IISS Asia Security Summit, Shangri-La Dialogue'.

[50] Cited in Reuters staff, 'China State Paper Warns of War Over South China Sea Unless U.S. Backs Down', *Reuters,* 25 May 2015.

[51] Cited in Matthew Doran and Bill Birtles, 'It Would Be a Shame If a Plane Fell from the Sky: China's Warning to RAAF over South China Sea Flights', *ABC News,* 20 December 2015.

[52] Benjamin Haas, 'Steve Bannon: "We're Going to War in the South China Sea ... No Doubt"', *The Guardian,* 2 February 2017.

[53] Anthony Fensom, '$5 Trillion Meltdown: What If China Shuts Down the South China Sea?', *The National Interest,* 16 July 2016.

[54] ibid.

[55] For an excellent account of this clash see Toshi Yoshihara, 'The 1974 Paracels Sea Battle', *Naval War College Review,* vol.69, no.2, Spring 2016, pp.41–65.

[56] Carl Thayer, 'Alarming Escalation in the South China Sea: China Threatens Force if Vietnam Continues Oil Exploration in Spratlys', *The Diplomat,* 24 July 2017.

[57] Kyle Mizokami, 'What Makes China's Fake Island Military Bases in the South China Sea So Dangerous', *The National Interest,* 12 February 2017.

[58] Amando Doronila, 'Is Obama Pledge Really Ironclad?', *Philippine Daily Inquirer,* 5 May 2014.

[59] Idrees Ali, 'Pentagon Says China Aircraft Intercept Violated 2015 Agreement', *Reuters,* 27 May 2016.

[60] Michael Green et al., *Countering Coercion in Maritime Asia,* p.220.

[61] Bonnie S. Glaser, 'Armed Clash in the South China Sea', Contingency Planning Memorandum no.14, Council on Foreign Relations, April 2012, p.1.

[62] John J. Mearsheimer, *The Tragedy of Great Power Politics,* W.W. Norton & Company, New York, 2001, pp.114–19.

[63] Robert S. Ross, 'The Geography of the Peace: East Asia and the Twenty-First Century', *International Security,* vol.23, no.4, Spring 1999, p.109.

[64] Shannon Tiezzi, 'Southeast Asian Countries Warm to US-Proposed Freeze on South China Sea Land Reclamation', *The Diplomat,* 5 August 2015.

[65] Ralf Emmers, 'China's Influence in the South China Sea and the Failure of Joint Development', in Evelyn Goh (ed.), *Rising*

China's Influence in Developing Asia, Oxford University Press, Oxford, 2016, p.159.

[66]   ibid, pp.160–1.

[67]   Ian Storey, 'Assessing the ASEAN–China Framework for the Code of Conduct for the South China Sea', *Perspective,* ISEAS Yusof Ishak Institute, no.62, 8 August 2017.

[68]   Leszek Buszynski and Christopher B. Roberts, 'The South China Sea: Stabilisation and Resolution', in Leszek Buszynski and Christopher B. Roberts (eds), *The South China Sea Maritime Dispute: Political, Legal and Regional Perspectives,* Routledge, Abingdon, 2015, p.204.

[69]   Jackie Calmes, 'Obama and Asian Leaders Confront China's Premier', *The New York Times,* 19 November 2011.

[70]   International Institute for Strategic Studies, *Asia-Pacific Regional Security Assessment,* pp.157–60.

[71]   Donald K. Emmerson, 'ASEAN Stumbles in Phnom Penh', *East Asia Forum,* 23 July 2012.

[72]   International Institute for Strategic Studies, *Asia-Pacific Regional Security Assessment,* pp.157–60.

[73]   Ely Ratner, 'Course Correction: How to Stop China's Maritime Advance', *Foreign Affairs,* vol.96, no.4, July/August 2017, p.69.

[74] Michael Green, Kathleen Hicks, Mark Cancian, Zack Cooper and John Schaus, 'Asia-Pacific Rebalance 2025: Capabilities, Presence, and Partnerships – An Independent Review of U.S. Defense Strategy in the Asia-Pacific', Center for Strategic and International Studies (CSIS), Washington, DC, January 2016, p.19.

[75] U.S. Department of Defense, 'Remarks by Secretary Mattis at Plenary Session of the 2018 Shangri-La Dialogue', 2 June 2018.

[76] Bilahari Kausikan, 'Standing up to and Getting Along with China', *Today*, 18 May 2016.

[77] See for example Hugh White, *The China Choice: Why America Should Share Power*, Black Inc., Collingwood, 2012.

[78] See 'Advance Policy Questions for Admiral Philip Davidson, USN Expected Nominee for Commander, U.S. Pacific Command', 2018.

[79] Gordon Lubold and Nancy A. Youssef, 'Likely U.S. Pacific Commander Has Spent Little Time in Asia', *The Wall Street Journal*, 2 March 2018.

[80] Sam Bateman, 'What Are Australia's Interests in the South China Sea?', *The Strategist*, 29 May 2015.

[81] Catherine Wong, 'U.S. Will "Compete Vigorously" in South China Sea, Defense

Secretary Jim Mattis Warns Beijing', *South China Morning Post,* 2 June 2018.

[82] Emily Rauhala, 'The South China Sea Fell Off Trump's Radar Last Year. He May Have to Pay Attention in 2018', *The Washington Post,* 1 January 2018.

[83] David Lawler, 'Donald Trump Attacks China on Twitter over Currency Manipulation and South China Sea Deepening Diplomatic Row', *The Telegraph,* 9 December 2016.

Chapter 5: Coming Cataclysm

[1] Cited in Bates Gill and Linda Jakobson, *China Matters: Getting It Right for Australia,* La Trobe University Press, Carlton, 2017, p.18.

[2] Reuters staff, 'China's Xi Says Political Solution for Taiwan Can't Wait Forever', *Reuters,* 6 October 2013.

[3] Cited in Charlotte Gao, '3 Major Takeaways from Xi Jinping's Speech at the 19th Party Congress', *The Diplomat,* 18 October 2017.

[4] Lim Yan Liang, 'NPC 2018: China President Xi Jinping Warns Taiwan Will Face "Punishment of History" for Separatism', *The Straits Times,* 20 March 2018.

[5] See for example Scott L. Kastner, 'Is the Taiwan Strait Still a Flash Point?: Rethinking the

Prospects for Armed Conflict Between China and Taiwan', *International Security,* vol.40, no.3, Winter 2015–2016, pp.54–92.

[6] For an excellent overview of Taiwan's history see Denny Roy, *Taiwan: A Political History,* Cornell University Press, Ithaca and London, 2003.

[7] The classic study of the First Taiwan Strait Crisis is Robert Accinelli, *Crisis and Commitment: United States Policy Toward Taiwan, 1950–1955,* University of North Carolina Press, Chapel Hill, 1996.

[8] For a useful summary of the Second Taiwan Strait Crisis see Robert L. Suettinger, 'U.S. "Management" of Three Taiwan Strait "Crises"' in Michael D. Swaine and Zhang Tuosheng (eds), *Managing Sino–American Crisis,* pp.268–76.

[9] Margaret MacMillan, *Nixon and Mao: The Week That Changed the World,* Random House, New York, 2007.

[10] Cited in Michael J. Green, *By More Than Providence,* p.351.

[11] Cited in James Mann, *About Face: A History of America's Curious Relationship with China, from Nixon to Clinton,* Vintage Books, New York, 2000, p.95.

[12] ibid., p.94.

[13] Andrew Scobell, 'Show of Force: Chinese Soldiers, Statesmen, and the 1995–1996 Taiwan Strait Crisis', *Political Science Quarterly,* vol.115, no.2, Summer 2000, p.232.

[14] Erik Eckholm, 'China Expresses Concern Over Arms Sale to Taiwan', *The New York Times,* 25 April 2001.

[15] Lin Chieh-yu, 'Chen to Thank Former AIT Boss', *Taipei Times,* 18 June 2004.

[16] Denny Roy, *Taiwan,* p.237.

[17] 'Beijing Offers Aid Package as KMT Ends Visit', *China Daily,* 3 May 2005.

[18] 'Ma "Most Handsome Leader in the World"', *Bangkok Post,* 17 April 2008.

[19] 'One-Minute Handshake Marks Historic Meeting Between Xi Jinping and Ma Ying-Jeou', *The Straits Times,* 7 November 2015.

[20] Reuters staff, 'China Military Carries Out Military Exercises in City Just Opposite Taiwan, Days After Elections', *Reuters,* 21 January 2016.

[21] Simon Denyer, 'China Responds to Taiwan Elections with Military Drills, Facebook Trolling', *The Washington Post,* 21 January 2016.

[22] Agence France-Presse, 'Taiwan Sees Fewer Tourists as Chinese Stay Away', *South China Morning Post,* 17 May 2017.

[23]   Demetri Sevastopulo, 'Trump Backs "One China" Policy in First Presidential Call with Xi', *Financial Times,* 10 February 2017.

[24]   Jeff Mason, Stephen J. Adler and Steve Holland, 'Trump Spurns Taiwan President's Suggestion of Another Phone Call', *Reuters,* 28 April 2017.

[25]   Aria Bendix, 'Trump Administration Approves Its First Arms Sale to Taiwan', *The Atlantic,* 29 June 2017.

[26]   Eva Dou, 'Xi Jinping Warns Against Dividing China After U.S. Passes Taiwan Law', *The Wall Street Journal,* 20 March 2018.

[27]   Marie-Alice McLean-Dreyfus, 'Taiwan: Is There a Political Generation Gap?', *The Interpreter,* 9 June 2017.

[28]   Fang-Yu Chen, Wei-ting Yen, Austin Horng-en Wang and Brian Hioe, 'The Taiwanese See Themselves as Taiwanese, Not as Chinese', *The Washington Post,* 2 January 2017.

[29]   Michael D. Swaine, 'China's Assertive Behaviour: On "Core Interests"', *China Leadership Monitor,* issue 34, Winter 2011.

[30]   Edward Cody, 'China Sends Warning to Taiwan With Anti-Secession Law', *The Washington Post,* 8 March 2005.

[31]   Cited in Toshi Yoshihara, 'Chinese Maritime Geography', p.50.

[32]   ibid.

[33]   Evan S. Medeiros, *Reluctant Restraint: The Evolution of China's Nonproliferation Policies and Practices,* NUS Press, Singapore, 2009, p.135.

[34]   Richard Bush, 'The United States Security Partnership with Taiwan', Asian Allies Working Paper Series, Paper 7, Brookings Institution, Washington, DC, July 2016, p.3.

[35]   Denny Roy, *Return of the Dragon: Rising China and Regional Security,* Columbia University Press, New York, 2013, p.210.

[36]   Nancy Bernkopf Tucker and Bonnie Glaser, 'Should the United States Abandon Taiwan?', *The Washington Quarterly,* vol.34, no.2, Fall 2011, pp.23–37.

[37]   Kyle Mizokami, 'China's Greatest Nightmare: Taiwan Armed with Nuclear Weapons', *The National Interest,* 4 March 2017.

[38]   President Donald J. Trump, 'National Security Strategy of the United States of America', The White House, December 2017.

[39]   'China Condemns US "Cold War Mentality" in National Security', *BBC News,* 19 December 2017.

[40]   Richard C. Bush and Michael E. O'Hanlon, *A War Like No Other: The Truth About China's*

Challenge to America, John Wiley & Sons, Inc., Hoboken, 2007, p.12.

[41] Ian Easton, *The Chinese Invasion Threat: Taiwan's Defense and American Strategy in Asia,* The Project 2049 Institute, Arlington, 2017, pp.97–105.

[42] Eric Heginbotham et. al., *The U.S.–China Military Scorecard: Forces, Geography, and the Evolving Balance of Power 1996–2017,* Rand Corporation, Santa Monica, 2015, p.48.

[43] Office of the Secretary of Defense, 'Annual Report to Congress: Military and Security Developments Involving the People's Republic of China 2017', 15 May 2017, p.76.

[44] Ian Easton, *The Chinese Invasion Threat,* pp.114–42.

[45] For further reading on the potential challenges facing the invading Chinese force see ibid, pp.143–94.

[46] ibid., pp.205–7.

[47] ibid., pp.135–6.

[48] Steven Lee Myers and Chris Horton, 'Once Formidable, Taiwan's Military Now Overshadowed by China's', *The New York Times,* 4 November 2017.

[49]   Eric Heginbotham et. al., *The U.S.–China Military Scorecard,* p.338.

[50]   Center for Strategic and International Studies, 'Dong Feng 21 (DF-21, CSS-5)', *MissileThreat: CSIS Missile Defense Project,* 13 April 2016.

[51]   Eric Heginbotham et. al., *The U.S.–China Military Scorecard,* p.337.

[52]   Austin Ramzy, 'When Leaders of Taiwan and China Meet, Even Tiny Gestures Will Be Parsed', *The New York Times,* 4 November 2015.

[53]   Xinhua News Agency, 'ARATS and SEF Key Talks', *Beijing Review,* no.29, July 2010.

[54]   'President Appeals for "Peace Agreement" with Taiwan', *China Daily,* 15 October 2007.

[55]   For further reading on the idea of a China–Taiwan Peace Treaty see Phillip C. Saunders and Scott L. Kastner, 'Bridge over Troubled Water? Envisioning a China–Taiwan Peace Agreement', *International Security,* vol.33, no.4, Spring 2009, pp.87–114.

[56]   'A Policy of "One Country, Two Systems" on Taiwan', Ministry of Foreign Affairs of the People's Republic of China.

[57]   Denny Roy, *Return of the Dragon,* p.201.

[58] C.C., 'Has "One Country, Two Systems" Been a Success for Hong Kong?', *The Economist,* 29 June 2017.

[59] Kelsey Munro, '"Disgusting" and "Extraordinary" Scenes as Chinese Delegation Shouts Down Welcome Ceremony', *The Sydney Morning Herald,* 3 May 2017.

[60] Grant Wyeth, 'The Sovereign Recognition Game: Has Nauru Overplayed Its Hand?', *The Diplomat,* 17 May 2017.

[61] Chris Horton and Steven Lee Myers, 'Panama Establishes Ties with China, Further Isolating Taiwan', *The New York Times,* 13 June 2017; Jess Macy Yu, 'Taiwan Angry as China Snatches Ally Away', *The Sydney Morning Herald,* 1 May 2018.

[62] Denny Roy, *Return of the Dragon,* p.206.

[63] Cited in Pan Zhongqi, 'US Taiwan Policy of Strategic Ambiguity: A Dilemma of Deterrence', *Journal of Contemporary China,* vol.12, no.35, 2003, pp.388–9.

[64] Denny Roy, 'Prospects for Taiwan Maintaining its Autonomy Under Chinese Pressure', *Asian Survey,* vol.57, no.6, 2017, p.1142.

[65] Scott L. Kastner, 'Is the Taiwan Strait Still a Flash Point?', pp.65–9.

[66]   See for example J. Michael Cole, 'If the Unthinkable Occurred: America Should Stand Up to China over Taiwan', *The National Interest,* 7 May 2015.

[67]   J. Michael Cole, 'Analysis: Chinese Envoy to the U.S. Threatens War Over U.S. Navy Port Calls in Taiwan', *Taiwan Sentinel,* 11 December 2017.

[68]   Hugh White, 'Will America Defend Taiwan?', *The Interpreter,* 5 May 2015.

[69]   J. Michael Cole, 'If the Unthinkable Occurred'.

[70]   J. Michael Cole, 'China's New Air Routes Near Taiwan: Why Now? To What End?', *Taiwan Sentinel,* 11 January 2018.

[71]   Michael Mazza and Gary Schmitt, 'The F-35: How Taiwan Could Really Push Back Against China', *The National Interest,* 18 January 2018.

[72]   Reuters, 'PLA Planes Fly Around Taiwan Again', *Taipei Times,* 19 December 2017.

[73]   Austin Ramzy, 'Taiwan Navy Accidentally Fires Antiship Missile, Killing Fisherman', *The New York Times,* 1 July 2016.

[74]   International Institute for Strategic Studies, 'Turbulence in the Taiwan Strait', *Strategic Comments,* vol.22, comment 23, August 2016, p.1.

[75] Mike Yeo, 'US State Department OKs License for Submarine Tech Sales to Taiwan', *Defense News,* 9 April 2018.

[76] Cited in James R. Holmes and Toshi Yoshihara, *Chinese Naval Strategy in the 21st Century: The Turn to Mahan,* Routledge, Abingdon, 2008, p.55.

Chapter 6: Can Asia Avoid Catastrophe?

[1] For further reading on this incident see Dennis C. Blair and David V. Bonfili, 'The April 2001 EP-3 Incident', pp.377–90.

[2] Coral Bell, *The Conventions of Crisis: A Study in Diplomatic Management,* Oxford University Press, London, 1971, p.14.

[3] ibid., p.18.

[4] Ja Ian Chong and Todd H. Hall, 'The Lessons of 1914 for East Asia Today: Missing the Trees for the Forest', *International Security,* vol.39, no.1, Summer 2014, pp.33–5.

[5] For further reading on this 'grand bargain' approach see Evelyn Goh, 'Is a "Grand Bargain" the Way Forward in Northeast Asia?', *Global Asia,* vol.11, no.4, Winter 2016, pp.58–65.

[6]   See for example James Woolsey, 'Under Donald Trump, the US Will Accept China's Rise – as Long as It Doesn't Challenge the Status Quo', *South China Morning Post,* 10 November 2016.

[7]   Cited in Alexander L. George, 'A Provisional Theory of Crisis Management', in Alexander L. George (ed.), *Avoiding War: Problems of Crisis Management,* Westview Press, Boulder, San Francisco and Oxford, 1991, p.22.

[8]   Stephan Fitzgerald, 'Managing Ourselves in a Chinese World: Australian Foreign Policy in an Age of Disruption', 2017 Gough Whitlam Oration, Whitlam Institute, Western Sydney University, 16 March 2017.

[9]   Hugh White, *Without America,* p.1.

[10]   Alexander Gray and Peter Navarro, 'Donald Trump's Peace Through Strength Vision for the Asia-Pacific', *Foreign Policy,* 7 November 2016.

[11]   See for example Tim Huxley and Benjamin Schreer, 'Standing Up to China', *Survival,* vol.57, no.6, December 2015–January 2016, pp.127–44.

[12]   Phillip Coorey, 'Australia Mulls Rival to China's "Belt and Road" with US, Japan, India', *Australian Financial Review,* 18 February 2018.

[13]   The White House, 'Dr. Condoleezza Rice Discusses President's National Security

Strategy', Waldorf Astoria Hotel, New York, 1 October 2002.

[14]   Richard Little, *The Balance of Power in International Relations: Metaphors, Myths and Models,* Cambridge University Press, Cambridge, 2007, p.4.

[15]   Michael J. Green, *By More Than Providence,* p.546.

[16]   For further reading see Jennifer Lind, 'Life in China's Asia: What Regional Hegemony Would Look Like', *Foreign Affairs,* vol.97, no.2, March–April 2018, pp.71–82.

FURTHER READING

Books

Accinelli, Robert, *Crisis and Commitment: United States Policy Toward Taiwan, 1950–1955,* University of North Carolina Press, Chapel Hill, 1996.

Allison, Graham, *Destined for War: Can America and China Escape Thucydides's Trap?,* Houghton Mifflin Harcourt, Boston and New York, 2017.

Ball, Desmond and Tanter, Richard, *The Tools of Owatatsumi: Japan's Ocean Surveillance and Coastal Defence Capabilities,* ANU Press, Canberra, 2015.

Bell, Coral, *Negotiation from Strength: A Study in the Politics of Power,* Alfred A. Knopf, New York, 1963.

_____, *The Conventions of Crisis: A Study in Diplomatic Management,* Oxford University Press, London, 1971.

Blainey, Geoffrey, *The Causes of War,* The Free Press, New York, 1973.

Bush, Richard C. and O'Hanlon, Michael E., *A War Like No Other: The Truth About China's Challenge to America,* John Wiley & Sons, Inc., Hoboken, 2007.

Buszynski, Leszek, *Negotiating with North Korea: The Six Party Talks and the Nuclear Issue,* Routledge, Abingdon, 2013.

Buszynski, Leszek and Roberts, Christopher B. (eds), *The South China Sea Maritime Dispute: Political, Legal and Regional Perspectives,* Routledge, Abingdon, 2015.

Campbell, Emma, *South Korea's New Nationalism: The End of "One Korea"?* Lynne Reinner Publishers, Boulder, 2016.

Cha, Victor, *The Impossible State: North Korea, Past and Future,* Harper Collins, New York, 2012.

_____, *Powerplay: The Origins of the American Alliance System in Asia,* Princeton University Press, Princeton and Oxford, 2016.

Choong, William, *The Ties That Divide: History, Honour and Territory in Sino–Japanese Relations,* Routledge for the International Institute for Strategic Studies, Abingdon, 2014.

Coker, Christopher, *The Improbable War: China, the United States and the Logic of Great Power Conflict,* Hurst & Company, London, 2015.

Easton, Ian, *The Chinese Invasion Threat: Taiwan's Defense and American Strategy in Asia,* The Project 2049 Institute, Arlington, 2017.

Emmers, Ralf, *Geopolitics and Maritime Territorial Disputes in East Asia,* Routledge, London and New York, 2010, p.54.

Friedman, George and LeBard, Meredith, *The Coming War with Japan,* St Martin's Press, New York, 1991.

Gill, Bates and Jakobson, Linda, *China Matters: Getting it Right for Australia,* La Trobe University Press, Carlton, 2017.

Goh, Evelyn (ed.), *Rising China's Influence in Developing Asia,* Oxford University Press, Oxford, 2016.

Green, Michael J., *Japan's Reluctant Realism: Foreign Policy Challenges in an Era of Uncertain Power,* Palgrave, New York, 2001.

_____, *By More Than Providence: Grand Strategy and American Power in the Asia Pacific Since 1783,* Columbia University Press, New York, 2017.

Green, Michael J., et al., *Countering Coercion in Maritime Asia: The Theory and Practice of Gray Zone Deterrence,* Rowman & Littlefield for the Center for Strategic and International Studies, Lanham, Boulder, New York and London, 2017.

Halberstam, David, *The Coldest Winter: America and the Korean War,* Hyperion, New York, 2007.

Hara, Kimie, *Cold War Frontiers in the Asia-Pacific,* Routledge, London and New York, 2007.

Hara, Kimie (ed.), *The San Francisco System and Its Legacies: Continuation, Transformation and Historical Reconciliation in the Asia-Pacific,* Routledge, London and New York, 2015.

Hayton, Bill, *The South China Sea: The Struggle for Power in Asia,* Yale University Press, New Haven and London, 2014.

Heinzig, Dieter, *Disputed Islands in the South China Sea,* Otto Harrassowitz, Wiesbaden, 1976.

Holmes, James R. and Yoshihara, Toshi, *Chinese Naval Strategy in the 21st Century: The Turn to Mahan,* Routledge, Abingdon, 2008.

Jackson, Van, *Rival Reputations: Coercion and Credibility in US–North Korea Relations,* Cambridge University Press, Cambridge, 2016.

Johnston, Alastair Iain and Ross, Robert S. (eds), *New Directions in the Study of China's Foreign Policy,* Stanford University Press, Stanford, 2006.

Kaplan, Robert D., *Asia's Cauldron: The South China Sea and the End of a Stable Pacific,* Random House, New York, 2014.

Little, Richard, *The Balance of Power in International Relations: Metaphors, Myths and Models,* Cambridge University Press, Cambridge, 2007.

MacMillan, Margaret, *Nixon and Mao: The Week That Changed the World,* Random House, New York, 2007.

Mahnken, Thomas G. and Blumenthal, Dan (eds), *Strategy in Asia: The Past, Present, and Future of Regional Security,* Stanford University Press, Stanford, 2014.

Manicom, James, *Bridging Troubled Waters: China, Japan, and Maritime Order in the East China Sea,* Georgetown University Press, Washington, DC, 2014.

Mann, James, *About Face: A History of America's Curious Relationship with China, from Nixon to Clinton,* Vintage Books, New York, 2000.

Mazarr, Michael J., *North Korea and the Bomb: A Case Study in Nonproliferation,* St. Martin's Press, New York, 1995.

McGregor, Richard, *Asia's Reckoning: China, Japan and the Fate of US Power in the Pacific Century,* Viking, New York, 2017.

Mearsheimer, John J., *The Tragedy of Great Power Politics,* W.W. Norton & Company, New York, 2001.

Medeiros, Evan S., *Reluctant Restraint: The Evolution of China's Nonproliferation Policies and Practices,* NUS Press, Singapore, 2009.

Mitter, Rana, *China's War with Japan 1937–1945: The Struggle for Survival,* Allen Lane, London, 2013.

Raine, Sarah and Le Miere, Christian, *Regional Disorder: The South China Sea Disputes,* Routledge for the International Institute for Strategic Studies, London, 2013.

Rosecrance, Richard N. and Miller, Steven E. *The Next Great War?: The Roots of World War I and the Risk of U.S.–China Conflict,* Belfer Center for Science and International Affairs, Cambridge, 2015.

Roy, Denny, *Taiwan: A Political History,* Cornell University Press, Ithaca and London, 2003.

_____, *Return of the Dragon: Rising China and Regional Security,* Columbia University Press, New York, 2013.

Samuels, Marwyn S., *Contest for the South China Sea,* Methuen, New York and London, 1982.

Sigal, Leon, *Disarming Strangers: Nuclear Diplomacy with North Korea,* Princeton University Press, Princeton, 1998.

Smith, Sheila A., *Intimate Rivals: Japanese Domestic Politics and a Rising China,* Columbia University Press, New York, 2015.

Storey, Ian and Cheng-yi, Lin (eds), *The South China Sea Dispute: Navigating Diplomatic and Strategic Tensions,* Yusof Ishak Institute of Southeast Asian Studies, Singapore, 2016.

Swaine, Michael D. and Tuosheng, Zhang (eds), *Managing Sino–American Crises: Case Studies and Analysis,* Carnegie Endowment for International Peace, Washington, DC, 2006.

Weissmann, Mikael, *The East Asian Peace: Conflict Prevention and Informal Peacebuilding,* Palgrave Macmillan, New York, 2012.

White, Hugh, *The China Choice: Why America Should Share Power,* Black Inc., Collingwood, 2012.

_____, *Without America: Australia in the New Asia,* Quarterly Essay, no.68, 2017.

Wit, Joel S., Poneman, Daniel B. and Gallucci, Robert L., *Going Critical: The First North Korean Nuclear Crisis,* Brookings Institution Press, Washington, DC, 2004.

Journal articles

Auslin, Michael, 'Don't Forget About the East China Sea', *East and South China Seas Bulletin,* no.2, Center for a New American Security, 3 May 2012.

Ayson, Robert and Ball, Desmond, 'Can a Sino–Japanese War Be Controlled?', *Survival,* vol.56, no.6, December 2014–January 2015, pp.135–66.

Bajpaee, Chietigj, 'Japan and China: The Geo-Economic Dimension', *The Diplomat,* 28 March 2016.

Ball, Desmond, 'Arms and Affluence: Military Acquisitions in the Asia-Pacific region', *International Security,* vol.18, no.3, Winter 1993–94, pp.78–112.

Bateman, Sam, 'What Are Australia's Interests in the South China Sea?', *The Strategist,* 29 May 2015.

Beckman, Robert, 'Scarborough Shoal: Flashpoint for Confrontation or Opportunity for Cooperation?', *RSIS Commentaries,* no.072/2012, 24 April 2012.

Bitzinger, Richard A. and Desker, Barry, 'Why East Asian War is Unlikely', *Survival,* vol.50, no.6, December 2008–January 2009, pp.105–28.

Blanchard, Jean Marc F., 'The U.S. Role in the Sino–Japanese Dispute over the Diaoyu (Senkaku)

Islands', *The China Quarterly,* no.161, March 2000, pp.95–123.

Byman, Daniel and Lind, Jennifer, 'Pyongyang's Survival Strategy: Tools of Authoritarian Control in North Korea', *International Security,* vol.35, no.1, Summer 2010, pp.44–74.

Chong, Ja Ian and Hall, Todd H., 'The Lessons of 1914 for East Asia Today: Missing the Trees for the Forest', *International Security,* vol.39, no.1, Summer 2014, pp.7–43.

Denmark, Abraham M., 'The Myth of the Limited Strike on North Korea', *Foreign Affairs,* 9 January 2018.

Friedberg, Aaron L., 'Ripe for Rivalry: Prospects for Peace in a Multipolar Asia', *International Security,* vol.18, no.3, Winter 1993–94, pp.5–33.

Gallucci, Robert L., 'The North Korean Threat: War, Deterrence and Diplomacy', *The National Interest,* 31 October 2017.

Goh, Evelyn, 'Is a "Grand Bargain" the Way Forward in Northeast Asia?', *Global Asia,* vol.11, no.4, Winter 2016, pp.58–65.

Gray, Alexander and Peter Navarro, 'Donald Trump's Peace Through Strength Vision for the Asia-Pacific', *Foreign Policy,* 7 November 2016.

Harrell, Peter and Zarate, Juan, 'How to Successfully Sanction North Korea', *Foreign Affairs,* 30 January 2018.

Holmes, James, 'The Sino–Japanese Naval War of 2012', *Foreign Policy,* 20 August 2012.

Huxley, Tim and Schreer, Benjamin, 'Standing Up to China', *Survival,* vol.57, no.6, December 2015–January 2016, pp.127–144.

Ikenberry, G. John, 'American Hegemony and East Asian Order', *Australian Journal of International Affairs,* vol.58, no.3, September 2004, pp.353–67.

Kaplan, Fred, 'The Worst Defense', *Slate,* 17 October 2017.

Kastner, Scott L., 'Is the Taiwan Strait Still a Flash Point?: Rethinking the Prospects for Armed Conflict Between China and Taiwan', *International Security,* vol.40, no.3, Winter 2015–2016, pp.54–92.

Kelly, Robert E., 'The Real North Korea Threat: A Forced Unification?', *The National Interest,* 16 January 2018.

Lind, Jennifer, 'Life in China's Asia: What Regional Hegemony Would Look Like', *Foreign Affairs,* vol.97, no.2, March–April 2018, pp.71–82.

Mazza, Michael and Schmitt, Gary, 'The F-35: How Taiwan Could Really Push Back Against China', *The National Interest,* 18 January 2018.

McLean-Dreyfus, Marie-Alice, 'Taiwan: Is There a Political Generation Gap?', *The Interpreter,* 9 June 2017.

Moon, Chung-in, 'A Real Path to Peace on the Korean Peninsula: The Progress and Promise of the Moon-Kim Summit', *Foreign Affairs,* 30 April 2018.

O'Neill, Tom, 'Korea's Dangerous Divide', *National Geographic,* vol.204, no.1, July 2003.

Osnos, Evan, 'Is the Political Class Drifting Toward War with North Korea?', *The New Yorker,* 8 November 2017.

Pan, Zhongqi, 'US Taiwan Policy of Strategic Ambiguity: A Dilemma of Deterrence', *Journal of Contemporary China,* vol.12, no.35, 2003, pp.387–407.

Panda, Ankit, 'A Great Leap to Nowhere: Remembering the US– North Korea "Leap Day" Deal', *The Diplomat,* 29 February 2016.

Rapp-Hooper, Mira, 'Uncharted Waters: Extended Deterrence and Maritime Disputes', *The Washington Quarterly,* vol.38, no.1, Spring 2015, pp.127–46.

———, 'The Cataclysm That Would Follow a "Bloody Nose" Strike on North Korea', *The Atlantic,* 31 January 2018.

Ratner, Ely, 'Course Correction: How to Stop China's Maritime Advance', *Foreign Affairs,* vol.96, no.4, July/August 2017, pp.64–72.

Reilly, James, 'China's Unilateral Sanctions', *The Washington Quarterly,* vol.35, no.4, Fall 2012, pp.121–33.

Roehrig, Terence, 'The Abilities – And Limits – of North Korean Early Warning', *Bulletin of the Atomic Scientists,* 27 November 2017.

Ross, Robert S., 'The Geography of the Peace: East Asia in the Twenty-first Century', *International Security,* vol.23, no.4, Spring 1999, pp.81–118.

Roy, Denny, 'Prospects for Taiwan Maintaining its Autonomy Under Chinese Pressure', *Asian Survey,* vol.57, no.6, 2017, pp.1135–58.

Saunders, Phillip C. and L. Kastner, Scott, 'Bridge over Troubled Water? Envisioning a China–Taiwan Peace Agreement', *International Security,* vol.33, no.4, Spring 2009, pp.87–114.

Schofield, Clive, 'A Landmark Decision in the South China Sea: The Scope and Implications of the Arbitral

Tribunal's Award', *Contemporary Southeast Asia,* vol.38, no.3, December 2016, pp.339–47.

Schreer, Benjamin and Taylor, Brendan, 'The Korean Crises and Sino–American Rivalry', *Survival,* vol.53, no.1, February–March 2011, pp.13–19.

Scobell, Andrew, 'Show of Force: Chinese Soldiers, Statesmen, and the 1995–1996 Taiwan Strait Crisis', *Political Science Quarterly,* vol.115, no.2, Summer 2000, pp.227–46.

Stashwick, Steven, 'South China Sea: Conflict Escalation and "Miscalculation" Myths', *The Diplomat,* 25 September 2015.

Storey, Ian, 'Assessing the ASEAN–China Framework for the Code of Conduct for the South China Sea', *Perspective,* ISEAS Yusof Ishak Institute, no.62, 8 August 2017.

Swaine, Michael D., 'China's Assertive Behaviour: On "Core Interests"', *China Leadership Monitor,* no.34, Winter 2011.

Tiezzi, Shannon, 'A China–Japan Breakthrough: A Primer on Their 4 Point Consensus', *The Diplomat,* 7 November 2014.

_____, 'Southeast Asian Countries Warm to US – Proposed Freeze on South China Sea Land Reclamation', *The Diplomat,* 5 August 2015.

Tonnesson, Stein, 'The South China Sea in the Age of European Decline', *Modern Asian Studies,* vol.40, no.1, February 2006, pp.1–57.

Tucker, Nancy Bernkopf and Glaser, Bonnie, 'Should the United States Abandon Taiwan?', *The Washington Quarterly,* vol.34, no.2, Fall 2011, pp.23–37.

Umbach, Frank, 'The South China Sea Disputes: The Energy Dimensions', *RSIS Commentaries,* no. CO17085, 4 May 2017.

Valencia, Mark, 'The Impeccable Incident: Truth and Consequences', *China Security,* vol.5, no.2, 2009, pp.26–32.

_____, 'The US–China Maritime Surveillance Debate', *The Diplomat,* 4 August 2017.

Yoshihara, Toshi, 'The 1974 Paracels Sea Battle', *Naval War College Review,* vol.69, no.2, Spring 2016, pp.41–65.

White, Hugh, 'Will America Defend Taiwan?', *The Interpreter,* 5 May 2015.

Reports

Bisley, Nick and Taylor, Brendan, *Conflict in the East China Sea: Would ANZUS Apply?,* Australia–China

Relations Institute, University of Technology Sydney, Sydney, November 2014.

Bush, Richard, *The United States Security Partnership with Taiwan,* Asian Allies Working Paper Series, Paper 7, Brookings Institution, Washington, DC, July 2016.

Center for Strategic and International Studies, 'Dong Feng 21 (DF-21, CSS-5)', *MissileThreat: CSIS Missile Defense Project,* 13 April 2016.

Cordesman, Anthony H., with the assistance of Charles Ayers, *The Military Balance in the Koreas and Northeast Asia,* Center for Strategic and International Studies, Washington, DC, 2017.

Cronin, Patrick M. (ed.), *Cooperation from Strength: U.S. Strategy and the South China Sea,* Center for a New American Security, Washington, DC, 2012.

Gill, Bates, *China's North Korea Policy: Assessing Interests and Influences,* United States Institute of Peace, Special Report 283, July 2011.

Green, Michael et al., *Asia-Pacific Rebalance 2025: Capabilities, Presence, and Partnerships – An Independent Review of U.S. Defense Strategy in the Asia-Pacific,* Center for Strategic and International Studies (CSIS), Washington, DC, January 2016.

Heginbotham, Eric, et. al., *The U.S.–China Military Scorecard: Forces, Geography, and the Evolving*

Balance of Power 1996–2017, Rand Corporation, Santa Monica, 2015.

International Institute for Strategic Studies, *Asia-Pacific Regional Security Assessment: Key Developments and Trends,* International Institute for Strategic Studies, London, 2017.

Jervis, Robert, *Unpacking a US Decision to Use Force Against North Korea: Issues, Options and Consequences,* 38 North Special Report, January 2018.

McInnis, Kathleen J., et. al., *The North Korean Nuclear Challenge: Military Options and Issues for Congress,* CRS Report prepared for Members and Committees of Congress, Congressional Research Service, 6 November 2017, p.34.

Office of the Secretary of Defense, *Annual Report to Congress: Military and Security Developments Involving the People's Republic of China 2017,* 15 May 2017.

PricewaterhouseCoopers, *The Long View: How Will the Global Economic Order Change by 2050?,* February 2017.

Trump, President Donald J., *National Security Strategy of the United States of America,* The White House, December 2017.

Tsirbas, Marina, *Saving the South China Sea Fishery: Time to Internationalise,* National Security College Policy Options Paper No.3, Australian National University, June 2017.

United States Office of the Director of National Intelligence, *The Future of the Indian Ocean and South China Sea Fisheries: Implications for the United States,* National Intelligence Council Report, 30 July 2013.

Welch, David A., *Crisis Management Mechanisms: Pathologies and Pitfalls,* CIGI Papers, no.40, September 2014, p.8.

Speeches

Fitzgerald, Stephan, 'Managing Ourselves in a Chinese World: Australian Foreign Policy in an Age of Disruption', 2017 Gough Whitlam Oration, Whitlam Institute, Western Sydney University, 16 March 2017.

Harris, Admiral Harry B., 'Address to Australian Strategic Policy Institute', Australian Strategic Policy Institute, Canberra, 31 March 2015.

Mattis, Jim and Chipman, John, 'Remarks by Secretary Mattis at Shangri-La Dialogue', East Asia Summit, Singapore, 3 June 2017.

Rudd, Kevin, 'It's Time to Build an Asia Pacific Community', Address to the Asia Society Australasia Centre, Sydney, 4 June 2008.

Turnbull, Malcolm, 'Keynote Address 16th IISS Asia Security Summit, Shangri-La Dialogue', East Asia Summit, Singapore, 2 June 2017.

Varghese, Peter, 'An Australian World View: A Practitioner's Perspective', Address to the Lowy Institute for International Policy, Sydney, 20 August 2015.

Dr Brendan Taylor is Associate Professor of Strategic Studies at the Australian National University. He is the author or editor of eight books, and his analysis of foreign and strategic affairs has appeared in leading policy journals throughout Australia and the world.

BACK COVER MATERIAL

A timely account of the four most troubled hotspots in the world's most combustible region

Asia is at a dangerous moment. China is rising fast, and its regional ambitions are growing. Reckless North Korean dictator Kim Jong-un may be assembling more nuclear weapons, despite diplomatic efforts to eradicate his arsenal. Japan is building up its military, throwing off constitutional constraints imposed after World War II. The United States, for so long a stabilising presence in Asia, is behaving erratically: Donald Trump is the first US president since the 1970s to break diplomatic protocol and speak with Taiwan, and the first to threaten war with North Korea if denuclearisation does not occur. The possibility of global catastrophe looms ever closer.

In this revelatory analysis, geopolitical expert Brendan Taylor examines the four Asian flashpoints most likely to erupt in sudden and violent conflict: the Korean Peninsula, the East China Sea, the South China Sea and Taiwan. He sketches how clashes could play out in these global hotspots and argues that crisis can only be averted by understanding the complex relations between them. Drawing on history, in-depth reports and his intimate observations of the region, Taylor asks what the world's major powers can do to avoid an eruption of war – and shows how Asia could change this otherwise disastrous trajectory.

***

'Clear, calm, rigorous and highly readable ... the perfect guide to the looming perils of the Asian Century.'
HUGH WHITE

'Gripping scenarios for major war in Asia – and the strongest case for the wise statecraft we will need to keep the peace.'
MICHAEL J. GREEN

A

38th parallel, *19*

A War Like No Other, *154*
see also Michael O'Hanlon; Richard C. Bush,

Abe, Shinzō (Japanese prime minister), *86, 89*
see also Asia-Pacific Economic Cooperation (APEC) 2014 Shangri-La Dialogue (2014),
and the Asian Infrastructure Investment Bank (AIIB), *78*
and the Belt and Road Inititiative, *77*
and the Japanese Air Defence Indentification Zone (ADIZ), *82*
and patrol boats for Vietnam, *117*
and Xi Jinping (Chinese president), *72, 146*
and the Yasukuni Shrine, *89*

Acheson, Dean (US former secretary of state), *19, 90, 198*

Agreed Framework (1994), *47, 51, 185, 191*
see also Clinton administration; George W. Bush (former US president),

Air Defence Identification Zone (ADIZ), *72, 78, 82, 155*
see also China; Japan,

Allison, Graham, *6, 8*
see also Cuban Missile Crisis; Thucydides Trap,

Anti-Secession Law (2005), *150, 151, 171*
see also China; Li Kexin (senior Chinese diplomat),

armistice agreement (1953), *20, 57*
see also China; Korean War (1950-53); North Korea; United Nations Command,

artificial islands, *110, 118, 119, 120, 129, 190, 194*

see also China; land reclamation; South China Sea,

ASEAN (Association of Southeast Asian Nations), *4, 5, 106, 110, 126, 127, 185*

see also East Asia Summit; Free Trade Area; South China Sea code of conduct; Special ASEAN-China Foreign Ministers' Meeting (2016),

ASEAN Defence Ministers' Meeting, *5*

ASEAN Regional Forum, *5, 85*

see also Li Zhaoxing (Chinese foreign minister); Taro Aso (Japanese foreign minister),

Asian Infrastructure Investment Bank (AIIB), *77, 78, 193*

see also China,

Asian 'Wars of the Roses', *6, 7*

see also Richard McGregor,

Asia-Pacific Economic Cooperation (APEC), *72, 166*

see also Shinzō Abe (Japanese prime minister); Xi Jinping (Chinese president),

'Asia's paradox', *17, 63*

see also Park Geun-hye (South Korean former president),

Asō, Tarō (Japanese former foreign minister), *85*

see also ASEAN Regional Forum (2006); Zhaoxing, Li (Chinese foreign minister),

Association for Relations Across the Taiwan Straits (ARATS), *162*

see also China; Taiwan,

Ayson, Robert, *83*

see also Desmond Ball,

B

Baker, James (US former secretary of state), *169*

Ball, Desmond, *2, 3, 83*

see also Robert Ayson,

Bannon, Steve, *119, 121*

Barrett, First Lieutenant Mark, *22*

see also Bridge of No
Return; Operation Paul
Bunyan,
Bell, Coral, *181, 182*
see also 'crisis slide',
Belt and Road Initiative
(BRI), *77, 113, 193, 194*
see also China,
Bishop, Julie (Australian
foreign affairs minister), *166*
Blainey, Geoffrey, *10*
see also 'wide war',
Bolton, John (US National
Security Adviser), *40, 58*
Bonifas, Captain Arthur, *22*
see also Bridge of No
Return; First Lieutenant
Mark Barrett; Operation
Paul Bunyan,
Brennan, John (CIA former
director), *39*
Bridge of No Return, *22*
see also Captain Arthur
Bonifas; First Lieutenant
Mark Barrett; Operation
Paul Bunyan,
BRP Sierra Madre, *96, 97, 131*
see also China; Fidel V.
Ramos (Philippines
former president); RVNS

My Tho; USS Harnett
County,
Bulletin of the Atomic
Scientists,
see also Doomsday
Clock; Martyl Langsdorf,
Bush, George H. W. snr
(former US president), and
weaponry to Taiwan, *146, 152*
Bush, George W. (former
US president), *5, 32, 33, 51, 55,
152*
see also Agreed
Framework (1994),
and weaponry to Taiwan,
145, 146
Bush, Richard C., *154*
see also A War Like No
Other,
Buszynski, Leszek, *125, 126*
Byman, Daniel, *29*
Cairo Declaration (1943),
66

C
Campbell, Kurt (Obama
administration), *107*
see also Fu Ying;
Scarborough Shoal,
Carter, Jimmy (US former
president), *142*

see also Taiwan Relations
Act 1979,
and Kim Il-sung (North
Korean former dictator),
42
and withdrawal of US
forces, *51, 58*
Cha, Victor, *24, 26, 40*
Chan, Lien (Taiwan former
premier), *146*
Chang Hsien-yi, Colonel, *153*
Chen Shui-bian, *145, 146, 147*
  see also Democratic
  Progressive Party (DPP);
  One China policy,
Chiang Ching-kuo (former
Taiwan president), *142, 144*
Chiang Kai-shek, General,
139, 140
  see also Chinese Civil
  War (1945-49);
  Kuomintang (KMT);
  Taiwan,
China, *64, 65, 79, 105, 116, 129*
  see also Declaration on
  the Conduct of Parties in
  the South China Sea
  (DoC); Ming dynasty
  (1368-1644); One China
  policy; Qing dynasty
  (1644-1911),

and the Air Defence
Identification Zone
(ADIZ), *72, 78, 155*
and the Anti-Secession
Law (2005), *150, 151, 171*
and the armistice
agreement (1953), *20*
and the artificial islands,
110, 118, 119, 120, 129, 190, 194
and Asian Infrastructure
Investment Bank (AIIB),
77, 78, 193
and Association for
Relations Across the
Taiwan Straits (ARATS)
of China, *162*
and the Belt and Road
Initiative (BRI), *113, 193, 194*
and the BRP Sierra
Madre, *97*
and the China-North
Korea relationship, *35, 36*
and the China-Taiwan
Economic Cooperation
Framework Agreement
(ECFA), *167*
and the 'Chinese lake', *128*
and Dongfeng 16
(DF-16), *155*
and Dongfeng 21D
(DF-21D), *161*

and the East China Sea, *74, 75, 76, 79, 81*

and the fishing-boat collision (2010), *71, 85, 89*

and the frigate radar lock (2013), *92, 93*

and guanxi, *5*

and the Japan-China Maritime and Air Communication Mechanism (2015), *89*

and the Korean Peninsula, *28*

and land reclamation, *107, 108, 183*

and Liaoning (Chinese aircraft carrier), *110*

and the 'Ministry of Traitors', *79*

and the Miyako Strait, *76*

and the People's Liberation Army, *121*

and Permanent Court of Arbitration at The Hague, *108*

and the pipeline construction, *112, 113*

and the Six-Party Talks, *48*

and the South China Sea, *106*

and the South China Sea code of conduct, *110, 125, 185*

and the Spratly Islands, *101, 104, 107, 108*

and Taiwan peace treaty, *164*

and Taiwan proposed peace treaty, *191*

and the Treaty of Peace and Friendship (1978), *69*

and the US spy plane collision (2001), *90, 180*

and the Yulin Naval Base, *113*

China National Party Congress (2007), *164*
　　see also Hu Jintao (Chinese former president),

China National Party Congress (2017), *136*
　　see also Xi Jinping (Chinese president),

China-Taiwan Economic Cooperation Framework Agreement (ECFA), *167*

Chinese Civil War (1945-49), *12, 139*
　　see also Chiang Kai-shek, General; Mao Tse Tung,

Chinese Communist Party, *36, 139, 154, 173, 175, 180*

Chinese National Offshore Oil Corporation, *110*
   see also South China Sea resources,

Clark, Christopher, *9*
   see also The Sleepwalkers: How Europe Went to War in 1914,

Clinton, Bill (US former president), *21, 42, 43*

Clinton administration, *47, 55*
   see also Agreed Framework (1994), and Taiwan Strait, *145*

Cloma, Tomas, *104, 105*
   see also Carlos P. Garcia (Philippines former vice-president); Kalayaan,

Coker, Christopher, *6*

Cold War, *2, 141*

Cole, J. Michael, *172*

'crisis slide', *181, 182, 183, 185, 186, 187, 199*
   see also Coral Bell,

Cuban Missile Crisis, *8, 13, 93, 181, 191*

see also Graham Allison; Robert McNamara (US former defense secretary),

D

Daesong-dong, the Freedom Village, *21*

Davidson, Admiral Philip S., *130, 131*
   see also US Indo-Pacific Command; US Senate Armed Services Committee,

Declaration on the Conduct of Parties in the South China Sea (DoC), *106, 125*

Demilitarized Zone (DMZ),
   see Korean Demilitarized Zone (DMZ),

Democratic Progressive Party (DPP), *145, 147, 164*
   see also Chen Shui-bian; Frank Hsieh; Tsai Ing-wen (Taiwan president),

Deng Xiaoping, *69, 84, 85, 136, 164, 165*

Diaoyu, *63*

Diaoyu Dao, *64*
   see also Uotsuri,

Dokdo, *63*
  see also Takeshima,
Doomsday Clock, *2, 199*
Dulles, John Foster (US former secretary of state), *67*
  see also Treaty of San Francisco (1951),
Dutch East India Company, *138*
Duterte, Rodrigo (Philippines president), *110, 116*

E
East Asia Summit, *5, 126*
East China Sea, *6, 74, 76, 79, 81, 90*
  see also China; Senkaku or Diaoyu Islands,
  and the conflicts in, *63, 72, 81, 83, 86, 87*
  and the consequences of conflict, *190*
  and the Japan-China Maritime and Air Communication (2015), *89*
  and the 'joint development zone' negotiations, *84*
  and the joint resource development, *124*
  and the Miyako Strait, *76, 113, 151*
  and trans-Pacific trade, *75*
  and the United States deterrence strategy, *89*
East China Sea ADIZ (2013), *72, 78*
Eisenhower, Dwight (US former president), *140*
Emperor Zhu Di, *101*
exclusive economic zone (EEZ), *105, 124*
  and Australia, *116*
  and China, *115, 116, 129*
  and Vietnam, *107, 120*

F
Fat Man atomic bomb (1945), *24*
Fitzgerald, Stephen (Australian former ambassador to China), *193*
'four-point consensus', *72*
  see also Asia-Pacific Economic Cooperation (APEC) 2014 Shinzō Abe (Japanese prime minister); Xi Jinping (Chinese president),

France, *101, 102, 104, 138*
   see also Paracel Islands;
   Qing dynasty
   (1644-1911); South
   China Sea; Taiwan;
   Vietnam,
Free Trade Area, *4*
   see also Association of
   Southeast Asian Nations
   (ASEAN),
Freidberg, Aaron, *2*
Fu Ying, *107*
   see also Kurt Campbell
   (Obama administration);
   Scarborough Shoal,

G
Gallucci, Robert (former
Clinton administration), *56*
Garcia, Carlos P.
(Philippines former
vice-president), *104, 105*
   see also Kalayaan,
Gates, Robert (former CIA
director), *26*
George W. Bush (former US
president), *51, 194*
   see also Agreed
   Framework,
Global Times (Chinese
newspaper), *118*

Green, Michael, *82, 198*
guanxi, *5*
   see also China,

H
Hagel, Chuck (US former
Defense Secretary), *86*
   see also Shangri-La
   Dialogue (2014),
Hainan Island, *98, 104*
   and Japan, *102, 104*
   and Lingshui Air Base, *179*
   and the US spy plane
   collision (2001), *90*
   and USNS Impeccable, *106*
   and the Yulin Naval Base,
   113
Harris Jnr, Admiral Harry
B., *107, 113, 130*
Hayashi Shihei, *65*
Hayton, Bill, *110, 112*
Hecker, Siegfried, *57*
   see also Los Alamos
   National Laboratory,
Hillary Clinton (US former
secretary of state), *98*
Ho, Admiral Cheng, *101*
   see also Emperor Zhu Di;
   Zhu Yunwen,
Holmes, James, *83*
Hoyt, Timothy, *7*

Hsieh, Frank, *164*
Hu Jintao (Chinese former president), *89, 162*

I
Imperial Japanese Navy, see Japanese Navy,
India, *3, 13, 75*
Indonesia, *120*
inter-continental ballistic missile (ICBM) test, *93*
  see also Vandenberg Air Force Base (California),
inter-continental ballistic missiles (ICBMs), *26, 27, 32, 43, 46, 188*
  see also North Korea,
inter-Korean summit (2018), *50*
  see also Kim Jong-un (North Korean dictator); Punggye-ri nuclear test site,
International Atomic Energy Agency (IAEA), *42, 50*
Ishihara, Shintaro (mayor of Tokyo), *72*

J
Jang Song-thaek, *35*
Japan, *10, 56, 60, 63, 64, 74, 75*

see also Hainan Island; Paracel Islands; Shinzō Abe (Japanese prime minister); Takeshima; Treaty of Mutual Cooperation and Security (1960),
Japan-China Maritime and Air Communication (2015), *89*
Japanese Ministry of Defense, *82*
Japanese Navy, *79, 81*
Joint Security Area (JSA), *20, 21, 22*
JS Izumo (helicopter carrier), *113, 117*

K
Kalayaan, *104, 105*
  see also Tomas Cloma,
Kausikan, Bilahari, *129*
Kijong-dong, the Peace Village, *21*
Kim Il-sung (North Korean former dictator), *19, 27*
  and General Douglas MacArthur, *20*
  and invasion of South Korea, *198*

and Jimmy Carter (US former president), *42*

Kim Jong-il (North Korean former dictator), *27, 55*

Kim Jong-nam, *33, 36*

Kim Jong-un (North Korean dictator), *27, 29, 35, 36, 40, 48, 50, 188*

   see also International Atomic Energy Agency (IAEA); Jang Song-thaek; Kim Jong-nam; Truce Village, Panmunjom, and the 'charm offensive', *39*

   and 'independent reunification' of Korea, *30*

   and North Korea denuclearisation, *57*

   and Song Tau Chinese (Communist Party international liaison), *36*

   and Xi Jinping (Chinese president), *35*

Kim Yo-jong, *39*

Kissinger, Henry (former US national security adviser), *69, 186*

   and Taiwan, *141, 142*

Koizumi, Junichiro (Japanese former prime minister), *82*

Korea,

   and 'America's forgotten war', *58*

   as a Japanese colony (1910-45), *18*

Korean Demilitarized Zone (DMZ), *16, 17, 18, 21, 23*

   and the armistice agreement (1953), *20*

   and the Association of Southeast Asian Nations (ASEAN), *4*

   and the Joint Security Area (JSA), *20, 21, 22*

Korean Peninsula, *6, 19, 28, 54, 122*

   see also 38th parallel; Korean War (1950-53); Pacific War (1941-45); Russo-Japanese War (1904-05); Sino-Japanese War (1894-95), and China, *35*

   and George W. Bush (former US president), *55*

and the Korean Demilitarized Zone (DMZ), *17*
and military deterrence, *190*
and the 'roadmap plan' (2005), *48, 185*
and the Sino-Japanese War (1894-95), *18, 64*
and the threat of war, *56, 188*
and the withdrawal of US forces, *30, 58, 195, 196*
Korean War (1950-53), *18, 22, 23, 24, 29, 35, 57*
   see also armistice agreement (1953),
Kuomintang (KMT), *139, 144, 145, 146, 164*
   see also Chiang Kai-shek; Lien Chan (Taiwan former premier); Ma Ying-jeou (Taiwan former president); Taiwan,
Kurihara, Kunioki, *71, 72*

L
land reclamation, *107, 108, 183*
Langsdorf, Martyl,
   see also Bulletin of the Atomic Scientists,

Leap Day Agreement (2012), *48, 191*
Lee Myung-bak (South Korean former president), *47, 52*
Lee Teng-hui (Taiwan former president), *144, 145*
Li Kexin (senior Chinese diplomat), *171*
Li Peng (Chinese former premier), *124*
Li Zhaoxing (Chinese former foreign minister), *85*
   see also ASEAN Regional Forum (2006),
Liaoning (Chinese aircraft carrier), *110*
Lind, Jennifer, *29*
Lombok Strait, *112*
Los Alamos National Laboratory, *57*
Luzon Strait, *113, 151*

M
Ma Ying-jeou (Taiwan former president), *164*
   and Xi Jinping (Chinese president), *146, 173*
MacArthur, General Douglas, *20, 176*
Macclesfield Bank, *99*

Makkassar Strait, *112*
Malacca Strait, *112*
Mao Tse Tung, *136, 141, 151*
   see also Battle of the
   Paracels (1974);Chinese
   Civil War (1945-49)
   Chinese Communist
   Party; Taiwan,
Matsu islands, *139, 140*
Mattis, James (US Defense
Secretary), *30, 76, 115, 128*
   see also Shangri-La
   Dialogue (2017);
   Shangri-La Dialogue
   (2018),
Mattis, James (US Defense
Secretary), *30, 76, 115, 128*
   see also Senkaku or
   Diaoyu Islands; US-Japan
   Security Treaty (1960),
McGregor, Richard, *6, 7*
   see also Asian 'Wars of
   the Roses',
McMaster, H.R. (US former
national security adviser),
40
McNamara, Robert (US
former defense secretary),
175, 191, 192
   see also Cuban Missile
   Crisis; The Fog of War,

Mearsheimer, John, *122*
Ming dynasty (1368-1644),
65, 101
'Ministry of Traitors', *78*
Miyako Strait, *75, 76, 113, 151*
Mizokami, Kyle, *121*
Moon Jae-in (South Korean
president), *50, 52*
   see also Truce Village,
   Panmunjom,
Munich Analogy, *196, 198*
Myanmar, *113*

N
National Museum of China,
62
Nixon, Richard (US former
president), *141, 142, 186*
Nixon administration, *68, 69*
Nodong-1 nuclear-capable
missile, *37*
North Korea, *22, 35, 54*
   see also Kim Il-sung
   (former North Korean
   dictator); Kim Jong-un
   (North Korean dictator);
   Pyongyang,
   and the armistice
   agreement (1953), *20*
   and the cyber hackers, *53*
   and denuclearisation, *57*

and the 'hermit kingdom', *28, 29, 36, 38, 51*
and inter-continental ballistic missiles (ICBMs), *27, 32, 43, 46, 188*
and Nodong-1, *37*
and the nuclear crisis (1993-94), *26, 42, 55, 180*
and the Six-Party Talks, *48*
and the Third Tunnel of Aggression, *23*
and the 'three generations policy', *29*
and the Treaty on the Non-Proliferation of Nuclear Weapons (NPT), *51*
and the United Nations Security Council (UNSC), *52*
and US military deterrence, *54*
and Yeonpyeong bombardment, *6, 24, 183*
and the Yongbyon Nuclear Scientific Research Center, *43*
Nye, Joseph, *8*

O
Obama, Barack (US former president), *76, 87, 121*
see also Obama administration; US-Philippines Mutual Defense Treaty,
and the East Asia Summit (2011), *126*
and the Rebalance strategy, *33, 169*
Obama administration, and Taiwan, *152*
O'Brien, Luke, *45*
O'Hanlon, Michael, *154*
see also A War Like No Other,
One China policy, *145, 148, 150*
Operation Paul Bunyan, *22*
see also Bridge of No Return; Captain Arthur Bonifas; First Lieutenant Mark Barrett,
Osumi Strait, *75*

P
Pacific War (1941-45), *18*
Paracel Islands, *99, 119, 122*
and the Battle of the Paracels (1974), *122, 151*
and France, *98, 101, 102*

and Japan, *10, 104*

and Vietnam, *105, 107, 113*

Park Geun-hye (South Korean former president), *17, 63*

   see also 'Asia's paradox',

People's Liberation Army, *121*

Permanent Court of Arbitration at The Hague, *108*

   see also China,

Philippines Perry, Commodore Matthew C., *115*

Philippines, *116, 120*

   see also Rodrigo Duterte (Philippines president); Scarborough Shoal,

   and the Chinese fishermen in Scarborough Shoal, *106*

   and the Permanent Court of Arbitration at The Hague, *108*

Potsdam Declaration (1945), *66*

Pratas Islands, *99, 104*

PricewaterhouseCoopers (PWC), and economic projections, *75*

'Propaganda Village', *21*

see also Kijong-dong, the Peace Village,

Punggye-ri nuclear test site, *50*

   see also inter-Korean summit,

Putin, Vladimir (Russian president), *39*

Pyongyang see North Korea

Qing dynasty (1644-1911), *65, 81, 101, 138*

Q

Quadrilateral Security Dialogue, *194*

Quemoy islands (Kinmen islands), *139, 140*

R

Ramos, Fidel V. (Philippines former president), *96*

   see also BRP Sierra Madre,

Ratner, Ely (US former adviser), *128*

Rebalance strategy, *33, 169*

   see also Barack Obama (US former president),

Rice, Condoleezza (US former national security adviser), *194* 'roadmap plan' (2005), *48, 185*

    see also Six-Party Talks, Roberts, Christopher B., *125, 126*

ROKS Cheonan, and the North Korean submarine, *24, 33, 183*

Ross, Robert, *5, 122*

Roy, Denny, *152, 167, 170*

Rudd, Kevin (Australian former prime minister), *5, 39*

Russia, *38*

    see also Soviet Union; Treaty of Friendship, Good-Neighborliness and Cooperation,

    and China's pipeline construction, *113*

    and East China Sea, *89, 90*

    and the Korean Peninsula, *28, 38*

    and the Six-Party Talks, *48*

Russo-Japanese War (1904-05), *18, 64, 65*

RVNS My Tho, *96*

Ryukyu Islands, *10, 12, 66, 68, 69, 76*

    see also Treaty of San Francisco (1951),

    and the Treaty of San Francisco, *67*

S

Scarborough Shoal, *99, 106, 116, 126, 128, 183*

South China Sea resources, *75, 110, 124, 191*

    see also China; Philippines; South China Sea; United States,

Senkaku, *63*

    see also Senkaku or Diaoyu Islands,

Senkaku or Diaoyu Islands, *63, 64, 65, 66, 67, 68, 69, 71, 81, 87*

    see also Diaoyu Dao; Dokdo; East China Sea; Hayashi Shihei; Koga Tatsushiro; Koga Zenji; Kunioki Kurihara; Shintaro Ishihara (mayor of Tokyo); Takeshima; Uotsuri,

    and Barack Obama (US former president), *76, 87*

    and the Chinese fishing-boat collision (), *71*

    and the freeze in high-level diplomacy, *85*

and Japan, *6, 72, 82*
and Taiwan, *12, 63*
and the Treaty of
Shimonoseki, *65*
and the United States, *93*
and the US-Japan
alliance, *129*
and the US-Japan
Security Treaty (1960),
76
Shangri-La Dialogue
(2014), *86*
Shangri-La Dialogue
(2017), *7, 115, 118*
   see also Malcolm Turnbull
   (Australian prime
   minister),
Shangri-La Dialogue
(2018), *128*
   see also James Mattis
   (US Defense Secretary),
Sino-Japanese joint
resource development
(2008), *124, 191*
   see also South China Sea
   resources,
Sino-Japanese trading
relationship, *77*
Sino-Japanese War
(1894-95), *18, 64, 81*

see also Qing dynasty
(1644-1911); Treaty of
Shimonoseki,
Sino-Japanese War
(1937-45), *62, 102*
Six-Party Talks, *48*
Song Tau (Communist
Party international liaison),
36
South China Sea, *12, 97, 98, 99,
126, 130, 131, 190, 191*
   see also Macclesfield
   Bank; Pratas Islands;
   Scarborough Shoal;
   Spratly Islands; United
   States; Zone of Peace,
   Freedom, Friendship and
   Cooperation,
   and 'accidental' clashes,
   121, 122
   and artificial islands, *110,
   118, 119, 120*
   and the 'Chinese lake',
   104, 127, 128
   and the consequences of
   US-China conflict, *119*
   and the Declaration on
   the Conduct of Parties in
   the South China Sea
   (DoC), *106, 125*
   and France, *101, 102*

and freedom of navigation, *115, 116, 132*

and land reclamation, *107, 183*

and wei-lu, *101*

South China Sea code of conduct, *106, 110, 185*

  see also ASEAN (Association of Southeast Asian Nations); Declaration on the Conduct of Parties in the South China Sea (DoC),

South China Sea resources, *75, 110, 124, 191*

  see also Chinese National Offshore Oil Corporation; Scarborough Shoal; Sino-Japanese joint resource development (2008); US Energy Information Administration,

South Korea, *23, 63*

  see also Lee Myung-bak (South Korean former president),

  and 1977 withdrawal of forces from, *51*

  and anti-Pyongyang propaganda, *23*

  and complacency about threat of war, *31, 32*

  and consequences of US military action, *45, 46*

  and missile defence, *56*

  and the Six-Party Talks, *16, 48*

  and the Sunshine Policy, *46, 47*

  and THAAD (Terminal High Altitude Area Defense), *55, 56*

South Vietnamese Navy, *96*

  see also RVNS My Tho,

Soviet Union, *2, 3*

  see also Russia,

Special ASEAN-China Foreign Ministers' Meeting (2016), *126, 127*

Spratly Islands, *98, 99, 101, 102, 104, 105, 107, 108, 120, 124*

  see also China; Japan; Kalayaan; Taiwan; Tomas Cloma; Vietnam,

Stalin, Josef, *19, 198*

Straits Exchange Foundation (SEF), *162*

submarine-launched ballistic missile (SLBM), *27*

Suganuma, Unryu, *63*

see also Senkaku or
Diaoyu Islands,
Sunda Strait, *112*
Sunshine Policy, *46, 47*

T

Taiwan, *76, 99, 146, 152, 160, 161, 192, 195*

see also Democratic
Progressive Party (DPP);
Dutch East India
Company; George H. W.
Bush snr (former US
president); George W.
Bush (former US
president); Henry
Kissinger (former US
national security
adviser); Kuomintang
(KMT); One China policy;
Qing dynasty
(1644-1911); Taiwan
Strait,
and the Asia-Pacific
Economic Cooperation
(APEC), *166*
and the Association for
Relations Across the
Taiwan Straits (ARATS),
162

and Chiang Ching-kuo
(former Taiwan
president), *142, 144*
and the China-Taiwan
Economic Cooperation
Framework Agreement
(ECFA), *167*
and 'Chinese Taipei', *166*
and the consequences of
conflict, *154, 155, 157*
and France, *138*
and General Chiang
Kai-shek, *139, 140*
and Lee Teng-hui (Taiwan
former president), *144, 145*
and Mao Tse Tung, *141*
and national identity, *149,
150, 170*
and the peace treaty, *164,
191*
and the Ryukyu Islands,
68
and Senkaku or Diaoyu
Islands, *12, 63*
and the Sino-Japanese
War (1937-45), *102*
and the Spratly Islands,
105
and the Straits Exchange
Foundation (SEF), *162*

and the Taiwan Relations
Act 1979, *142, 154*
and the Taiwan Travel
Act, *148, 174*
and the Treaty of
Shimonoseki, *64*
and the United Nations,
165
and the US National
Security Strategy (2017),
153, 154
and World War II, *139*
and Xi Jinping (Chinese
president), *136*
and Zheng Chenggong
(Chinese warlord), *138*
Taiwan Relations Act 1979,
142, 154
   see also Jimmy Carter
   (former US President),
Taiwan Strait, *139, 140, 141, 144,
145, 160, 161, 192, 195*
Taiwan Travel Act, *148, 149, 174*
   see also Donald Trump
   (US President),
Takeshima, *63*
   see also Dokdo,
Tatsushiro, Koga and the
Senkaku or Diaoyu Islands,
65, 66, 71

THAAD (Terminal High
Altitude Area Defense), *55,
56*
   see also United States,
The Economist, *77*
The Fog of War, *175*
   see also Robert
   McNamara (US Defense
   Secretary),
The Sleepwalkers: How
Europe Went to War in
1914, *9*
   see also Christopher
   Clark,
Third Tunnel of Aggression,
   see North Korea,
'three generations policy',
   see North Korea,
Thucydides Trap, *6, 7, 8*
   see also Graham Allison,
Tillerson, Rex (US former
secretary of state), *40, 118, 119*
Treaty of Friendship,
Good-Neighborliness and
Cooperation, *38*
Treaty of Mutual
Cooperation and Security
(1960),
   see US-Japan Security
   Treaty (1960),

Treaty of Peace and Friendship (1978), *69, 85*
  see also China; Japan,
Treaty of San Francisco (1951), *10, 12, 67*
  see also John Foster Dulles (US former secretary of state); Ryukyu Islands,
Treaty of Shimonoseki, *64, 65, 66, 138*
  see also Sino-Japanese War (1894-95),
Treaty on the Non-Proliferation of Nuclear Weapons (NPT), *51*
Truce Village, Panmunjom, *50*
  see also Kim Jong-un (North Korean leader); Moon Jae-in (South Korean president),
Truman administration, *140*
Trump, Donald (US President), *30, 32, 51, 174, 188, 199*
  and 'America first' policy, *46, 132, 169, 172, 188, 199*
  and 'peace through strength', *193, 194*
  and the period of strategic patience, *57*
and the Taiwan Travel Act, *148, 149, 174*
and withdrawal of US forces, *58, 195, 196*
and Xi Jinping (Chinese president), *36, 37*
Trump administration,
  and the 'bloody nose' military option, *43, 45*
  and freedom-of-navigation operations, *110, 132*
Tsai Ing-wen (Taiwan president), *147, 148, 174*
  see also Democratic Progressive Party (DPP),
Turnbull, Malcolm (Australian prime minister), *7, 118*
  see also Shangri-La Dialogue (2017),

U
Uotsuri; Yasukuni Shrine,
  and the Air Defence Identification Zone (ADIZ), *78, 82*
  and colony of Korea, *18*
  and the fishing-boat collision (2010), *71, 85, 89*

and the frigate radar lock (2013), *92, 93*

and the Japan-China Maritime and Air Communication (2015), *89*

and the Japanese Navy, *79, 81*

and JS Izumo (helicopter carrier), *113*

and the Korean Peninsula, *28*

and missile defence construction, *37, 38, 56, 57*

and the post-World War II 'pacifist clause', *81*

and the Pratas Islands, *104*

and purchase of the Senkaku or Diaoyu islands, *72*

and Ryukyu, *68*

and the Senkaku or Diaoyu Islands, *82*

and the Six-Party Talks, *48*

and the South China Sea, *116, 117, 118*

and the Spratly Islands, *10, 104*

and the Treaty of Peace and Friendship (1978), *69*

and the US-Japan alliance, *12, 86, 92*

and the US-Japan Security Treaty (1960), *68, 76, 87, 129*

United Nations, *33, 42, 50, 52, 115, 116, 165*

see also International Atomic Energy Agency (IAEA),

United Nations Command, *19, 20*

see also armistice agreement (1953),

United Nations Convention on the Law of the Sea, *116*

United Nations Security Council (UNSC), *52*

United States, *110*

and consequences of military action, *45, 46*

and freedom of navigation, *115, 116, 132*

and the Korean Peninsula, *28*

and military deterrence, *54, 190, 192*

and Operation Paul Bunyan, *22*

and the Ryukyu Islands, *12, 67*

and Scarborough Shoal, *116*

and the Six-Party Talks, *48*

and South China Sea, *115, 116, 117, 127, 128*

and THAAD (Terminal High Altitude Area Defense), *55, 56*

and the Treaty of Mutual Cooperation and Security (1960), *68*

and the United Nations Convention on the Law of the Sea, *116*

and the US spy plane collision (2001), *90, 180*

and the US-Japan alliance, *12, 86, 92*

and the US-Japan Security Treaty (1960), *68, 76, 87, 129*

Uotsuri, *64*

  see also Daioyu Dao,

US Congressional Research Service report, *41*

US Energy Information Administration, *110*

US Indo-Pacific Command, *130*

  see also Admiral Philip S. Davidson,

US National Security Strategy (2017), *153, 154*

US Senate Armed Services Committee,

  see also Admiral Philip S. Davidson,

US 'strategic perimeter', *19*

US-China Group of Two (G2), *4*

US-Japan alliance, *12, 86, 92, 129*

  see also Treaty of Mutual Cooperation and Security (1960); US-Japan Security Treaty (1960),

US-Japan Security Treaty (1960), *68, 76, 87, 129*

  see also Senkaku or Diaoyu Islands; Treaty of Mutual Cooperation and Security (1960); US-Japan alliance,

USNS Impeccable, *106*

US-Philippines Mutual Defense Treaty, *121, 128*

  see also Barack Obama (US former president),

USS Harnett County, *96*
USS Ronald Reagan (US super-carrier), *117*
uti possidetis, ita possideatis, *124, 126*

V

Vandenberg Air Force Base (California), *93*
  see also inter-continental ballistic missile (ICBM) test,
Varghese, Peter (Australian former diplomat), *118*
Vietnam, *105, 107, 119, 124*
  see also exclusive economic zone (EEZ); Paracel Islands,
  and France, *101*
  and the Spratly Islands, *120*

W

Wang, Lieutenant-General Guanzhong, *86*
  see also Shangri-La Dialogue (2014),
Wang Wei, *179*
White, Hugh, *8, 172, 193*

  see also Without America: Australia in the New Asia,
'wide war', *10, 181, 187*
  see also Geoffrey Blainey, Without America: Australia in the New Asia, *8, 193*
  see also Hugh White,
World War I, *182*
World War II, *4, 10, 16, 19, 26, 66, 96, 104, 139, 185, 196, 198*
  see also Munich Analogy,

X

Xi Jinping (Chinese president), *196, 198, 199*
  and the China National Party Congress (2017), *136*
  and Donald Trump (US President), *36, 37*
  and Kim Jong-un (North Korean dictator), *35*
  and Ma Ying-jeou (Taiwan former president), *146, 173*
  and the 'new model of great power relations', *7*
  and Shinzō Abe (Japanese prime minister), *72, 146*
  and Taiwan, *136*

and the wall for border and ocean defence, *113*

Y

Yalta agreements (1945), *66*

Yasukuni Shrine, *60, 89*
  see also Shinzō Abe (Japanese prime minister),

Yeonpyeong, and bombardment by North Korea, *6, 24, 183*

Yongbyon Nuclear Scientific Research Center, *43, 47*

Yulin Naval Base, *113*

Yushukan military history museum, *60*

Z

Zenji, Koga and the Senkaku or Diaoyu Islands, *71*

Zheng Chenggong (Chinese warlord), *138*
  see also Qing dynasty (1644-1911); Taiwan,

Zhu Yunwen, *101*
  see also Emperor Zhu Di,

Zone of Peace, Freedom, Friendship and Cooperation, *124, 125*

Made in United States
North Haven, CT
22 February 2023

32989507R00174